TOO MUCH
TOO LOUD
TOO FAST

Doing life with God while battling
Hurry, Busyness, Noise,
& Distraction

Craig Knudsen

Too Much, Too Loud, Too Fast: Doing Life with God While Battling Hurry, Busyness, Noise, and Distraction

ISBN: 978-1-7322171-0-2 (paperback)

Published June, 2018
Interior design by Deborah Stocco
Cover design by Christine Lee Smith

Craig Knudsen, 1955–

Table of Contents

The mantras of "I'm so busy" and "I have no time" and "I'm so tired" have become a liturgical prayer ending in, "Lord, have mercy."

- Tim Chester, *The Busy Christian's Guide to Busyness*

Introduction: God's Dream for Doing Life with Him

As I've interfaced with normal, everyday men and women over four decades as a pastor, public school teacher, and working with teenagers as a Young Life Area Director, I've noticed that there is a common feeling of defeat and failure when it comes to taking on many spiritual practices. It seems that anyone in any stage of life has a jam-packed schedule with a multitude of responsibilities. Most feel like it would be impossible to add anything else to their life. They barely have enough energy to watch the evening news, let alone read their Bible.

In this book, I want to help those of you with jam-packed schedules, those who feel trapped by the speed of everyday life. I want to show you how you can experience God *within* the normal days of life. I believe you can experience Jesus' whisper of "You are my treasure and I enjoy doing life with you every day," in the midst of a regular day.

An Invitation to Dance

It was our 35th wedding anniversary. My wife, Karen, and I had saved up for two years to go to Jamaica and stay at an all-inclusive resort for a week. The weather was beautiful. We went sailing in a little skiff and swimming in the warm water. We rented a cabana which included the

1

service of a waiter bringing us lunch, beverages, and snacks. Each night, we had a choice of various styles of restaurants: Italian, Japanese, European, Hispanic, or American.

Every evening, local musicians came and sang near the restaurants. No matter the original style of the songs they performed, everything was played to a reggae beat. It didn't matter if it was "Close to You" by the Carpenters or "You've Got to Hide Your Love Away" by the Beatles. Everything was reggae.

On the last night of our trip, Karen and I were eating and listening to the music when they started playing, "I Can't Help Falling in Love with You" by Elvis Presley...in reggae style. Karen looked at me and said, "Let's dance."

I wanted to say, "Here? Now? In front of all these people?" But I saw the look on her face and replied, "Sure, honey." We rose from the table, stepped to the side, and began slow dancing like normal, awkward white people.

As we danced, we sang the words to each other. It was truly an "Ahhhhh, isn't that romantic?" moment. We said, "From now on, this is our song."

Later on, I pondered one of the verses: "Take my hand. Take my whole life too. For I can't help falling in love with you." I thought, "This is a picture of Jesus inviting me to do the dance of life with Him, each moment of every day. He's inviting me to embrace His whole life of grace (undeserved favor), and love (believing that I matter deeply to Him), and to live in the truth that He can't help falling in love with me over and over again."

The words to that song are how God feels about you! It's God's constant choice, forever and ever, to love you.

Don't get me wrong. He doesn't do this dance with me because of my stellar, morally perfect life. As with dancing, I can trip over my size 15s, step on my partner's feet, and do the moves all wrong. But Jesus doesn't trade me in for a new partner when that happens. He doesn't give a look of disappointment if it takes me a long time to get the dance right. Instead, with every trip and misstep, I look into His face. He smiles, and He needs no words to say, "I would never trade you in. Let's practice some more because I can't help falling in love with you over and over again. Just take my hand again and embrace a life with Me that we enjoy forever."

An Image from Junior High Dance Class

When I was in junior high school, my parents signed me up for cotillion: a "learn to formal dance" program for young people. It was the heyday of 60's rock 'n' roll, but in cotillion we were stuck with the foxtrot and the waltz. We were forced to wear ironed, perfectly-creased black dress slacks and polished shoes and a bright red sport coat. Did I mention it was the 60's: the age of ripped jeans, long hair, tie-die T-shirts, and sandals?

Needless to say, we all hated it. At the start of every session, the boys sat on folding chairs lined up on one side of the room. The girls were on the other side of the room. When signaled, each boy was to walk in a straight line across the floor to a girl in the vicinity of that straight-line walk, bow, extend our right hand, and say, "Would you like to dance?" At this point, the girl had a choice to make. Do I lift my hand and place it in this young man's hand or not? In the class, she was told to take it or risk being told to dance alone in front of everyone. She took the boy's hand.

Now, I know this might be a tough analogy for the men reading this book to swallow, but go with me here: *Dancing is an analogy of "doing life with Jesus."*

Jesus is inviting us to live each moment of each day believing that He is so close to us that it's like dancing with Him. God intended our lives to be lived with the confidence that He is *with* and *within* us each day, moment by moment, as if we were dancing with Him. He leads the dance. We follow His lead. As we do this dance of life with Him, He transforms our hearts and minds to more closely resemble the "dance of heaven" rather than the "dance of the world." In a figurative sense, every day Jesus walks towards us, bows, and asks, "Would you like to dance with Me today? Would you like to do life with Me today?" We have the choice: to simply lift our hand and place it in His, or to keep our hands to ourselves, which is essentially saying, "I'd rather do the dance of life by myself. Thank you very much."

Fortunately, this doesn't deter Jesus from asking us to dance with Him over and over again.

Pastor Ed Noble said it this way: "Jesus has taken 9,999 steps toward us. He leaves the 10,000th step for us." This is true when someone takes their first step to become a Christ-follower. It's also true in any step we take, as people already following Christ, to place ourselves in a position to experience Jesus and grow further into thinking, feeling, and acting like He would if He were in our place.

His hand is out. The one step He asks is that we take His hand. And when we do, we begin to see that all His commands, all His calls to obedience, are not dictatorial edicts handed down because God loves to tell us what to do. No. Rather, they are signposts to the way life works best. His dream for each of us is *not* that we'd think, "I guess I have to do these spiritual practices in order for Him to like me." No, Jesus' dream is that, *as* we take His hand every day and do life with Him, eventually we'd become people who would *want* to connect with Him by doing some of the practices in this book, because we know we will experience Jesus' presence and whispers of love and encouragement when we do them. As we experience Jesus being so "for us," we end up wanting to be like Him. We want to act like He did. We want to speak like He would if He were in our place. We learn to feel like He feels about anyone He brings across our path. It ceases being a "have to" thing.

God's strategy He's assigned Himself:

- To convince us
- To woo us
- To tell us; show us; demonstrate to us *that you and I are loved by Him* beyond our wildest dreams!

*He desperately wants us to know, "I can't help but fall in love with you."
Why? Because you and I are God's:*

- One of a kind
- Never to be duplicated ever again
- Uniquely made
- Cherished
- Adored
- Absolute treasure
- Someone He loves and adores with a passion beyond measure. A sinner for sure, but also a child of His; a permanent member of His family.

We must come to an understanding and then an embracing of this truth: *we are loved by God* with a passion way beyond the passion with which we love our own children, spouses, family, or close friends. Ask yourself, what wouldn't you do for your children? Well, then, what wouldn't God do for *you*, His unique, treasured child? ANSWER: There's *nothing* God wouldn't do to show you His love and grace, to constantly whisper to you that He is present with and within you always.

So, how do we increase our capacity to see, feel, and embrace for ourselves the truth that we matter to God so deeply? How do we recognize His wooing of us? How can we be constantly reminded and assured that we are *loved by God*? How can we get to a place of eagerness to love Him with all our heart, soul, mind, and strength?

The answer is simple. Our part in all this is *learning* and *practicing*.

I want to open your eyes to what "taking Jesus' hand" might look like. I'd like you to understand and embrace the truth that you don't have to be a scholar, pastor, church staff person, or an extremely involved volunteer to put your hand in Jesus' hand and to respond to His invitation to dance through life with Him.

Or, put another way, how can we come to recognize God's messages to us in our everyday life? How can we sense His strong leadings, promptings, or whispers in almost every moment of every day? Again, it's by learning and practicing.

Definition of "God's Presence"

Throughout this book I will use the phrase "God's presence." Sometimes, that's a hard term to get our minds around. So, whenever you read that phrase, think of His presence to you in this way:

God is...

- with and within you...
- in front and in back of you...
- to the left and the right of you...
- above and below you.

The "Dance Steps" We Do with Jesus: Spiritual Practices

There are many possible dance steps to learn in doing life with Jesus every moment of every day. Dance steps are an image for *spiritual practices*. In other words, as we do the dance with Jesus, there are some particular dance steps that may feel much more natural to you. You're more excited when you do them. In the same way, there are certain spiritual practices in this book that will come naturally to you, and others you might have to practice a bit harder to nail down and enjoy. But all of the practices ("dance steps") in this book are legitimate ways we can connect with Jesus, and ways to enjoy His constant presence with and within us.

Spiritual practices are "taking the hand of Jesus" experiences. They are the "our effort" part, the part where we practice learning to dance to Jesus' tune of how life works best. We must make some *effort* to experience Jesus. The goal of this book is to help you *experience God in everyday life!*

The "Classic" Spiritual Practices

Certainly, you can experience God's presence in church: through singing, through worship, through prayer, through listening to teaching. You can experience Jesus' presence *with* you and *within* you when you read, meditate on, ponder and practice Jesus' example and teaching found in the Bible. You can experience God alone: in private and/or in silence. You can embrace His presence when you're in a small group, or by serving and helping in your local church. I'm not minimizing that at all. You keep that up! God is saying, "Way to go!" on all that.

But I've found that so many people simply cannot (or in some cases, will not) carve out the time to do these classic spiritual practices: meditation, prayer, fasting, study, simplicity, solitude, submission, service, confession, worship, guidance, and celebration. Many Christ-followers know that these classic spiritual practices can be difficult because of time crunches, distractions, and busyness. And I'll be honest: some of these practices do involve large blocks of time. Many people feel like they disappoint God and He is not very happy with them because they can't seem to fit these practices in. They want to do it, but simply can't in their current life stage. As a result, they feel that Jesus is in a constant state of mild disappointment with them because they haven't cracked open their Bible in three months, or prayed in a week, or even thought about God for a couple of days.

Adapting the Spiritual Practices

What if (in addition to doing our best with the classic spiritual practices) there were some types of practices we could do *in the midst of the busy schedules we already have?* What if some of the classic practices could be adapted to modern life? What if there were some additional practices that Jesus Himself did that might fit into our modern world of hurry, busyness, noise, and distraction?

There are practices like that. And this book will introduce them to you and give you the tools you need to do them. Some of the practices I'll suggest are: *noticing, receiving, treasuring*, and *advanced preparation*. The working mom with three children can do any one of these. So can a retired senior citizen, a single adult, and couples with no children. But a huge part of experiencing

Jesus through any of these practices is that we must ruthlessly battle the Four Great Enemies to experiencing Jesus in our day.

The Four Great Enemies of Life with God

What are the greatest deterrents to lifting our hand to place it in Jesus' hand and do the dance of life with Him? What are the Four *Enemies* that want to steal away our joy, and our awareness of God's love for us? These enemies come from the strategy of Hell. They are subtle. They work away at us slowly. They are popular and embraced by our culture. They seem *normal* to our everyday lives. These enemies are:

- *HURRY*
- *BUSYNESS*
- *NOISE*
- *DISTRACTION*

Imagine trying to dance "fast," or to say to Jesus, "Sorry, I can't dance with You, I have too much in my schedule to do something like dancing." Imagine us saying to Him, "WHAT? I CAN'T HEAR YOU. I HAVE THESE EARBUDS THAT ARE PLAYING OTHER MUSIC IN MY HEAD!"

Or imagine us not even responding to Him because we don't notice Him. Why? Our heads are down; we're too distracted because we're playing with our cell phones.

This Is a Guilt-Free Book

Now, instead of making you feel guilty about what you're not doing as far as the classic spiritual practices I mentioned before, I'd like to introduce you to some practices and experiences which will make you enjoy and look forward to them. You'll learn to believe and experience that God is present with you every moment of every day (remember, "with and within; above and below"…etc.). They'll remind you that He is extending His hand saying, "I'd love to do the dance called 'Life' together."

And these practices are things you can do in your normal, everyday life:

- Getting ready for the day (showering, brushing teeth, eating, dressing, etc.)
- Doing your job
- Noticing everyday objects like your cell phone, credit cards, and driving
- Taking the dog for a walk
- Playing with your children
- Going to sleep at night.

Fighting these great enemies to experiencing Jesus will take *practice*. I believe that these are practices that people can do *in the midst* of packed schedules, school, work, families, social lives, and fun. But you will have to start somewhere. This book is about practices that you can train yourselves in, in order to experience Jesus' presence in normal day-to-day life!

Go Easy on Yourself

The spirit behind all of the practices in this book is to "go easy on yourself." I have failed if, after reading this book, you feel like you have to "take on" more practices or behaviors in order for God to like you more or to make you feel like you're more pleasing to Him. I have failed if, after trying and then discarding some of these, you feel that Jesus is "disappointed in you." Think of a parent and their child. If the child tries to learn to ride a bike, the parent won't get disappointed and walk away when they fall down—even if they fall down over and over again! No, the parent would hold them, comfort them, and help them get up and try again, until bike riding becomes a natural thing. I believe that experiencing Jesus in everyday life can become a very natural thing—like riding a bike. But just like riding a bike, it takes some practice to learn. So please, go easy on yourself.

> **The huge supposition of today's world is that devotion equals activity. The more we love Jesus, the more we will do for Him. Those who love Jesus the most will do the most.**[1]

Combating hurry, busyness, noise, and distraction is *not* a monumental task. In fact, Jesus said it was "easy." What does "go easy on yourself" look like? It looks like staying with any given practice for about six weeks, in order for it to become an automatic habit. Don't try to do all of them or even several of them all at once. Initially, just *start with one* that appeals to you. I am totally confident and absolutely convinced that you'll experience Jesus' still small voice saying, "Well done," when you do.

Think of this as "training" as opposed to "trying."[2] If you wanted to learn the piano, you start with scales, not Beethoven. So start your training with *small amounts of time* being intentional with one of the practices and soon you'll find that your "experience of Jesus" level will increase. Soon, without even being aware of it, you'll realize, "I'm in His presence all the time, in anything I'm doing, with anyone I'm with, in the normal-everyday stuff that comes my way!" Soon, you will have learned to dance in time with Jesus—all day and automatically—and really enjoy it! That is Jesus' dream for you and me!

Jesus said (my translation), "My yoke (anything you might 'take on' to connect with Him) is easy. My burden (anything that is 'our part' in connecting with God) is light." That means that Jesus is not making it hard to grow into increasing measures of Christ-likeness. It does mean that we have to make some effort in all this.

Earning vs. Effort

Dallas Willard wrote, *"Grace is always opposed to earning, not to effort."* What that means is that experiencing God whispering to you that you are His beloved (grace) is not an "I have to earn it by good behavior" type of thing. We don't *deserve* or *earn* God's love and favor. It is simply given.

The "effort" on our part to experience God's love and grace is taking on any of the classic spiritual practices and/or any practices in this book, one small step at a time, one small piece at a time. The ongoing growth towards thinking, feeling, and acting like Jesus is a result of engaging in any of these practices in any moment of any normal day or night. In other words, we practice placing our hand in Jesus' hand every moment of every day.

So, what are some of the dance steps we can learn in order to experience Jesus' love and closeness?

In each section of this book, after describing one of the Four Enemies to experiencing life with God, I suggest a few practices that anyone can do to battle these enemies of life with God *and* to experience God in normal, every-day life. These practices are "some other options" (*not replacements*) for the "classic spiritual practices." And let me be clear, there is *no substitute* for two of the classic spiritual practices: the *Bible* and *prayer*. Without these, your life with God will stay in the gate of the airport and never get to "lift off."

I believe the practices that I describe in the rest of this book are so simple that they can be done by a married parent with three children in elementary school, who are involved in school plays and soccer leagues and have home-work every night. They can even be done by a single parent juggling all those same challenges! I believe these practices can be done by childless couples who are career-minded and have to spend much more time at work than the normal 40-hour work week. I believe these practices will help single people connect with God—even if at the same time they're going to school, holding down two part-time jobs, and volunteering in their community. I believe these practices can be done by empty-nesters who might be battling health chal-lenges or decreasing energy levels. They can be done by adolescents. They can be done by the "veteran Christ-follower" who has been a Christian for over 20 years. They can be done by newer believers.

These practices are for everyone.

I hope you'll come away from the following chapters with a sense that, indeed, Jesus was right, following and experiencing Him is easy and His "ask" for the 10,000th step is not a *heavy-difficult* thing, but a *light* step. Learning to dance with Him is not a burden of guilt.

It's fun.

Life in the fast lane,
Everything, all the time.

- The Eagles

Part 1: Too Fast!

Enemy #1: Hurry

One of the things I do for a living is to officiate weddings. I officiated 72 weddings in 2015 for couples from all walks of life. It's a blast. I often do multiple weddings on the same day.

But one day in particular taught me a lesson about hurry.

It was a supposed to be a two-wedding day. The first wedding was at 1 p.m., and the second was at 5:30 p.m., and it was a 50-minute drive from the first wedding. No problem. Plenty of time in between.

Then, I got a last-minute call from a couple in Oklahoma asking if I could officiate their wedding at Balboa Park at 3:30. Balboa Park is one of the "wonders" of San Diego. It's about two square miles in size and parking there is terrible on a Saturday. It's usually a 10-15 minute walk to get to any of the 10 locations for weddings inside the park. If I added this third wedding, I'd be fine coming from the first wedding to the second, but getting from Balboa Park to that third wedding with a 5:30 start time was going to be tight.

Doing the math, I thought, "Okay, if I tell this last-minute couple that they *have to* start their wedding on time, I'll be done by 4 p.m., on the road by 4:15 (taking into account the walk to the parking lot), have 50 minutes of driving, and I'll get to the third wedding by 5:05 or so...I'm good to go." (By the way, I'm usually at least a half-hour early to every wedding I officiate, so I had a feeling I was taking a huge gamble.) I called the couple back and told them that they absolutely must start their wedding on time. They assured me over and over again that they would.

The three-wedding day arrived. The 1:00 p.m. wedding went well. I arrived at the 3:30 wedding site at 2:45. Soon, it's 3:00 p.m., then 3:15 p.m., then 3:20 p.m. I'm standing around with the groomsmen wondering where the bride is. The groom got on the phone with his fiancée, "Where are you guys?"

The bride said, "We're on the freeway approaching the park."

Now, it's 3:30. The groom called the bride again, "WHERE ARE YOU GUYS?"

"We're on the entrance road to the park."

Now, driving down that road on a Saturday can take at least 10 minutes, because the number of cars there on a weekend cause frequent traffic jams.

At 3:45 the groom told me, "They're close."

I asked, "How close?"

"Any minute now."

My anxiety thermometer was rising steadily. 3:55 p.m. comes. I was seriously considering handing my notebook to the best man and saying, "You officiate. Just read this. You'll be fine." When I told him that he might have to officiate, he looked like he'd seen a ghost. He clearly did *not* want that to happen.

At 4:00 p.m., the bus shows up with the bridal party. Backing out of the party-bus door first is the mother of the bride, who has a tray of boutonnieres for the groomsmen and the dads. Okay, there goes another 10 minutes. We finally get lined up ready to enter and I see a guitar in one of the groomsman's hands. I asked, "What's that for?"

"It's a surprise, the groom is going to sing his vows to her."

"Oh, okay," I said, but I'm thinking, "How long is *that* going to take?" (As you can tell, I was really "into" their ceremony at this point.)

We all entered and I'm semi-fast talking my part up to the vows. Then the groom straps on the guitar and starts singing to her. Tears are coming out of every tear duct of every guest. The wedding party members, the bride, the parents are all crying a river while he's singing. Except me, of course. Because all I'm thinking about is the next wedding I have to get to ASAP.

So, I'm holding the mic for him, smiling as he sings a love song to her... but inside I'm thinking, "Another chorus...*really?* I think she gets it. You love her. We all get it. Can you wrap this up *please?*"

I usually stick around for 10 minutes or so after a wedding to congratulate the couple, parents and family, but this time I did a fly-by wave while hustling up the stairs, "CONGRATULATIONS, GUYS." I fast-walked to my car. It's 4:40. Okay, if I push the speed limit, I can make the 50-minute drive and arrive right at the 5:30 start time. Not ideal but at least I won't be late.

Half way up the freeway, traffic comes to a halt: there was a *car fire* in the middle lane. I'm gripping the wheel in anxiety. I'm calling the wedding coordinator saying, "I could be a little late. Please don't sit the people down. Let them enjoy the drinks being served beforehand. Better yet, let them enjoy several drinks!"

I arrive at the wedding 30 minutes late. I'm *never* late. And the guests were seated, who knows for how long. I heard later the bride was going to ask an uncle in attendance to officiate...off the cuff. I pull in, the coordinator says, "It's okay, Craig, we're good." She must have seen my face frozen in a state of anxiety and embarrassment.

Now, I use these small-sized black three-ring notebooks during any ceremony I officiate. They are all different, based on the wedding the couple wants. My habit is to stack the notebooks in chronological order for the day on the seat next to me in the car. After each wedding is complete, I toss that notebook into the back seat of my car so I won't grab the wrong one. In my hurried state from the previous wedding, I simply tossed the previous wedding's notebook on the seat next to me, so, when I got out for this last wedding ....you guessed it...I grabbed the wrong notebook. So I'm all mic'd up. The procession begins. I open my notebook and my stomach dropped to my feet. I have the notebook from the previous wedding. *Panic* ensued.

I personalize each wedding I officiate, so they are not all the same. I can see my car right at the curb, about 25 yards away. I consider leaving the front, going over to the car and switching it out, but after being 30 minutes late, I couldn't find the courage to leave the front. The mother

15

of the bride was staring daggers at me anyway.

So, here I am, I have the wrong wedding notebook. My first thought is, "What are their names?" I recalled the groom's name: John, but for the life of me I couldn't remember the bride's. So when the bride starts coming down, when all the guests are turned to see her, I lean over to the best man and ask, "Hey man, how do you *pronounce* the bride's first name?" (Sneaky huh? not "What is her name? But how do you *pronounce* her first name?")

He looks at me like I'm an idiot and says, "Jennifer."

"Oh, Jennifer... right." (Like it would be Jen-*eee*-fer, or Jeni-*fer*).

So I dodged one bullet. The welcome and the brief message went fine. I had that in front of me from the previous wedding, but then we get to the vows and I have no idea what vows they picked, so I think, "I'm going with the traditional vows and hope they don't remember what they really chose. I've read those vows hundreds of times. I can recall them, no problem."

But I *blank*. All I could remember was "sickness and in health." So the bride got one version of what I could remember of the traditional vows. The groom got another version. The ring exchange went well. They didn't want a prayer, so the end of the ceremony is coming when I have to introduce the couple's new last name and I can't remember the groom's last name. So, during the kiss, I always step to the side so the photographer can get a picture without a 6'8" gorilla standing there doing the geeky-smiley-face in the photo. So when I step to the side I lean into the best man again and ask, "How do you *pronounce* their last name?" (Trying to be sneaky again).

He looks at me again with the "what kind of a dork are you" face and says, "*Smith*."

I step back into view and announce their new name: "Ladies and Gentlemen, it is now my pleasure to introduce: The *new* Mr. and Mrs. John and Jen-*eee*-fer...Smythe..." (I'm kidding...I said it correctly.)

I spent the next half hour apologizing to anyone I met.

I call this "the wedding day from hell" because I'll never forget how much of a panicked *hurry* I was in.

Hurry Sickness

The spiritual writer Dallas Willard was asked at one time what the greatest obstacle to experiencing God is. He said:

If you want to experience Jesus' presence on a daily basis, you must ruthlessly eliminate hurry from your life.[1]

Wait a minute, you might say, I thought I was supposed to ruthlessly eliminate sin and moral failure from my life, not hurry! Yes, but hurry is just as insidious a destroyer of life with God as those others.

Our world is in constant pursuit of speed and hurry. We want faster drive-up ATM's, faster functioning cell phones, quicker service in restaurants, faster ways to make meals, and to spend less time at traffic lights. We can record our favorite TV shows so that when we watch we can speed through the commercials (my personal favorite "speed item"). Some of us remember that the internet used to be "dial-up" and we'd wait for what seemed like an eternity to get on the web (something like 30-45 seconds). We now demand *instant access* to anything on our cell phones.

Worse yet, as I learned on the wedding-day-from-hell, our urge to hurry pushes us to *do* more—more than we're actually capable of doing. We speed so fast that we think we're superheroes.

But we're not.

We have everyday expressions used to promote more speed: *I'm going as fast as I can; Speedy recovery; Hurry up!; Mad dash; Get a move on; ASAP; the sooner, the better; step on it; shake a leg; get cracking; I've got to run; I don't have much time; just a second; right away; how soon can I expect it; running late; running scared; run down; running out of time; grab a bite; on the run; it'll only take a second; fast food.*[2]

17

It's the strategy of the evil one to make us feel that we have to rush. The devil's strategy for winning souls is to get us to "hurry ourselves" through life, making us feel like we don't have time for God. I wonder if the devil, in his annual speech to his demonic minions said, *"Stop dangling obvious sins in front of people. They can see those coming. Sure, some will fall to them, but our overall strategy needs to change. If we can make everyone feel like they have to hurry, they won't have the time or feel the need to slow down and listen for that still small voice which is our Enemy, Jesus. If we can make them feel like they don't have time for God, we will win their souls...because they will* hurry themselves *all the way to their grave."*

There is diagnosed phenomenon called "Hurry Sickness."

Hurry Sickness: Behavior pattern characterized by continual rushing and anxiousness; an overwhelming and continual sense of urgency. It's a sickness in which a person feels chronically short of time, thus tending to perform every task faster and getting frustrated with any kind of delay. "Hurry sickness comes from an insatiable desire to accomplish too much or take part in too many events in the amount of time available."[3]

Hurry sickness is the constant need to do more, faster, even when there's no objective reason to be in such a rush. We seem to be blinded by our desire for ceaseless motion, achievement, results, and success. We can work ourselves into a state in which we cannot believe we are pleasing God unless we are busy with a dozen jobs at the same time. Eventually, hurry sickness really can make you sick, since it increases the body's output of the stress hormone cortisol, which suppresses the immune system and has been linked with heart disease.

I was officiating a wedding recently and the father of the bride had moved, several years prior, from San Diego to Montana. I asked why. He said, "I couldn't take the pace of life anymore. I felt pressured by the need to stay on top of things, rush around and fulfill my obligations. I was always tense and nervous." He had lived in Montana for years. I asked him what it felt like to come back to San Diego for the wedding. He said, "When I'm driving on the

ask questions

freeway, I have a death-grip on the steering wheel. I'm sweating and anxious as people whiz by me. The pace is unbelievably fast in every aspect of life here."

Slow down. Take a deep breath. What's the hurry? Why wear yourself out? Just what are you after anyway?

- Jeremiah 2:25, The Message.

The Hurried Child

Parents can get trapped into forcing a child to grow up faster. But do we force wine to age faster? Do we force a tree to grow faster? What happens when you hurry a golf swing? Does forcing love to come sooner work? Is forcing tomorrow to come today something we have control over?

When the great children's psychologist Jean Piaget toured America, after he had explained the stages of cognitive development he had discovered in children, he was asked one question more than any other: "Dr. Piaget, we are impressed with your research, but could you tell us how we can make our children go through these stages faster?"[4]

Time limits on exams like the SAT force students to go as fast as they can. Students who get anxious under time limits are penalized unfairly. What difference does it make how fast you can produce the right answer, as long as you produce the right answer? Unless you're preparing for a career on Jeopardy, does it really matter? Timed testing is just another example of the bias in our world that favors speed.

"Spare Time"... Are You Kidding Me?

There used to be a thing called "spare time", which was greatly anticipated and enjoyed by those who had it. Six decades ago people pondered, with relish, what they would do with their spare time. After the clothes were hung up to dry, the dishes were washed, the family's one and only car cleaned, the dinner cooked and the rugs dragged outside and beaten with a broom, maybe the family would enjoy a movie. Or maybe an afternoon of bowling, or miniature golf, or a picnic.

As the years progressed, technological breakthroughs supplied us with new household appliances that today we take for granted: clothes dryers that steam the wrinkles out, dishwashers that clean not only the dishes but also the pots and pans, drive-through car washes that wash and wax the car, micro-wave ovens to warm up a pre-packaged dinner, and self-propelled robotic vacuums that suck up dust and dirt while you're away from home.

All of these valuable time-savers are meant to give us more spare time. Unfortunately and ironically, with all these high-tech wonders, we have less and less spare time. "A recent *USA Today* national survey revealed that the vast majority of Americans feel they are busier this year than last year and they were busier last year than the year before. For better or for worse, the pace of life is speeding up to make us feel trapped in a 'time crunch'" (Breaking Busy, Ali Worthington).

Symptoms that Indicate You Might Have Hurry Sickness:

- At a grocery store, if you have a choice between two check-out lines, you note the number of people in each line and multiply this number by the number of items per cart. You imagine yourself in the other line…the "alter-you." If the "alter-you" leaves the store while the "real-you" is still in line, you feel depressed.
- Counting the cars in each lane at a traffic stop and getting in the lane that has the fewest number of cars. If each lane contains one car, you read the year, make, and model of each car to guess which will pull away most quickly.
- Accidentally putting your clothes on inside out or backwards.
- Repeatedly pushing the "close door" button on an elevator. (In over half the elevators made, the button isn't connected to anything. Even if they worked, the time saved would be about three seconds.)
- Eating lunch at your desk while checking emails and talking on the phone.

- Habitually interrupting other people.
- Having the urge to do something else while microwaving something for 30 seconds.
- Feeling the need to "stay connected" every minute of the day or night on your phone, iPad or computer.
- Easily distracted by minutiae and not slowing down enough to take time to ask big, important questions.

Results of Hurry Sickness

Our bodies were not meant to endure living at breakneck speed. Sooner or later, physically, mentally and/or emotionally we fall apart. Our bodies were not meant to endure continual stress. Spikes in blood pressure eventually stay spiked. The heart wears out, we become irritable, angered and easily upset, sometimes to the point of crying, from frustration and exhaustion.

One of the results of a "hurry-filled" day at work is that those needing our love the most, those to whom we are most committed, end up getting the leftovers. We just don't have much gas in our tank at the end of the day. This is part of what author Lewis Grant calls "sunset fatigue"[5]—all those end-of-the-day behaviors that signal hurry sickness:

- We rush around at home in a constant state of hurry and anxiety.
- We feel as if we always have to be available for people. When they call, we have to answer. When they email, we have to write back immediately. When they text and we don't text back right away, they get frustrated and wonder where we are. When they want to meet, we clear our schedule.
- We speak sharp words to our spouse and children, even when they've done nothing to deserve them.
- We walk fast. We drive over the speed limit. We talk and think too fast. We fail to listen because we're doing "hurry-talking." We interrupt people because they talk too slow or we need to present our ideas rather than really listening to theirs.

- We eat fast, not really chewing and savoring. We've even invented an entire industry around food and hurry called "fast food" where we don't eat at a table, but we eat our meals while driving around in a car, as God intended.
- Idle moments bother us because we think that we are wasting time by not doing anything productive.
- We hurry our children along by setting up mock races *("okay kids, let's see who can take a bath the fastest")*, which aren't about them at all, but really about our own need to get through it.
- We tell our family that everything should slow down in a week or two. But the "week or two" never comes. We find ourselves living for "two weeks from Tuesday," but soon realize this has become a way of life. We're always living for "two weeks from Tuesday."
- We flop into bed with no sense of gratitude and wonder for the day, just exhaustion.

The most serious sign of hurry sickness, though, is a diminished capacity to love. For love and hurry are fundamentally incompatible. Love always takes unrushed segments of time, and time is the one thing hurried people don't have. When I get hurried, I begin to resent the very people I love most.

Do I Have "Hurry Sickness?"

Here are some questions to ask yourself to determine if you might have "hurry sickness":

- On a regular basis, when you wake up at night, does your mind start racing and you can't get back to sleep?
- If you had "blank sections" in your schedule simply to "be," would you automatically feel guilty and unproductive?
- If someone asked you what you did with your day, would you feel the freedom to say, *"Nothing?"*

Times When We *Should* Hurry…In an Emergency:

- When a young child is about to put their hand on a burning stove or run into traffic.

- When someone is injured in a traffic accident.
- When someone is in danger of drowning in the ocean.

From the Bible:

- When God is about to destroy Sodom and Gomorrah, Lot urges his family members, "Hurry and get out of this place" (Gen. 19:14, NIV).
- When Joseph urges his brothers to get his father Jacob, he orders them to hurry home and bring him back (Gen. 45:9).
- Moses urges Aaron to *hurry* and make an atonement offering to God in response to a rebellion against Moses and his leadership (Num. 16:46).

Hurry makes sense in an emergency and emergencies happen. The problem is that when we find ourselves living with a *constant sense of urgency*, we get stuck there. Every situation seems like an emergency.

Dangers of "Time Management"

Time management books, seminars, and TV shows focus our attention on the immediate. But the immediate is not always, or even often, the most important. *God made days.* Hours, minutes, and seconds are human inventions. There are no words for seconds or minutes in the Bible.

Imagine book titles like: *Getting 26 Hours Out of Every Day* or *Thirty Days to a Better Life*. These "time topics" would have meant nothing to Jesus or the biblical authors. They didn't divide the day into 24 hours. *They never thought of time as a thing to be spent or maximized or organized.* The Bible tells us to "number our days," not our hours or minutes.

Over the triple doorways at the Milan Cathedral are three sayings:

1. Over one door is "All that pleases is but for a moment."
2. Over another door is "All that troubles is for a moment."
3. Over the central doorway are the words, "That only is important which is eternal."[6]

What lasts into eternity? God's words and people.

23

Hurry and Our Journey with God and People

The bottom line truth is: *We can't hurry life with God*. More specifically, we can't hurry prayer, Bible reading, Bible study, solitude with God, silence with God, and hearing from God.

We can't *hurry* relationships either. We can't do "fly-bys" or "skim" relationships with God, our spouse, our family, and friends. They aren't enemy territory we're trying to strafe with our fighter jets. We can't have in-depth marriages, in which deep communication results in greater intimacy, by hurrying through our conversations with our spouses. We can't have significant and close relationships with our children if they feel we "don't have time" to be totally present to them or to play with them. We will live in a constant state of *being preoccupied* when we are with our spouses, children, friends, and family if we constantly feel like we need to get on to the next thing or if we relentlessly check our cell phones so we don't miss anything.

In other words we can't form deep relationships in a hurry. And that includes our relationship with God. I believe it is possible to "hear from God." Maybe not in an audible voice, but through *strong inner leadings, promptings, nudges and impressions*, in which we intuitively sense, "that could be God speaking to my soul." If we are in a constant state of rush and hurry, we will miss a lot (if not all) of what God is attempting to communicate to us. And He is communicating constantly (as we will see). And most all of His messages to us are messages of love; messages of grace; directed at us personally in whatever state of life we find ourselves.

The truth of our lives with God is this: *God visits us in MOMENTS,* in ordinary pockets of time. But in a life of "too much" or "too fast" or "too loud" or "too distracted," we can miss them. What might some of those moments look like?

- God reminds me of someone to call or write.
- I see my neighbor and I feel a nudge to go over and chat.
- I walk past a homeless person and I'm prompted to give.
- I'm prompted to deal with an uncomfortable situation.

- A conversation triggers something I must deal with in my heart.
- When a light-hearted conversation suddenly shifts with just a look or tone of voice that signals "sadness."

Recognizing these "promptings" from God come when we're not hurrying. Even *serving* Jesus in a hurry can get in the way of our relationship with Him.

What if we were to ruthlessly counter-attack our culture's (and the devil's) relentless push to hurry our lives with God and each other? What practices could we infuse into our lives that would counteract our culture's relentless desire for speed? We can battle hurry by incorporating (at various times and situations):

- SLOWING
- WAITING
- BEING USELESS
- TREASURING

Let's look at these four practices now.

Slow down, you move too fast
You got to make the morning last...just,
Kickin' down the cobblestones
Lookin' for fun and feelin' groovy.

- Simon and Garfunkel, 59th Street Bridge Song

Chapter 1: The Practice of SLOWING

TWO FRIENDS OF MINE, RANDY and Lyne, were in Europe. Part of the experience of Europe involves walking down streets, stopping at cafés, visiting art galleries, and eating new kinds of food. After a long day of doing all this while walking, they were both tired. They came upon an old European church. They heard a boys' choir rehearsing inside. They went in, sat down and listened for quite a while. Lyne told me, "I was transported to a place where I could let go of the 'to-dos' and I was simply 'being.' I didn't want it to end."

The Spiritual Practice of Slowing

Reducing the speed at which you do life creates space in your schedules for unrushed moments with God and people. It is giving time to simply "BE…ing."

Warren Buffet, an American business magnate, investor, and philanthropist, who is worth $73.3 billion and gives away 99 percent of his income every year, has an office without a computer. He sits in his Omaha, Nebraska office, and he thinks.

Bill Gates takes two weeks off every year to go to a cabin in the woods to…think.[1]

What is a 10-year-old boy doing when he simply watches a frog that he's stalked for 20 minutes? He's pondering. He's *thinking*.

To experience God we have to slow down. For some, this will be as radical a change as going vegan or as radical as going without your cell phone for a day. Slowing can have a "game-like" quality to it once you get past your dislike of it at first. How about a fast from honking? What about eating your food slowly, actually doubling your chewing time before swallowing? What about choosing the longest check-out line at the grocery store? And then letting someone go ahead of you? Go one day without texting, posting, Instagramming, or FaceTiming for the purpose of *slowing* down to sense God's whispers to you. How about leaving 10 minutes earlier for every errand, appointment, soccer practice, school drop-off, and social gathering, all for the purpose of creating enough of a "time cushion" that you don't feel rushed.

What if we actually drove the speed limit or drove in the slow lane because we had plenty of time? I wonder if our minds might turn towards God more because we aren't turning our freeway experience into a scene from *Grand Theft Auto*.

Another word for slowing is *savoring*. Savoring is to taste, smell, and enjoy with pleasure; to relish; to delight in. The quality of the remainder of our lives on earth will be greatly determined by how well we can keep a "savoring pace." There is a major foe that we must face and defy if we are going to live at a savoring pace: *ourselves*. In other words, the greatest hindrance to eliminating busyness in our lives is our own mindset: the mindset that we matter only in terms of our productivity and speed.

One practice of savoring (or slowing) is "holding sightings" with our eyes for several seconds longer than we normally would. Our modern pace usually has us linger on something for about 10 seconds and then we move on. Do we expect God to whisper to us only in the time frame we want to give Him? God's not in a hurry. So by savoring, we are giving Him the opportunity to speak to us while we're slowing. Lingering enables us to "see slowly" rather than to "see fast." Savoring counts as a spiritual practice because whatever or whoever God puts in front of us is a possible "God sighting" that we can catch if we just slow down.

We have to have enough unhurried time in our lives to be attentive to the promptings and nudgings from God. Slowing enables us to notice God's very real but often hidden activity around us, in us, and among us.[2]

Slowing and Our Interaction with People

The apostle Paul wrote to the Colossian church, "Make the most of every opportunity." (Colossians 4:5, NLT). People think this is about what we *do*. It's not. It's about being alert in conversations with people. Being "alert" is looking for "openings." An "opening" is when someone shares something just a bit more intimate than their opinions about sports teams and the weather. These "openings" sound something like, "I wish I would have thought of that when my child did the same thing." That's an opening to ask, "How's it going being a mom for the first time?" Another opening might happen around the barbeque when a friend says with a small tone of sadness, "Man, that date you had with your wife sounded like it was a lot of fun." That's an opening to ask, "So, what do you and your wife like to do for fun together?"

You might be thinking, "Craig, that's not a very deep follow-up question." If so, you might be someone who wants to hurry the conversation. These "openings" for deeper conversation only come after spending time with people and starting conversations with ball scores and the weather. People don't talk about personal issues in a hurry! *It takes time because it takes trust.* And trust comes when we've won the right to be heard. Football, politics, TV shows and potty-training may be the topics of conversation for quite a while before someone will open up about their marriage, their wayward child, or their soul. *That* is what "making the most of every opportunity" looks like.

Interruptions as "Divine Appointments"

My whole life I have been complaining that my work was constantly interrupted, until I discovered the interruptions were my work.[3]

— Henri Nouwen

Everyone is interrupted. Moms are constantly interrupted by children who have no filter or awareness for waiting. It doesn't matter if she's talking to someone on the phone or talking with the neighbor on the sidewalk. Inevitably, their child will run up to her and with an unfiltered voice yell, "MOMMY! MOMMY!" Dads are interrupted this way as well. Granted, many times the child needs to learn to wait, but the interruptions continue. Parents know that interruptions come with the territory.

Supervisors, bosses, leaders, executives, pastors, department heads, and any other kind of overseer knows that their agenda has to be held loosely. Fires need to be put out. Employee questions arise unannounced. Phone calls come from higher-ups and they don't care what you're doing. Interruptions are part of the game of life.

Jesus was interrupted constantly. Numerous times, the Bible records that Jesus was simply walking along, or speaking to a group of people, or enjoying a meal, and:

- A woman entered the dinner area, started crying, poured oil on Jesus' feet, and dried His feet with her hair. That's a dinner conversation stopper.
- A woman who had been caught in the act of adultery was thrown to the ground in front of Jesus.
- A leper approached Jesus out of the blue while He was carrying out travel plans to another town.
- While speaking to a roomful of people, four young men removed the roof above Jesus and lowered a paralyzed friend of theirs down in front of Jesus so that He might heal him.

I could go on and on. But judging by Jesus' reactions, it seems that interruptions were "holy moments" in which Jesus took the sudden opportunity to teach something to the people around Him, or stop what He was doing or saying in order to heal a poor soul. Being interrupted became moments for affirming someone, forgiving someone, teaching someone, or telling a story relating to the interruption. Remember the catalyst for telling the parable of the Prodigal Son? It was people observing that Jesus liked to hang around with regular people who knew they didn't have their life together.

When you read any book, there are paragraph breaks, commas, semi-colons, periods, margins, dashes, and colons. Each of them is a pause, which allows the words to sink in. It's critically important to schedule pauses into our days: pauses when we read the Bible, pauses when we pray, pauses between appointments, pauses because we just need a break from having *too much* in our lives. Hurry and busyness crowds out those pauses. When our lives are in a rush because we schedule as much as we can into our days, we start taking out paragraph breaks, periods and commas from our days. We edit out the spaces and eliminate the margins.

When I was pastoring, at times I was "zoned in" on preparing a message, or running a leadership meeting or a worship team meeting. Then, one of my children would call or Karen would call. In the early years, I'm pretty sure they felt "brushed off" or they picked up that they were interrupting and they needed to get off the phone.

After a few years, I realized that if anyone had the right and permission to call whenever they needed to, it was my family. That circle of "permissible interruptions" extended to my close friends, leaders of the church, and soon, anyone who called. I figured out that if I really didn't want to be interrupted, I'd go to Burger King, grab a booth in the back, turn the phone off, and dive into what I needed to do.

I discovered that the *key to welcoming interruptions* was seeing them as *divine appointments*. Every intrusion on my time had the potential to be a *here's what Jesus would do if He were in my place* opportunity. And what would He do with interruptions? He would ask how the person was doing, and then listen to them. In these situations, Jesus would be thinking, "Is there any way I can affirm them, comfort them, teach them, or encourage them even though that isn't why they were interrupting me?"

How did I find the energy to see these divine interruptions in this manner? Well, how was Jesus able to see them as opportunities to reveal what God was really like? *Because Jesus wasn't in a hurry!* Therefore, I shouldn't be either. Slowing down the pace of my life, and not taking on more and more, gave me the space to slow down my interior worry factor about the things I needed to get done. Soon, at every interruption I'd say to myself, "God, I know this is a divine interruption. You have brought this person my way at this moment. Help me to treat them as a message from You."

Imagine every mother and father seeing their children's interruptions this way. Imagine the spirit of a work environment where the employees may interrupt their boss and know they will be valued, heard, listened to, and treated with warmth and kindness.

How does one find the energy for this? Again, *slowing* is what gives us the perspective to see life this way. *And*, you will be modeling Jesus, because that's how He'd handle interruptions if He were in your place.

Slowing and Our Relationship with God

In every moment of every day, God is whispering to us, "I appreciate your service for My Kingdom deeply, but do you know that I not only *love* you, I *like* you, and guess what: *I enjoy you. I celebrate you. I am pleased with you!*"

I've found that Christ-followers have a very difficult time picturing God feeling this way about them. We think He "expects" a certain behavior, or that He's more pleased with us when we jam our already-packed schedules with ministry-serving opportunities. The truth is, He sees you as His one-of-a-kind, never-to-duplicated, marvelous, cherished treasure, whom He loves with an unimaginable passion. He is attentive to your every thought, dream, and desire. And there's nothing that you could do to make Him love you any less or more than He does at this moment. So, "taking on" more serving opportunities—thus creating more hurry and busyness—does not help.

Very few Christ-followers or secular people believe this however. I think it breaks God's heart that we think we have to demonstrate our love for God in some way. What earthly father would demand that of his child? What father would tell his child, "Here's how it works, my son, my daughter: at the end of each day I want to see a list of what you've accomplished for the day and if it's satisfactory, I won't punish you in any way. I may even say 'thank you,' but remember, we do the same thing tomorrow."

A true father loves his child simply because they *are*, not because of what they *do*. Similarly, this is the way God feels about you. It's the devil who broadcasts the message of "You'd better perform for God," trying to replace God's message of, "You are my beloved, just as you are."

Being still is not the absence of activity; it's the rejection of hurry.

How might we appropriate this wonderful truth into our lives? Having enough *unrushed segments of time* would open up the possibility of hearing Jesus whisper these truths to us. One thing is for sure, we won't adopt this truth for ourselves while hurrying. Evil does *not* want us to know or embrace this wonderful truth: that God's undeserved favor (grace) and His passionate love is a constant truth coming your way. The devil wants us to blow past this truth. He'd like nothing better than for us to think, "Well, that's nice, but I have to pick up my kids from soccer practice. I'll think about this later."

The solution is an aggressive, all-out assault against *hurry*!

Giving Yourself Permission To Slow Down

I was asked to do a day-long retreat for a church staff. As each person came in, I greeted them and chatted with some in order to get a read on how some of them were doing. What I sensed in many of them was exhaustion. Some were starting to get sick. Some had a chronic low-grade fatigue. As we dialogued, I said to some of them, "You know, one of the most spiritual things you could do today is *take a nap*."

Some said, "*Really?*"

"Yes," I answered, "*Really!* Do you think God doesn't want you to rest? God Himself rested on the seventh day after making the universe! And that was a lot of work!"

We rarely give ourselves permission to *slow down*. It's as if we think being unproductive has become one of the "Seven Deadly Sins," right there on the list along with lust, gluttony, and greed! Our culture *never* encourages slowing, only speeding. Trust me, you'll feel very uncomfortable at first, but if practiced enough, the "hurry factor" will slow to the point where you'll begin to *notice* the many ways God is communicating with you at every moment of every day.

Some Simple "Slowing" Practices:

- Choose to walk more slowly. While doing so, be aware of your surroundings, of the sights, sounds, and smells, and ask God to bring anything to your attention He wants you to notice.
- Pause before answering.
- Eat more slowly; savor your food.
- Drive more slowly.
- Stand in a longer line rather than a shorter one.
- When something catches your attention (e.g., flowers, a sunset), linger.
- Stop a few times each day for one minute or two to remind yourself that God is with and within you.
- Take mini "cease times" during the day (7–15 minutes) to refocus your mind and heart towards God.
- Take a power rest (15–20 minutes). Close your eyes. Be still. Ponder one of God's attributes (His graciousness, love, kindness, provision, power, etc.).
- Sleep a healthy length of time (6 ½–8 hours).
- Develop some activities that help you slow down: walking on the beach, taking a bubble bath, lying in a hammock, playing with your dog, flying a kite, hand-watering your yard, hiking, riding a bike, cooking, camping, surfing, blowing bubbles, juggling, gardening.

The Key to Slowing: Practice, Practice, Practice

God is all about increasing your intimacy with *Him*. And intimacy takes unrushed segments of time. It takes slowing down enough to *enjoy* God and people. It takes a quietness in your soul.

The key to making "slowing" a part of your DNA is to realize it will take time. It takes six weeks of practice for any habit to develop in us, like quitting smoking, taking up a regular prayer practice, or walking for 15 minutes every day.

It takes *practice* to experience God. It will take at least that long to embed "slowing" into your life.

More Slowing Practices

Here are some ways to begin practicing slowing that can be done anytime, anywhere, in any situation...especially your normal everyday life:

1. The "take on" – "take off" Practice

Some of you reading this are probably volunteers. Maybe you volunteer in a church, as a Little League coach, as a tutor in a classroom or a dispenser of food to the homeless. You've "taken on" these things in your life. Wonderful! But have you "taken off" anything in your schedule? Ever?

When I was a Senior Pastor, some new initiative or program would need to be started or addressed. I knew it would take several weeks of time and energy. It was an addition to my already jammed schedule of leadership meetings, individual appointments, message and church service preparation, staff meetings, administration, and interruptions. At one point, my spiritual director said, "Okay, Craig, so you're taking on this project, what are you taking off your plate?"

I said, "Nothing, I'm just adding it on."

"Do you think that's a healthy thing to do?," he replied. "Sounds like you'll increase your busyness, increase the speed of your life, and decrease any degree of margin you might have for experiencing God. You'll only increase the 'hurry factor' by taking on this thing. So, I ask again, what are you taking off your plate if you're going to take on starting this new program?"

He was right.

But did I follow his advice? No, and because I didn't, this decision and many other decisions of "taking on" without "taking off" landed me in the hospital after having a seizure that the doctors determined was due to stress and exhaustion. My life as a Senior Pastor ended soon after that.

Service for God can contribute to hurry sickness. Service for God can replace any type of self-care. By not doing self-care, I negated my ability to enjoy God, my wife, my family, and my friends in the name of "service for Jesus." Sounds noble, but Jesus wasn't asking me to do this. I took this on myself. When we "take on" without "taking off" it makes it difficult to slow down enough to enjoy God; to recognize that every heartbeat, every breath, every step we take is a gift from Him. Every ocean wave, snow-capped peak, and flowering field is a gift that God made for you and me to enjoy and to marvel at. Every apple, carrot, Hershey Bar, and slice of cherry pie that brings a smile of culinary joy to your face, makes God smile. Why? Because He loves to see us *enjoy* things. And if we've "taken on" too much, we'll have to hurry to handle the "too-much" and there goes the slowing down to enjoy.

2. Practice PLAY!

Play slows us down. It doesn't accomplish anything. It's simply *fun*.

Several years ago, I started a Christmas tradition called "Bonus Christmas." Most every family battles the "what do we do after the breakfast and presents are done" dilemma. A friend of mine suggested an afternoon of 5-7 stupid/silly contests which neutralize any skill level one player might have over another. The games are:

   a) Paper airplane thrown for distance from the balcony.

   b) Shoe perched on the toe: kick for distance. (Picture my son whipping his shoe over the fence of the neighbor's yard into their pool. We gave him automatic victory for that.)

c) Build the tallest tower from the same amounts of toothpicks and marshmallows.

d) Hang thin baggies taped on hangers all over the garage rafters and shoot an air cannon at each one. Thirty second time limit. Most hits wins.

e) Superball bounce into containers. I'd take the screen off the second story window, put a long table below it with a piece of plywood on it. I'd then set out all sorts of containers and apply point values to them based on difficulty (trash cans, buckets, paper cups, boxes). Each contestant would bounce 15 superballs from the second story window off the table and into the containers.

When it's all over and scores are tabulated we have a BONUS CHRIST-MAS WINNER. Prizes are "same value" gift cards (no higher than $25) to Target, Starbucks, Home Depot, and places my children have told me they like.

The "winner" gets to choose first, then second place chooses. Everyone gets the same value of prize.

When I started this years ago, I didn't know how it would go, but now it's part of our Christmas DNA. "We're doing Bonus Christmas, right Dad?" ask my 32, 30 and 28-year-old children and their spouses. I answer, "Yes, we are, children."

Doing "Bonus Christmas" slowed down Christmas Day. Often, after the breakfast is eaten and presents are open and it's only 10 a.m., families might be thinking, *"I wonder if there are any new movies playing at the theatres?"* Our family has done that. But we have to be careful about replacing hours of simply enjoying one another's company with staring vacantly at a giant screen. More introverted families might enjoy playing cards, dominos, a jigsaw puzzle, or going on a quiet walk. Still together, but less bustle and noise. In these activities you're still enjoying togetherness, just in a different way.

For many, the effort needed to practice *slowing* may be a radical shift in how you do life. It may mean pulling your children out of the many options for youth sports, after-school programs, children's theatre, dance and more. There's evidence that children are being denied the major avenue by which socialization occurs as they grow up: PLAY! Academic curricula once used in kindergarten are now being pushed down to the preschool level. It's "hurrying" the child. Preschool experts say that education's push for academics is not helping but actually hindering children from growing into well-adjusted human beings.

Do children need to participate in three sports every year? No!

Do children need down time where they aren't "accomplishing" anything, but simply playing? Yes!

Do adults need sections of time where they can simply "be" and not "do?" Yes!

Do couples need unrushed segments of time for in-depth conversation about how they are feeling, what's going on in their soul, and what's most on their mind? Lemme think: *Yes!*

Play is just as essential for adults as it is children.

I was a Young Life staff person for many years. We made play into an art form for teenagers. We found that fun broke down the walls of resistance to "matters of faith" in a huge way. Laughter brought down kids' defenses. When defenses are down, conversations go deeper and people are more open to consider the "God thing." Instead of figuring out ways to increase your child's productivity, teach them that you love to play. Parents don't always have to be in a "teaching mode." You can simply *play* with them. You'll be putting relational money in the bank and later on, you will have won the right to be heard. Play teaches people that you enjoy their presence simply for who they are, not what they can produce. So.......*play!*

In addition, *play* reveals the face of Jesus. Trying to modify someone's behavior to Christian tenets does not. Arrogantly declaring that Christians are *in* and everyone else is *out* because we have Jesus and they don't, does not reveal Jesus' heart and mind. Listing acceptable and unacceptable behaviors in order to make people feel ostracized does not reveal Jesus to people.

But when Christ-followers have fun, *that* catches folks off guard. They see we aren't *serious* all the time. Play teaches our children, family members, and friends that, while being a Christ-follower is a serious thing, it doesn't mean we can't have fun. Play slows us down enough so we can have fun and laugh at ourselves and not take ourselves so seriously. I've embarrassed myself often in the Bonus Christmas games. I believe it's helped tremendously for my children to see that being a Jesus-follower does not mean you have to become a *fun-killer* type person. So folks, I hereby give you permission to build PLAY into your life. Joy will pull your mind towards God faster than anything you've ever experienced before.

Slowing allows for unrushed segments of "play time."

3. Adopt SLOWING Vocabulary to Your Life

Cement a new vocabulary into your heart, soul and mind to counteract the culture's vocabulary of *speed, hurry, busyness,* and *noise!*

Incorporate words like: *strolling, dawdle, relish, cherish, treasure, loiter, amble, meander*, and *saunter*. As you do that, *see what God brings to your attention*. What if, in doing these slowing things, we might *learn to be astonished*: at a tree, a bird, a child, the ocean, a flower, your hand…and realize, God made all of it, not just to serve a function, but *simply for you to marvel at and enjoy*. Because you're slowing, you might ponder these things that are right in front of your eyes and you might sense God whispering, "You know, I made what you're looking at for you to enjoy. Not just to serve a function. It is a gift from Me to you. I love to bring a smile to your face."

4. Then…Practice the New Vocabulary

Saunter or dawdle somewhere. Name that place "my dawdling place." If you have the time to drive to a place that is life-giving to you—the beach, hills, mountains, desert, forest—do it! Wherever you go, ask God, "Bring to my attention what You'd like me to notice, relish, cherish or treasure," whether it's something you see, or something else that may be a pressing matter in your brain. Adopt a training regimen of loitering, ambling, and meandering. And simply look around. See what God brings to your attention! It could be something you see, or it could be something totally unrelated that He says to your spirit. Whatever it is, you have made yourself available to be spoken to by God. Chances are, there is something He'll communicate to you. If you slow down enough you will learn to be astonished.

5. Practice "Wasting" Time!

Our culture considers "wasting time" a mortal sin. I believe Jesus did a lot of what could have been called "wasting time." While Jesus walked from place to place—and while He wasn't doing the things that are recorded in the Bible—I wonder if, in His meanderings, He ended up noticing:

- A farmer planting seed.
- A fisherman throwing his nets.
- A woman sweeping a house.
- A shepherd herding his sheep through a gate.
- A farmer separating the wheat from the chaff…

…and turned each of them into a story (parable) about the love and grace of God, or the preciousness of people, or how life with God works.

Jesus' pace of doing life must have been (on several occasions) in the category of "wasting time." And while going slow and wasting time, He noticed these things and turned them into memorable stories about God, grace, heaven and hope.

6. Practice Personalized FUN!

At one point in my career as a pastor, I landed in a counselor's office suffering from the first of three "burn-outs" in my 30-year ministry career. Each burn-out was the result of doing very little (if any) self-care. If you are in the helping industry (paid or volunteer), this is probably the biggest danger you will face: ignoring your well-being for the sake of others. Sounds noble, but it's very dangerous.

One session the counselor asked me, "Craig, what do you do for fun?"

(Long period of silence.) "I don't really know."

"Why not?" he asked.

"Well, when I'm not doing 'pastor stuff' I'm helping my wife with our six, four, and two-year-old children. And after they are in bed, I'm in my office studying Greek and Hebrew so I can get my Master of Divinity Degree. Who has time for fun?"

Then he said, "Craig, let's say you had some time, what have you always *wanted* to do; not *needed* to do, but *wanted* to do?"

I said, "Learn to surf."

"What's stopping you?" he asked.

(Very long pause.) "I guess...me."

"That's right. You are not giving yourself permission to have fun; to do something that would bring you joy. Your life is all duty, obligation, service, and giving to others. In this lifestyle, what's the first thing you eliminate from your life?"

The answer was, *"Fun!"*

So, I started surfing. I slowed down my schedule of appointments and commitments and created space in my week for some fun. Here's what I discovered: Fun drew me to God. When I caught my very first wave and stood up and didn't fall, the thrill, the joy, the exhilaration caused me to scream, *"THANK YOU GOD!"*

I had to learn that God, my Father, was screaming with me, "Craig, I made that wave, in part, so you would be able to ride it, and I could watch you and cheer for you. My heart is full because you experienced some joy today. My son, I made you with that desire to surf. I celebrate you when you're surfing just as much, and maybe even more so, than when you're 'doing something for Me.' So Craig, I want you to have some *fun* simply because you're my child, and children have fun. Give yourself permission to have fun!"

So from then on, I did. And whenever I have fun doing anything (including surfing!), I not only get refreshed in my soul, but I experience God in a way that is different from serving, ministry and giving. I learned to receive fun! But I had to slow down enough to create space to do it.

41

Be Careful, You Good-Hearted People

Motivated by a heart for God; driven by a desire to help the poor, the hungry, the homeless, the mentally challenged, and dysfunctional families, good-hearted people care for others at the expense of caring for themselves. This is a formula for burn-out. Complicating matters for Christ-followers is a mindset of sacrificing oneself for Jesus' sake.

We forget that Jesus had "down time" (days of travel between towns, and purposeful retreats away from people to be alone with His Father). These were times when He was not "on" (having to be fully present to heal, teach, lead, listen, and deal with crowds). There is no record of what Jesus might have done strictly for the sake of having fun. But if he was fully-human as well as fully-God...well...humans have fun! Jesus must have had fun. Why? Fun refreshes the soul. Fun re-energizes us. Fun is *life-giving*, not *life-draining*. Jesus needed fun to refresh and re-energize Himself too! I wish I could have been there to see what He did for fun.

So, do you have some fun scheduled into your week? Your month? Your year? Do you hurry through vacations, feeling you have to keep a schedule even there? What are we teaching our children when we don't slow down to have fun? Is life all about duty and service and achieving and acquiring and getting ahead and increasing income? We are not "work automatons." When others label fun as a "wasting time" endeavor, will we ruthlessly battle our culture's bent towards constant production? Will we learn to rest in the truth that we are loved by God when we're not producing?

What's Stopping Us From Practicing Slowing!

So, who is or what is stopping you from giving yourself permission to take some baby steps into the practice of slowing? The only answer: YOU! Remember the word "ruthless." Be ruthless about combating hurry with *slowing*. Give yourself permission to carve out the time for strolling, wasting time, play and fun.

I guarantee you'll experience God along the way.

Final Practices To Try

1. Go on a *slow* walk. Look around and do some noticing. (See Chapter Five for more on *noticing.*)

2. Practice a period of time each week that others might call "wasting time" and try to *do* nothing—or to do something fun.

What's harder than sexual righteousness?
Rest righteousness!

- John Kossler, Radical Pursuit of Rest

Chapter 2: The Practice of BEING USELESS

AT THE END OF MY career as a senior pastor, I had a seizure and landed in the hospital for three days. After all the tests were done, the doctors concluded that it was caused by exhaustion, stress, and fatigue. When I came home from the hospital, I spent over a week mostly sleeping. My wife told me, "You're done being a pastor." She was right (as usual). I had worked myself to a point where I resented meetings, individual appointments, and interruptions. I had no energy in my emotional tank. I needed five months completely off of work, and when I started working again, I had to take on a completely different kind of career. My story is one of many stories of how men and women end their jobs by getting to this point of exhaustion. I neglected God's command to *be useless* on a regular basis. I neglected to *rest*.

"Non-Rest" Statistics

USA Today reports the following "non-rest" statistics:
- Thirty-five percent of employed adults say the internet, e mail, and cell phones have *increased* the amount of time they spend working.
- Forty-one percent of Americans did *not* take a single vacation day in 2015. Fifty-five percent did *not* use all of their vacation days.
- More than one third of employers require employees to work on Thanksgiving. Thirty-nine percent will require employees to work on Christmas Day or New Year's Day.

- Forty one percent of employers will have staff working on Labor Day.
- Unlike nearly every other first-world country, the U.S. offers no (or very little) paid leave for parents. New Zealand, France, Spain, and Russia are just some of the countries to offer at least 14 weeks of maternity leave…paid in full.
- Just to be fair, the U.S. isn't the most overworked country. Turkey wins that prize, with Mexico not far behind. The U.S. doesn't even make the top five. In 2014, we came in 16th (with our workers averaging about 34.4 hours of work per week).

Constant work is the behavior of someone who thinks everything depends on them. REST is the behavior of someone who looks to God to provide.

- Tim Chester, The Busy Christian's Guide to Busyness.[1]

Our culture assumes that vacation is the answer to busyness. Our society has adopted a pattern of 48 weeks of work and four weeks to rest (or for many people, only two). In other words, we are overworked for most of the year and then "binge rest" for two to four weeks. This is not how God made us to live. He made us to have a weekly pattern of work (six days) and rest (one day).[2]

There is a new drug called Provigil that takes away the need for sleep. It can keep you awake and alert for two days. Doctors aren't sure how it works. There have been no studies about its addictive or long term effects. Sales are over one billion dollars a year.

- The Secret Life of Sleep, quoted in Addicted to Hurry, by Kirk Byron Jones.

Denying ourselves sleep makes us appear more productive. There is an assumption in many Christian circles that it's godlier to get up early to pray than it is to sleep. Granted, the New Testament records that, on occasion, Jesus would get up early to pray. So, there are times when that may be needed, especially when facing challenging or important circumstances. We are told that saints of old rose at 5 a.m. to pray (forgetting that they went to sleep when it got dark).

Here's what happens to me when I rise early to pray: I get tired, fatigued, irritable, and selfish; and I'm more prone to sin on less sleep. People have different sleep needs, but I better have at least seven hours of sleep or I'm *crrrrrranky!* God made us to need sleep. People who think they can operate with little sleep are defying God's created order. God's first priority for a despondent Elijah was plenty of sleep and hearty meals (see I Kings 19:5-8). Next time someone makes you feel inadequate because of their early rising, think of Colossians 2:23:

Such regulations indeed have the appearance of wisdom, with their self-imposed worship, their false humility and harsh treatment of the body, but they lack any value in restraining sexual indulgence. (NIV)

Here's another one: "In vain you rise early and stay up late, toiling for food to eat—for he grants sleep to those he loves." Psalm 127:2 (NIV). The New Living Translation says, "It is useless for you to work so hard from early morning until late at night," and the ERV says, "The Lord provides for those he loves, even while they are sleeping."

Getting up early is a waste of time if you think you can use the extra time to achieve your goals, solve your problems, or control your life. Denying yourself sleep reveals a lack of trust in God.

We Have a Limited Capacity

The cell phone has a *limited* capacity. It can only hold so much information. It can only perform a few functions simultaneously. It has a limited battery life. When the battery is low it gives a warning and if I ignore the warnings, the cell phone doesn't work anymore.

It would be great to know and respect one another's capacity. Our phones help us understand our personal capacity. Our "battery" (energy level) needs to be re-charged. We have a finite capacity for storage and functionality. Different activities of life drain our "energy battery" at different rates. Figuratively, each of us is a brand of phone that is unique and operates differently.

So, we have a unique capacity level depending on our personality, experiences, and seasons of life. People and events are constantly draining us. Think of gas mileage on different types of cars and trucks. Some have great mileage, some only get 12 miles to the gallon. It depends on how you drive the vehicle as well. Like the cell phone, we have to re-charge or we'll shut down. Like a vehicle, we have to "gas-up" or we'll run out of energy.

How Hurry (and Busyness) Causes People to "Crash and Burn"

Senior Pastor of Willow Creek Community Church in Chicago, Bill Hybels, once said there are three dials on the dashboard of our lives:

1. The physical dial

2. The mental dial

3. The emotional dial

When he had a "crash and burn" experience, due to exhaustion, his counselor described the three dials listed above. Bill's *physical dial* was on "F" (Full). He ran regularly, lifted weights, and more. His *mental dial* was on "F" as well. He regularly read, studied, memorized, and meditated on biblical truth and on the writings of many authors on matters of leadership, the church, and connecting with God. He prayed often and regularly as he did ministry each day.

But, he confessed that he had completely ignored his *emotional dial* for years. He couldn't bring himself to take a day off. He was teaching in four services every weekend and teaching a different message at a mid-week service as well. That's two preparations and five deliveries of messages *per week!* Add to that all the responsibilities of a senior pastor: hiring, firing, and guiding staff; leading an elder team, working with volunteers, raising money, guiding a worship team, casting vision, encouraging, confronting, challenging, and more.

He found himself with a chronic low-grade anger and frustration when things didn't go well or the staff did not do their jobs. He had no patience. He had no energy to linger with people. He found it hard to listen to people's issues and struggles, simply because he had nothing to give them.

So, he landed in a counselor's office. He got some real help. He radically changed the way his church did ministry, and took up sailing, which was something that he was passionate about that helped enable him to "re-charge" emotionally. The elders of the church took responsibilities off his plate and delegated to others. He developed a "teaching team" to get relief from the relentless onslaught of Wednesdays and weekends.

His needle on his emotional dial started swinging to the right towards "FULL." He started to have margin in his life. The page of his day wasn't filled from top to bottom and side to side with never-ending responsibility. He started to have space in his schedule. He gave himself permission to do self-care. He took a day off. He started to pay close attention to the state of his soul and took steps to protect his own relationship with Jesus, his wife, and children. He let go of feeling responsible for other people's lives with Jesus.

Like Bill, many of us are completely out of touch with what they are feeling. (And that would be most men. They wouldn't know a feeling if it hit them.) Again, because our lives are in such a *hurry* and we're so *busy*, we don't give ourselves time and space to ponder what it is we might be feeling. In order to get in touch with our inner world we need to have space in our schedules—and those spaces need to be longer than 15 minutes.

Enrolling in the School of "Be-ing"

Having *space for God* means we need to have *time for God*. We have to enroll in the school of "*be-ing*." Most of us have graduated with honors from the school of "*do-ing*." Like Bill, we have a hard time embracing the truth that we are cherished and adored by God when we're not producing, achieving, or serving Him. Yet, He does cherish and adore us—no matter what. So much of having a healthy emotional state is having regular times when we *stop*: stop working, slaving, solving, servicing, and being obligated. Instead, we must schedule rest: in our day, our week, our month, and our year. Why don't we give ourselves permission to rest, stop, and recreate? We feel like "it all depends on me." A busy life has no room for a day off. And even if we take it, our fun is filled with busyness. Busyness results in hurried conversations. We want our children to talk faster so we can deal with it faster. We don't take time to "depth" (deepen) conversations or relationships because we have things to do.

By "depth-ing" I mean taking the time and making the effort to ask questions that go further than the surface level of conversation. Depth-ing helps move the conversation from sharing news to sharing feelings. This takes some intentional "question asking" on the part of the listener. For example, if someone shares about having a bad day, depth-ing is asking things like, "What was it about your day that made it bad?" After the person shares the facts, you could say, "Wow, how did that make you feel?" By being unhurried, we feel we can focus on the person in front of us, taking the time to make them feel really heard.

It is a sign forever between me and the people of Israel that in six days the Lord made heaven and earth, and on the seventh day He rested and was refreshed.

- Exodus 31:17, ESV (emphasis mine).

God knew that one of the first things human beings would neglect is *rest*. So, God created a "cease day" even for Himself (Genesis 1). Then, at the Exodus, with Moses and the gang, God *commanded* that rest be built into every week because we didn't stick with the model of creation. Believe it or not, the *Sabbath* (rest, ceasing labor) is the *first thing God declared to be holy*! If we go back to the creation account, we discover that the sum total of humanity's first full day on planet earth entailed the sole activity of resting (Gen. 1:26-2:3). Day one of life with God and with one another was not about getting anything done. It was an entire day of enjoying the new world God had just made.

If God rested, we certainly can. Jesus told us that God made this rest day for *humanity*. Unfortunately, as the "cease day" was practiced over the decades in ancient Israel, instead of bringing refreshment, it birthed fear. The "*stop* day" had morphed into a "what you could and could not do" sort of day.

Radically religious people devised an extensive set of rules to determine if someone was breaking the Sabbath (the "being useless" day). The rest day was now about avoiding certain behaviors that might be considered work. It had become about appeasing God, who was assumed to be holding a clipboard as He watched us, giving demerits for doing what was considered labor by the religious authorities. *Rest* had become a chore, not a gift.

> **Adultery is scorned, maybe even disciplined. Lust (think pornography) is shameful. But we hardly bat an eye when someone uses Sunday as they would any other day of the week.**[3]

When real *rest* happens, it can keep us from being seduced and assimilated by the world. God knows what's best for the people He created, and what's best is a rhythm of work and rest. The best thing for our lives, the best medicine for our well-being, is to take an entire day to cease doing, even doing for God. Instead God desires that we rest, sleep, savor, worship, enjoy creation, enjoy people, or whatever it is that recharges our emotional batteries, living into the truth that God didn't make us "human do-ings" but "human be-ings." Rest's purpose is receiving, not necessarily giving. It is a day to gain perspective regarding anything: your relationship with God, your parenting, your marriage, your pace of life, your job, your well-being, your direction in life, or simply a day in which to have some genuine FUN!

Giving Yourself Permission to *Take* Rest

Most Americans need to feel "productive." At the end of our day, we measure our worth by what we have done: tasks accomplished, work hours put in, errands run, or housework done.

The most important step in experiencing rest is to give ourselves permission to take it. We need to *embrace* rest. We have to be convinced of the need for rest. Then, we have to carve out the time in our weekly schedules for rest and protect it with our lives, because our lives—our vibrant, healthy lives—depend on it. We have to carve out small, medium, and larger sections of time for *uselessness*. When we rest, we're useless. Will we give ourselves permission to be useless for periods of time, even a whole day? Creating space for rest is just as important as scheduling meetings, appointments, and talking with a friend. In order to do this, we have to be *ruthless* with our time and schedules.

Rest: Doing "Life-Giving" Things

Rest unplugs us from our hurried lives. By taking rest, we are declaring, "Rest is for life-giving endeavors that fit my unique make-up."

"Life-giving" is a state of being where you feel energized, alive, excited, and even happy. You know a certain activity is life-giving because you smile automatically when you do it. You feel a sense of joy in your heart. "Life-draining" activities are things that, when you are done with them, you want to take a nap because you're exhausted. These activities drain energy from you at a fast rate. It doesn't mean they are wrong or unnecessary. We all have things in our lives that we simply *have* to do. But life-giving activities are the "want-to" choices we make for our well-being.

In other words, give yourself permission to do "self-care."

Self-Care is never a selfish act – it is simply good stewardship of the only gift I have, the gift I was put on earth to share with others…me! Anytime we can listen to our true self and give it the care it requires, we do it not only for ourselves, but for many others whose lives we touch.

- Parker Palmer

Each of us must experiment to find out what brings us "life-giving energy." Our "thing" will be different than someone else's. The temptation will be to do what others are doing without doing ruthless self-examination on how God wired *you* up. You are not the same as your spouse or your friends. What gives them joy might not be what gives you joy. And when you find out what it is that truly gives you a sense of rest, a replenishing of energy, *lean into that*. Do *that* more often than anything else. He's made you to get rest in *that* particular way because He wired you up that way.

So What Is It that Recharges Your Emotional Batteries?

Off-road vehicles, fixing stuff, laying on the beach and reading a novel, eating at your favorite sandwich shop, playing with your dog, cooking or baking, sailing, road biking, gardening, watercolor painting, calligraphy, lying in a hammock, wake boarding, fishing, blowing bubbles, juggling, flying a kite, swimming, or rollerblading. We have to become convinced that God enjoys our play as much as our work, maybe even more so because His dream is that we'd enjoy the life He's given us, not just the duty He's given us.

My "being useless" day will look different than yours. The important thing is to discover and then craft *your* ideal "cease day." When someone asks you for some time with you on *your* Sabbath day, you can say, "Sorry, I'm booked at that time." They don't need to know what that "booking" is. You need to guard your rest with your life, or burn-out, irritability, chronic low-grade fatigue, and resentment will be your unwanted companions.

An Example of Individualized Rest

When I marry couples, the first time I meet with them mostly involves listening to their story. I ask about their career path, their families of origin, how they met, the engagement story and what character traits they appreciate about each other.

Two years ago, a groom started sharing his story. In over 40 years of ministry I have never heard a more brutal story of every category of abuse and neglect. The couple took me up on my offer of free premarital counseling for as many times as they wished. They lived in Chicago so we Skyped each time. One of the results of this man's story of physical, mental, emotional, and psychological abuse was a strong need to please his fiancée, so he worked hard at his job. He worked long and hard seeking to receive a "well done" from his fiancée as often as she would give it because he never got one from his family of origin.

At one point, I asked both of them what they did for rest. Blank stares. After pondering for a bit, he said, "I've always loved playing soccer."

I said, "What's stopping you from joining a recreation league and having some weekly fun with a sport that makes you feel good?"

He got the point.

Then I asked his fiancée that same thing. She said, "I've always loved sewing." I responded to her like I did her fiancé.

At the time, I didn't know if they'd actually do it. But one year later, they happened to be in town and called me to have lunch. When we met I asked them how the "rest thing" was going. Lo and behold, they were both doing the two things that truly relaxed them and energized them.

They were resting while they were doing something. That counts because it's how God made them to get rest.

An Image of Our Lives: A Wagon Wheel

A picture of a healthy life can be drawn with an Old West wagon wheel. Imagine the hub and the spokes and the rim that rolled along the ground. If the hub was weak or off-center, the wheel would look like one of those clown wheels that makes the ride anything but smooth. A wheel with the proper center, and spokes attached to the hub and rim, rolls along well.

Think of the hub as the central thing in your life. Think of the spokes as all the different components you have in your life. Think of the rim as how your life connects with the world. Key question: What do we put in the center of the wheel? What is strong enough to bear the weight of all the spokes? Imagine the spokes being things like:

- you
- your spouse
- your children
- your career

- money
- fun
- church
- volunteering
- any cause you are passionate about.

What is a hub that is strong enough to make sense of and give meaning to all those things and more? ANSWER: anything other than God at the hub is inadequate to hold the spokes in place. Anything other than Jesus as the hub is not strong enough to give meaning to marriage, parenting, handling money, and more.

Some people put their family as the hub. Some put their career in the center, or their spouse, or money. Most put themselves at the hub. But none of those things are big enough, strong enough, and pervasive enough to hold the spokes in place. Life goes well when Jesus has all the aspects of our lives tied into Him; when we invite Him to be the center of our lives. Anything else in the center of our lives will let us down and disappoint us. We ask too much of those things when we ask them to give our whole life meaning. They are not strong enough to help us make sense of why we were made and what gives our lives genuine purpose.

Why is this important with regards to rest? When we invite Jesus to be "the center," we learn what is best for us from Him (and not from the other "hub options" like ourselves, our spouse, and our children). If what's best for us comes from Jesus, and He orders, "You need *rest*," we must submit ourselves to His wisdom for us. His wisdom says, "You must rest one day in the course of your week. I'm the hub. I'm the center. I know how life works better than anyone. I created life. I created you. Now, take me up on my formula for a healthy life for you. Keep that 'cease day' holy. Guard it with your life!"

A Healthy View of "Being Useless"

The key question is, "What refreshes you?"

55

Here's God's instruction:

It is a sign forever between me and the people of Israel that in six days the Lord made heaven and earth, and on the seventh day he rested *and was refreshed*.

- Exodus 31:17, ESV (emphasis mine).

Wow! Even God rested. He worked hard, and then He ceased His creation work.

What refreshes you is now the guideline for which activities you engage in on your "cease day." The religious people of Jesus' day made the Sabbath about rule-keeping, thus making people more nervous, forcing them to work (again) at keeping these rules. This was not rest and it certainly wasn't refreshing.

So the questions become, "What's *refreshing* for you? What's fun and energizing for you? What's the right kind of rest for you? What is it that recharges your emotional batteries?" You'll have to do some research on yourself to conclude which things bring you joy. Just to start, it might be a good exercise to name three activities that refresh you.

Here are some more useful questions to consider:

- Do *passive* activities refresh you? This would be things like sleeping, napping, or reading a novel.
- Do *active* activities refresh you? This would include things like jogging, biking, surfing, hiking, playing outdoor games, pick-up basketball, water skiing, painting, drawing, or sketching. (CAUTION: if any of these feel like an "obligation," it's not Sabbath day stuff.)
- Do *relational* activities re-energize you? Barbeques, card games, Super Bowl parties, coffee with friends. My wife returns from some time with her friends and she can't get to sleep. I return from time with people and I'm done.
- Do *private* activities bring you a sense of experiencing God? Do you get a sense of "rest" by being alone? I can do extended time alone and be happy as a clam. I'm talking days, not just hours. Parents can

model for their children that life will go on without work, without their cell phone, without an agenda.

The purpose of any of these "being useless" activities is to create enough "pause" in our week to think about what matters, and what matters draws our hearts and minds to Jesus. I find that when I surf, I am automatically thinking of Jesus, thanking Him for the opportunity, praising Him for creating waves, in part, for me to enjoy. I have grown to sense that God is smiling and cheering for me when I catch a wave, even though I'm not "producing" for Him.

Where's Church in All This?

Besides rest, God asked us to *remember* on the "being useless" day. He orders us to remember that every heartbeat, every breath, and every step is a gift from Him. Jesus commands us to remember who paid the debt for our moral failures on the Cross. He tells us to remember that He's alive and well because He's resurrected from the dead. We are commanded to remember who holds our lives, the world and all of history in His hands.

Attending and being involved in a church can keep us mindful of these things that really matter. Participating in the Lord's Supper is a constant reminder of the most important thing Jesus did: He gave His body and blood for our sin. He went so far as to be tortured and murdered unjustly. He was willing to pay the debt we could not pay by our good behavior. Jesus bought us back with His life. We now know we are loved by God. Jesus is the bridge between us to God. We have a restored relationship with Him when we take that step of faith to entrust, yield, and submit our lives to Him. We are to remember all of that.

How do we get reminded of all this? What causes us to reflect on all this? Church helps. Therefore, showing up at church is important. And, the church has the responsibility of providing the atmosphere where Jesus can be experienced. If Jesus is the hope of the world and the church is the vehicle entrusted to make that known in a compelling and attractive way, then church better not be boring. Jim Rayburn, the founder of Young Life, the high school ministry to unchurched teenagers, coined a motto for the staff, "It's a sin to bore people with the gospel." He insisted that every time we gathered teens together, a 15-minute message must be challenging, understandable, and applicable to everyday life. I never forgot that. Church should be interesting, it should touch people's emotions, it should be fun and understandable.

What's Your Job in This "Rest Thing?"

We have our responsibility and so does the church. If we are both doing our job, then *remembering* what matters most in our lives happens. We end up remembering important questions like:

- For whom am I living? Myself or Jesus and people?
- Whom do I ultimately serve? My own agenda or Jesus' agenda?
- What is the guiding principle of my life? Self-fulfilment or serving? Taking or giving?
- What's going on in my heart and mind? Thoughts and feelings of guilt? Of disappointment in myself? Resentment? Anger? Gratitude? Safety? Concern? Worry? Am I bringing this all to my God who desires to not only hear me but also take action to help? Or am I looking to solve my own issues because I'm a smart person?

So, church matters. Being in a small group matters. Reading and studying the Bible matters. Prayer matters. Because all of this causes us to pause and remember what ultimately matters.

What are some ideas for incorporating rest into your week, even your day?

Ideas for Resting

1. A fast from virtual connection.

(Fasting is denying something from your life in order to focus your attention on experiencing God's presence *more*). This might also be called: *The Practice of Unplugging or Disconnecting.*

A friend of mine was lamenting the fact that her teenage daughter was always texting on her phone. He came upstairs to say good night and she was furiously texting away. "Who are you texting at 10:00 p.m. at night?" he asked her.

"Dad, I'm saying goodnight to all of my friends."

He thought, "Really? Is that necessary? Does this happen every night?"

"Yes, there's only 20 or 30 of them."

We'll discuss the cell phone when we get to the section on distraction, but suffice it to say, the cell phone does not give us rest. In fact, it is a relentless *interruption* to rest. What if you turned it off whenever you're meeting with someone, having family time, or having a backyard barbeque with friends? Is every text so important that it has to be answered immediately?

> **Digital technology has turned our world into one where we are never alone and always on the job. Digital culture has broken down the natural boundaries that used to exist between work and rest. All we need to do in order to pursue rest is disconnect from the digital world.**[4]

Whatever day your Sabbath day is, imagine what it would be like without texting, Twitter, phone calls, surfing the net, or Facebook. What if you used six hours to do what really recharges your emotional batteries, without interruptions?

2. A television fast.

The average amount of time the average American spent consuming media of any kind (TV, surfing the web, using an app on your phone, Face-Time, listening to radio) was *nine and a half* hours per day in 2015. And in 2016, it's up to 10 hour and 40 minutes per day! Ouch!

It will take a huge, intentional effort to push back on those statistics. Electronic media is having more influence per day on our children than all their schooling and parents' parenting combined!

Like you, I have some favorite shows I like to watch. But a good case could be made that I have *too many* favorite shows. Some authors suggest that families have a TV fast for a week and substitute board games, conversation, recreational reading, or writing to the children you might be sponsoring through World Vision or Compassion International. At the end of the week, talk amongst yourselves. "Did you miss it? Was it hard to do at first? Did you find yourself not knowing what to do with yourself? Do you end up liking it more than you thought?" Maybe you will end up doing this once a quarter. You might set aside one day a week for a television fast and instead make it "family night" or "couple's night" or "exercise night" or "board game night" or "reading night." Be as creative as you wish.

I understand that most of you reading these words work very hard at your jobs and "jelling" in front of the TV is a way of "checking out" and escaping the relentless responsibilities of life. I do this too. I am not advocating NO TV forever. Some advocate this, but I would simply suggest monitoring your amount of TV viewing time. Is TV time replacing people time, parents with children time, or friends-with-friends time? And ask yourself the question, "Is the amount of TV I'm watching 'lifegiving'? Is TV really re-charging my emotional batteries, helping me to get more fired up about life and what matters? Or am I just lazy about doing what is really energizing to me when I have free time?" Honestly, I'm that lazy guy lots of time. Like you, I'm a work in progress.

I'd suggest tackling *one* media mechanism at a time. One evening might be a "no cell phone" night. Another night might be a "no-TV" night, substituting TV with some form of people interaction. Set a half-hour alarm on your phone when surfing the web or FaceTiming and then STOP! Find an alternative to electronic contraptions, like working out, reading, or taking up a hobby. The point: we have to find a way to halt the domination of media, cell phone, and online activity that are consuming the precious time we have been given on earth by God. Most likely, TV does not provide *true rest* for us. We must find some other means to find rest for our hearts, minds and souls.

3. Practice mini-moments of uselessness.

The one minute *mini-uselessness* break. As I mentioned earlier, begin the habit of *stopping for a couple of minutes* throughout your day simply to remind yourself that God is with and within you; to your right and left; above and below you; in front and back of you. You might whisper a prayer, "God, I am loved by you. You are here. Help me to embrace that for myself."

You might remind yourself that He is attentive to all that you're thinking and feeling. You could set your cell phone to chime every half hour to signal this practice for you. When it goes off you might ask God, "Is there anything You want to whisper to me, show me, or assure me about?" Maybe you might pray, "Jesus, I'm grateful that I'm your cherished one. I am a treasure to you, not a problem. Help me to live into that."

(Note: this practice is suggested for families with young children, because in that situation any sort of lengthy break never really happens.)

The 10-15 minute *mini-uselessness break*. Maybe you already have scheduled breaks throughout your day. In that case, practice "turning off" the speedometer on your day and just *stop*. Close your eyes, and when all the agendas come to mind simply think, "Ok, that's one thought. I'm going to put that aside for now and rest from that." You could have a pad of paper next to you and write down the to-dos that come to mind, then lay it aside and continue to rest. (Again, this might be most helpful with parents of young children because your "ceasing time" at home will most likely be filled with family stuff.)

Take a *power rest* in which you remain silent and focus on God's love and grace for you, while being dead still. If you fall asleep, that's what you needed.

Sleep a healthy length of time: 6½–8 hours. Allow yourself naps.

The *most of the day* uselessness.

Start small and move to bigger. Start with a six hour cease/stop day and move it towards a sunset-to-sunset Being Useless *Day. The guiding principle for how to incorporate this into your weekly schedule: SOMETHING IS BETTER THAN NOTHING.* Don't feel like you have to start with an entire day. Start small and let it grow.

A Note to Parents with Families of
Young or Teenaged Children

I'm a father of three, so there was a season of life where finding time, space, quiet, and rest was hard. At times, I felt like I'd let God down. I'd go days without thinking of Him. Weekends were filled with soccer practices, school plays, kids' friends over to play, and endless car transportation taking them hither and yon. When someone mentioned rest, I laughed. When the children were infants and toddlers, the constant lack of sleep produced what I called a "chronic low-grade fatigue" where I never felt completely rested.

How do you remove yourself from the "being useful" game in this section of life that can go on for at least 10-15 years? Pastors get paid to have blocks of time to connect with God, but the average Joe and Joan don't have that luxury. The practices I've described in this chapter are ones that families and parents can do in the middle of this era of life. God's *not* disappointed in you because you haven't had time to read your Bible or pray with any sense of a coherent thought. He knows your situation and loves you in the middle of it. In fact, God never expects us to be at some other place other than where we are now. I'm not talking a geographic place, but the place where we are with our minds, hearts, souls and life situation. In other words, what's most on your mind is where God wants to meet you, even if that "place" is trying to get your child potty-trained. We can find rest when hurry and busyness are pushing us. It may just take a little intentionality on our part.

Some Questions and Exercises for You

1. What are three activities that "refresh" you? (Print out the answer; put it on your home page; look at it often. Take steps to put it into your week.)

2. What tends to keep you from taking time to do refreshing things for yourself? Are there any downsides to the type of rest you are drawn to? (For example, if golf is your refreshment, the downsides might be that it takes many hours, costs a fair amount of money, and your spouse has to take care of the kids for a long period of time.)

3. If you actually practiced a "Being Useless Day," what would be difficult for you to stop doing in terms of striving, earning, producing, and preparing? Why?

I say to myself, "The Lord is my portion
(the One who I have confidence in),
therefore I will *wait* for Him."

- Lamentations 3:24, (TNIV), emphasis and paraphrase mine.

Chapter 3: The Practice of WAITING

We Hate to Wait

WHETHER IT'S:

- waiting to get into an examination room in a doctor's office
- waiting at a traffic signal
- waiting in line at Costco checkout
- waiting for paint to dry
- waiting for your car to be ready while being repaired
- waiting for medical test results…

…we hate to wait.

In the movie, *The Princess Bride*, the Spanish swordsman Indigo Montoya is waiting at the top of a sheer cliff while Westley, the hero, slowly climbs up. At one point Indigo says, "I do not suppose you could speed things up?"

Wesley answers, eventually, "I'm afraid you'll just have to wait."

Indigo mumbles, "I hate waiting."

This is a summary statement of our culture. We hate to wait. Waiting disrupts our desire for speed. Waiting interrupts our "hurry" state of being.

We get frustrated when someone doesn't text back immediately, or emails aren't answered for a day. Some people think that waiting for the microwave to cook something takes too long. We hate that it takes so long for our laptop to boot up; we hate how long it takes for something shipped to arrive at our home.

You probably hate to wait…so do I.

I have to get my skin checked twice a year for skin cancer. In the past three years, I've waited an average of 45 minutes to get into an examination room. At one appointment, I waited over an hour, was finally put in an examination room, and then waited another 20 minutes. Finally, I opened the door in my boxers (which they'd asked me to strip down to) and loudly spoke down the hall, "Is anyone coming in here in the near future?" The doctor stuck her head out with a bite of a sandwich in her mouth and said, "Oh my gosh, I forgot you were in there." Can you say, "Ticked off"?

At one point, I told the receptionist about the constant pattern of extreme lateness on behalf of this skin doctor. Her answer was, "The best thing to do is schedule yourself for the first appointment of the day at 9:00 a.m., then you'll get in on time." I thought, "First, there was no apology. Second, it's now up to me to schedule an appointment when it's convenient for them, not me." Needless to say, I'm looking elsewhere for another skin guru—one who sees my time as being as valuable as his or hers is.

Believe it or not, real, live people from the Bible hated waiting too. Over and over again, this question is voiced:

"How long, O Lord; How long?"

Did you know that in Revelation (the last book in the Bible) there's a snapshot of heaven in which all the Christ-followers who've been killed for their faith are all together asking in one loud voice, "HOW LONG, O LORD?" In other words, "How long are you going to let this world spin out of control? How long are You going to let the powers of the world kill Christ-followers? How long are you going to let evil influence people, leaders, cities, and countries? How long, O Lord? HOW LONG?"

I am not exactly a pillar of patience when it comes to waiting for things like test results that will tell me if someone I love has cancer. The medical profession can be as slow as a slug, in some cases. Parents wonder, "When is my child going to grow out of this stage?" And need I mention that young children want everything NOW?

At one point, when each of my daughters turned 13, a switch went off inside them and suddenly I felt like I was living with two strangers. I asked my wife, "Whose children are these and where did our real ones go?" For about four years of their adolescence, it seemed like I'd lost my daughters. I can say the same thing about my son. In each case, I had to wait for my children to mature and grow into adulthood. Waiting for that to happen was not easy. Karen and I had to deal with bad behavior choices, hurtful words, and snippy attitudes while we waited.

It makes you wonder how God feels, waiting for us grown-ups to actually grow up. My wife, a preschool director, often asks parents, "Why do we expect adult behavior in a two-year-old when we sometimes do the same behavior as the two-year-old?" Does God feel, "Wow! That was really immature for your age!" Maybe it was. But instead of demeaning and punishing us, He chooses to wait, thinking, "Okay, we have some more work to do in that area of your life. Let's stay with this for a while. I'll work with and within you so that the good, God-like behavior becomes a natural response for you. In the meantime, I'll wait."

Why Waiting Is a Spiritual Practice to Combat Hurry

Why is waiting a spiritual practice? We aren't really *doing* anything, just *being* in each moment while waiting for *God* to do something. It doesn't seem we're accomplishing anything when we're waiting. We don't have much to show for it afterwards. What if someone asked us, *"What avenue of connecting with God do you find yourself in these days?"*

"Well," we'd say, "I'm just waiting."

I wonder if the unspoken response might be, "What's that accomplishing?

67

You're not really *doing* anything." But, in my opinion, we're doing plenty!

Why does God make us wait?

- Is it because He doesn't want us to see Him as simply a genie in a bottle?
- Is it because He wants us to experience delayed gratification?
- Is He using the "waiting situation" to teach us patience, or some other virtue?
- Is He testing whether we will love Him when we don't get exactly what we want exactly when we want it and in exactly the way we want it?

I don't know. I wonder if God waits to answer us in situations in which we wouldn't like His answers. Would we really like His answers to questions like:

- Why did You let my son die of brain cancer?
- Why did You not stop my spouse from cheating?
- Why did You allow my boss to fire me?
- Why do you not stop earthquakes, tsunamis, and people shooting people in schools, churches, and airports?
- Why did you allow Hitler to gain power and kill millions of Jews?

Near the end of my time as a Senior Pastor, a 19-year-old boy started getting headaches. When they didn't stop for five days and they increased in pain, his parents took him to get x-rayed. The results: three tumors in his brain. One was able to be taken out. The others were inoperable. Treatments didn't work. He died six months later. I stood by his bedside as he died and then helped with a small service with the parents and family over his dead body. Many, if not thousands of people prayed for him, asking God for healing. We waited. He died.

We tend to think of waiting as "waiting until." Waiting until is usually a time of antsy impatience, muttering "C'mon, c'mon." In other words, we feel like waiting is just enduring. Granted, it is partly that. So when the

Bible writes, "Wait on the Lord," (Psalm 27:14, KJV), it intends more than knotted-up, anxious, clock-watching impatience. It means something more like "standing on" God. It means yielding to Him, depending on Him, and trusting that He will never lose His grip on us (or people we care about who are in crisis). So, in response we are to "Be still, and know that [He is] God" (Psalm 46:19, NLT).

Waiting and Never Seeing the Answer to Our Prayers

Sometimes we wait for years and a situation or an issue is seemingly never resolved. One day in a class I was taking, a seminary professor shared that he'd been praying for his son to take even a small step toward investigating who Jesus is and toward the whole Christ-following thing. He told us that his son had actually gone to a church service recently. The professor had been praying for him for 30 years.

Sometimes we even die before a situation is resolved. I know many parents who died and their prayers for their children were not answered while they waited. Couples pray for their marriage to come back from the brink. Divorce eventually happens while they waited for God to act. Some ask for employment. Some ask for a child to recover from an addiction. Some ask for a potential spouse to come their way. They wait. And it doesn't happen. What's up with that?

What is God Up To in Making Us Wait?

Answer #1: I don't know.

Answer #2: Maybe He's using waiting to increase our *trust* in Him, deepen our *love* for Him, and not necessarily for *what* He can do for us. Maybe His ultimate dream is that we would love Him for Him. Maybe in waiting, we grow in ways we never would have without having to wait.

Imagine a marriage in which each partner only stays in the relationship for what the other can *do* for them. If the one spouse doesn't do what the other expects or wants, then they both bail. What happened to, "for richer for poorer, in sickness and in health"? Will spouses love each other to the end when one of them faces Alzheimer's, dementia, paralysis, cancer, disabilities, or senility? Will partners hang in there while they wait for cancer to take their life away? Will they wait not just days or months, but years?

Bruce was a Junior High Principal for years. He married Loreene when they were quite young. After 50 years of marriage, Loreene started to forget things, then slowly slipped into Alzheimer's. For nine years, Bruce took care of her: fed her, bathed her, dressed her, talked to her, helped her until eventually he wasn't physically capable anymore of doing everything she needed. But even after that, he visited her for hours while she was bedridden in a nursing facility. He'd take her for walks in her wheelchair while he walked with a cane. They'd sit by a fountain and he'd tell her stories of their children, their friends, and past events.

Soon, she couldn't talk. You could tell she was no longer "there." But Bruce didn't give up. He continued to see her for most of the day, simply to be with her, to be present to her. After nine years of waiting for the inevitable, Loreene passed from this earth to the arms of Jesus in heaven.

Bruce is one of my heroes. His monumental heart of love and tenderness to Loreene, who eventually became a woman he didn't know, was colossal. He *waited* in hope that a miracle might happen. But it didn't. He still waited, and while he waited, he served, loved, endured, hung in there, and was completely "others oriented." He really was doing what Jesus would do if He were in his place. He was Jesus incarnate to Loreene.

Bruce waited. Loreene died. His faith wasn't destroyed. In fact, he felt it was an honor to care for her to the end. He dreamed of Loreene dancing on the streets of heaven...healed...whole...happy. Bruce hung on to *hope* while he waited.

Waiting is Practicing Hope

In a letter to a church, Paul wrote these words:

"[Love] always trusts, always *hopes*, always perseveres"
- I Cor. 13:7, NIV (emphasis mine).

This means that when we invite Jesus to form in us a heart that reflects His heart, we will hang onto the truth that God can be trusted. Hope is not a wasted endeavor, because we're trusting Jesus while we wait. We hang in there when we don't get what we want in the timing we want. Trusting and hoping is not easy when people we love die. It's hard to persevere in believing that God is still good when tragedy comes our way.

This is "varsity Christ-following." This is not "Screw you, Jesus, because you didn't do what I wanted." This is "I trust You Lord, because I know you are good, loving, and gracious. I will not quit when I have to wait for what I want. And even if I never get what I'm asking for, and I have to wait to the end and still not see what I wish for, I will still follow you."

Can you see now, why waiting is a spiritual practice of the highest order? In waiting, we may not have the energy to read our Bibles or even pray more than, "God help me." Because most of the time, waiting is *not* about days, weeks or years. *It's about hope.*

Hoping doesn't mean we can't express our raw emotions to God. A heart full of hope can still say things like:

- "I am broken Lord. I can't even pray. I can barely get out of bed. But I'm still here."
- "God, I don't see any purpose or goodness in this, but I still trust you."
- "God, I'm angry at you. What were you thinking? This is just crappy."
- "God, how much more do you think I can stand?"
- "Jesus, what are you doing? What's going on? Are You really good?"

I had these questions about Loreene. I had these questions about that

19-year-old with the brain tumor. I still do. The parents of that teenager could barely get out of bed for weeks after he died because they were so devastated.

What's the point of God having us *wait*:

- for a prayer to be answered?
- for a sign that God is working in someone's faith journey?
- for any sign that recovery from addiction is happening?
- for a spouse to change a behavior that's threatening their marriage?
- for an autistic child to be able to speak their first word?

What's the point of waiting for all this?

ANSWER: *At least as important as the things we wait for, is the work God wants to do IN us as we wait.* [1]

Parents have dreams for their children. Children have dreams for their parents. Friends have dreams for their friends. Lots of those dreams have to do with wanting God to be discovered and embraced by those we love. What happens when those dreams don't come true in the timing we're hoping for… or when they never come true? We can get stuck in these questions and not realize that God is always doing "reconstruction" in *our* hearts, minds, and souls towards further and increasing Christ-likeness. As we witness a loved one go down the road of tragedy, rebellion, or dumb choices, God is doing something in us while all that is going on. In all these situations, I need to increase my trust factor in God that He has those people in His hands. *And my job is to pray and wait.*

There's a phrase in the Bible:

"Rejoice in the *hope* of the glory of God!"[2] In other words, we will be revealed as having a glory just like God, because God is doing a work *in* us while we *wait*.

I Peter 1:7 says it this way: "*Our faith* (trust in God's trustworthiness) is *gold* that must be purified by *fire*" (my paraphrase).

That's what waiting is about: *gold* (that's the infinitely precious *you*) refined and purified by *fire* (the tough things that come our way). Long-enduring and waiting faith is *gold*. Fire refines precious gold. Suffering is fire for our souls. There is an anguish in waiting for God to keep His promises. What is He doing while we wait? He is *making our character pure*; meaning, He's forming us into people who know what really matters in this life. He's shaping us into people that increasingly reflect His own character.

To wait graciously requires two virtues: *humility* and *hope.*

Humility

Humility comes from a firm conviction, belief, and then a living out of this truth: He is God, I am *not*. He is the creator, I am the created one. Who am I to think I know what He's thinking? His thoughts aren't my thoughts. They are *way higher* than mine. His ways, methods, and timing are not what I would do. Why? Because His ways, methods, and timing are His. Once again, He's a lot smarter than I am.

**We exist for God's sake. God does not exist
for our sake.** *(See Romans 11:36.)*

Only the humble can wait with grace. Why? Because only the humble know they have no demands they can lay on God and this world. They know life is a gift and not a right. Humility is having a sober, clearheaded grasp of the place we occupy in God's world. We are His valued, cherished master-pieces. We are all on level ground with kings and presidents, all-star athletes and Nobel Prize winners. Who are all of those famous people in God's world? Another created person like us. In God's presence we are all on level ground.

The humble know that each cellular transfer of oxygen into the blood-stream is a gift from God. Each day is a Christmas present from Him. The humble yield to God's great power and wisdom and they wait on God. While we wait, God invites us to pour out our frustration, anger, disappointment, bitterness, and sadness in unedited prayers. The world hates waiting. Waiting gets *no applause* from the world! But still we wait.

Hope

To wait graciously also requires *hope…*

Hope is essential to waiting. Why wait unless there is something worth waiting for? The world reasons that since there is no eternal *hope* to wait for, why wait for anything else?

Christ-followers can fall prey to this "no hope" thinking. We may pay lip service to *humility* and *hope*, but when it comes to how we deal with our difficult marriage, failing health, or a bleak professional future, we live as though there is no tomorrow that shines with God's promises. We act as though there is only the here and now. We forget that *ultimate healing* of any kind is in *heaven*.

Two Old Testament Believers Who Waited

Let's look at two people, of many in the Old Testament, who had to *wait*: Abraham and Job. They each display waiting at its best and its worst.

Abraham

Abraham, at age 75, was told by God that through him, hundreds of thousands of people would eventually form a nation. God chose him to be the start of that nation. Then God invited Abraham to look at the stars at night. When he did, God said, "That's not even close to how many people will end up following me and yielding their life to Me." At the time, there was nobody to follow in Abraham's footsteps because Sarah couldn't bear children. Abraham was 66 when God told him about the stars. Waiting for decades for this baby boy to come only made it harder for Abraham to believe even one star would happen, let alone hundreds of thousands.

Circumstances being what they were, Abraham struggled with hope; hope that he would eventually have a son to continue the family heritage. God waited until Sarah was 90 years old to enable her to get pregnant. Abraham was 99. When Abraham was 100 and Sarah 91, they became parents for the first time. I know…weird. But I think God waited so long to give them a son so that there was no way they could say, "We did this."

Abraham and Sarah waited 25 years for God to come through on His promise of a son. Abraham's struggle was with hope. Will God follow through on His promise? Could it really be true that Sarah will have a son when she's 91? That seems like a forlorn hope...but it happened.

Job

Job's struggle was with *humility*. The man had everything. And God allowed it to be taken away. He felt that God was being unfair. What had he done wrong? In his mind, nothing. He demanded an audience with God Himself. So Job waited with a heart of "God owes me," a heart of "I didn't deserve that."

He felt he could straighten God out on a thing or two. He felt that God owed him an explanation as to why all the tragedy came his way. "Why were all my children killed, all my possessions taken, and I'm left with nothing but heartache?" Job felt he'd done nothing to deserve this, so he decided to tell God that he was owed an explanation to the "why did this happen" question. After all, he was a great man.

See the lack of humility. God comes on the scene at the end of the story and asks Job a series of questions that only God could answer, like, "Who created weather, Job? Who made the sun, Job?" Job's arrogance and ego quickly melted into a puddle of humility. God won't answer Job's "why" questions because He doesn't have to and because most likely Job wouldn't understand the answers. He learned humility.

Abraham and Job learned at the hands of the Good Teacher: God Himself. There is no cheating when it comes to learning to wait. There is no article entitled "Ten Easy Ways to Learn to Wait." If we're going to learn we simply must...*wait!*

But While We Practice Waiting...

What are two character traits that are increasingly formed in us while we WAIT? *Patience* and *Endurance.*

1. *Love is Patient* (I Corinthians 13:4). Maybe you've heard this opening

75

statement of the greatest description in history of what real love looks like in real life. When you are called on to wait, for anything, it will require patience. And we don't live in a patient society. We live in a "hurry" society.

God is constantly forming Christ-followers into a reflection of Him. How patient is Jesus? Pretty patient, but even He once said something like, "Man, how long is it going to take before you people 'get it' about the whole 'God-thing'?" In saying that, Jesus gave us permission to complain about how long things are taking. We can say to God, "Ahhhh, any time now God. Any time." We can say, "God, this has gone on too long. Do something for crying out loud."

But, even while we are invited to cry, whine, complain and demand, God may still make us wait, for His own good reasons (which we'll never know). But one thing can't help but happen: *We will learn patience. We will learn to wait on God's timing. Or we'll simply walk away from God.*

Patience as a character trait can be practiced all the time by doing things like:

- Waiting in the longest checkout line
- Waiting in a waiting room for the doctor
- Waiting in traffic.

But the patience we're talking about here is long-term patience, and there are no tricks to going through this. It simply must be gone through.

2. *Love endures all things* (I Corinthians 13:7). Love sees the long view, yet our culture lives in the short view. But it takes time to wait on God with a mindset to grow into the type of love-characteristics that God possesses. Caring for and waiting for a loved one to pass away takes gargantuan enduring. This type of love must fire up for the long haul.

I have a friend who lost his daughter when she was only 33 years old. We are close friends. We meet most every week to talk through how he's doing with his daughter's unexpected death.

"Where was God in all this?" he asks.

"I don't know," I say.

My friend and his wife will never recover from this blow. They will wake up every day and think of her. The acute pain may subside over the first five years, but some form of pain will never completely disappear.

Question: Am I going to walk with my friend for the long haul, or give it about five months and then expect him to be "over it?" I hope I won't do the latter. Love does long-haul waiting. Love does long-haul "coming alongside" people. The one doing the loving may have to wait a long time for any "results" to happen, but that's not the point.

God waited a long time for me to become a Christ-follower. He waited a long time while He kept putting people and circumstances and experiences in front of me that could only be called "God-things." I missed most of them and frankly, couldn't be bothered. But God is in the business of doing long-haul love with us.

So, in what areas of your life do you find yourself waiting on God? Whatever just came to your mind, that is a big part of God's "with-ness and within-ness" in you. The only real practice for building up our capacity to wait is to trust: trust that God is doing something in us and something in our circumstances. Our job is to concentrate on what He's forming in us in the midst of those circumstances. So, a prayer might be: "God, form in me an increasing capacity to wait on You and to trust You. In the meantime, I'll leave the circumstances to You."

Final Question to Ponder

What are you waiting for in humility and hope? Ask God to give you the capacity and patience and endurance to hang onto hope while you wait.

You are God's:
Never-to-be-duplicated-ever-again,
Absolutely-valued-beyond-measure,
Cherished, Delighted-in, Cheered-for
Precious treasure of unmeasurable worth,
Whom He loves and adores with a passion
unmeasured.
You are His child; loved, protected,
and safe in His hands.

- From Larry Warner, my spiritual director.

Chapter 4: The Practice of TREASURING

TREASURING IS SOMETHING WE DO whether we know it or not. Even God treasures things. After each day of creation, God paused, looked at all He'd created and said, "Man that's gooooooood!" After creating the first human beings, Adam and Eve, God paused a bit longer and said, "Wow! They are *very* gooooood!" God stopped; He did not rush on to the next day. He stopped, lingered, gazed, and took a long look at each creation wonder and after who knows how long of giving such a long, pondering look, He quietly whispered, "Oh, how good is that! That is sooooo good! I did gooood!"

I've been fortunate enough to have vacationed in Hawaii and in the Caribbean. I am drawn to water more than to the mountains. My wife is the opposite. (Typical.) I like to snorkel, swim, and surf. Whenever I'm in any of these environments, my practice of treasuring God and His passion for beauty skyrockets. I can't help but be drawn to think of Him in these environments of unbelievable beauty. In other words, I do a little treasuring.

I have three children. At many moments during their upbringing, I paused for a few extra moments and treasured them. Sometimes, it was prompted by their part in a school play. Sometimes the treasuring happened in a moment of excellence on sports team or dance company. Sometimes I treasured their ability to read, write, or communicate. These, and many others, were things they *did*. But sometimes, I'd just watch them while they slept. They weren't doing anything. I'd sit on their bed, put my hand on their shoulder, and linger. Soon, I was marveling at their uniqueness: that they were God's "never to be duplicated again" treasure of immeasurable worth. And God entrusted me to be their dad. Wow. I still treasure every moment with them.

Triggers for Treasuring

- What causes us to stop our hurry and pull us up short with a, "Wow! That is awesome!" Or, "Wow, God, only You could have created or orchestrated something so beautiful!"
- Being in the room when your child is born?
- Watching a sunset?
- Walking through a forest?
- Sitting by an Alpine lake?
- When your child makes a loving, gracious choice?
- When someone close to you reaches a goal?
- When someone gets their one-year pin at an AA meeting?
- On your child's wedding day?
- While your family is singing in the car together?
- When someone confesses to you something intensely private and personal?

Treasuring is the practice of pausing long enough to "value" or to "see the preciousness of" a person, a situation, a circumstance, a relationship—or even a hardship.

Treasuring is "re-seeing," "re-hearing," and "re-experiencing" things over and over again in our mind and we ponder their value and meaning in our hearts.

Treasuring is about experiences where we see God's hand at work, or He helps us to see what He's up to, or we see that He's brought a gift into our lives, and we say or think, "God brought this my way. It's a great treasure."

Mary

One of the places in the Bible where treasuring is most clear is in Mary's role in the birth accounts of Jesus. The *summary statement* of Mary's life from the time she was told she'd give birth to God Himself in human form, to the time when Jesus launched out into His public ministry at age 30, is:

Mary *treasured* all these things in her heart! *(See Luke 2:51.)*

She treasured it all. Here's what she treasured:

- An angelic visitation announcing Mary's impending pregnancy, which would occur without sexual intercourse, and being told the child would be God's Son.
- A weird "pregnancy companion," Elizabeth (her aunt or cousin, age 60), now three months along with a baby who would be John the Baptist. Mary spent several months with her aunt because she's the only one who really "got" this kind of "unplanned pregnancy." Elizabeth was the only one, when Mary told her how she got pregnant, who didn't give her that "have you been drinking" look.
- She treasured Joseph staying with her after she told him that he wasn't the father *and* it wasn't another guy.
- She treasured the dream in which God gave Joseph the orders to "stay with her" in this weird "unwed mother" thing.
- She treasured the visits of the shepherds, the prophecies over her baby when she took Him to the temple, the strange wisdom of her child as He grew.

We might be hard-pressed to find much to treasure in the actual "birth story." After all, Mary and Joseph (because of orders from Caesar) had to travel to their town of birth to register (a census). From Nazareth to Bethlehem is a *70 mile trip*, walking. It is possible Mary rode a donkey for part of the journey. Riding a donkey is nothing like riding in a Cadillac, especially when you're nine months pregnant. I'd like to see any woman have to do that five-day journey on foot or riding a donkey today. It shows me that Mary was one tough lady.

When they arrive in Bethlehem, there's no hospital, no hotel rooms, just an inn. There's a NO VACANCY sign out front but Joseph asks the innkeeper just in case there was a late cancellation. There wasn't, but the innkeeper saw Joseph's downcast face, glanced over Joseph's shoulder and saw the pregnant Mary, and felt some compassion. "Tell you what, I have a cave out back where I keep the animals. You can bunk there if you want." Joseph said, "We'll take it." So, a dark cave with cows, chickens, goats, and lambs is the birthing room for the Son of God.

There's no baby shower, no stroller, no bassinet, no Pampers, no baby monitor, no crib. Mary uses an animal feeding trough for Jesus to sleep in. Were any relatives or friends there to do Lamaze or take photos? Was anyone outside the cave in the so-called "waiting room" ready to celebrate a woman having her firstborn child? No. The only real witnesses to the birth were things that went "Mooooo" and "Baaaaaa."

So What's to Treasure in That?

In our day and age, if what happened to Mary happened to us, I think the "Complaint Box" would be full. But there's no record of Mary whining for better accommodations or better *anything*.

She had a place, some shelter to give birth. I'll bet she treasured Joseph's company. Maybe she treasured just a little privacy for bringing the King of the Universe into the world. Either way, Mary treasured the birth experience deeply, as most women do.

Mary treasured the surprise visit from some shepherds to see Jesus. They were told by some angels that they'd see God's Son in the flesh if they took one step of faith and then another towards this cave. Imagine Mary and Joseph's surprise when they hear a knock on the cave wall, "Sorry to intrude but has anybody in here given birth recently?" Mary and Joseph look at each other and think, *How did they know?*

The shepherds tell their story. "We were just doing our normal watching-the-sheep thing. It was the night shift when suddenly we were blinded by a bright light and angels told us about you and your baby. Then we were serenaded by thousands of angels singing a song about the specialness of your son." Mary and Joseph are blown away. God gave them some people to celebrate with. She treasured that "shepherd surprise party."

Then another surprise party. Three star gazers/astrologers show up. *Knock, knock.* "Anybody in here just have a baby boy?" Another glance from Joseph and Mary towards each other. "Come in," they say. These guys have travelled hundreds of miles following a star (of all things) and they bring *gifts*, not "onesies." They brought Mary and Joseph valuable gifts that funded their journey to Egypt and maybe much of their time there. In other words, God *provided* for Mary and Joseph. These pagan astrologers end up paying for travel expenses, but also for the long-term financing of living in a foreign country as aliens. Mary certainly treasured that.

Finally, Joseph and Mary brought Jesus into the Temple area to be consecrated. Every firstborn male was dedicated to God back then. Two rather strange characters found Joseph and Mary in the temple area: Simeon and Anna. They tell the proud parents, "Your child is very, very special." What parent wouldn't love hearing that? I'd never forget it.

...and it's after this last incident that the writer says that Mary "treasured *all* these things in her heart" (emphasis mine).

Remember, treasuring is "re-seeing," "re-hearing," and "re-experiencing" things over and over again in our mind's eye as we ponder their value and meaning in our hearts. Treasuring is about experiences where we see God's hand at work, or He helps us see what He's up to, or we see that He's brought a gift into our lives, and we say or think, "God brought this my way. It's a great treasure."

Mary experienced a lot of "being stopped in her tracks," and "pulling up short" moments, with God's constant attentiveness to her plight of bringing Jesus into a world that would eventually kill Him. *The key to her treasuring is that she took the time to STOP, LINGER, and REFLECT on the significance of each event, small or large.*

As I mentioned earlier, I officiate weddings for part of my income. I'm completely reliant upon a couple scrolling through the many "officiant options" out there, being attracted to my website, and then taking the initiative to contact me with a "cold call." With every notification of interest in my services, I can't help but pause and whisper, "Jesus, you are incredible that you would provide, yet again, for us." This is another form of practicing treasuring. Over time, I risk the danger of becoming casual about this and thinking, *Yeah, I'm pretty good at this. I've got great reviews on the internet. I'm experienced, I'm poised, and I always make a couple's wedding personal and fun. Yeah, I'm kind of "all that."* In this mindset, there is the potential for hurrying past this kind of provision God brings my way, instead of continually practicing pausing, reflecting, and then treasuring God's gracious acts of providing income for our needs.

Practicing Treasuring

It takes continued practice to make treasuring a fundamental response to all that God brings our way. What is it about treasuring that helps us "practice God's presence"? In other words, if you take a moment to stop, take an extra moment to notice all the things God brings your way in the course of a day, if He brings to your attention something that you might want to *pause* and *reflect* on for a moment or two, what does pausing to treasure *do*?

It makes you realize that God brought something good your way... specifically, as a personalized *gift* for *you*! It could be a friend, a job, an opportunity, a church, a "break," an encouragement of some sort, something in nature, or an inner leading from the Holy Spirit. Pausing to treasure what God brings our way is a form of recognizing Him as the *giver of all good things*; recognizing that He knows us and our situation (whether our situation is good or not so good).

How can we practice *treasuring*?

1. Have your finger over the "pause button" throughout your day!

We must believe that God brings us "God moments" every day. Things that are holy moments. And they can be very ordinary:

- A brief interchange with a 3-year-old
- A moment of transparency from a friend
- The produce department in the grocery store. ("God, you made all these fruits and vegetables. What an imagination!")

All of these moments require hitting the "pause button" on the *hurry* pace of life. If you find yourself in a "task mode" (i.e., in a hurry), this stuff is easy to miss. If I had to put a phrase to this, I would call it *The Practice of the Pause*. Hurry blows by the impressions God is trying to give us. The "pause" enables us to hear Him, sense His leadings, and notice His goodness towards us.

2. Intentionally slow down your eyes and ears!

It changes everything when you carry with you the truth that everyone you lock eyes with is God's one-of-a-kind, never-to-be-duplicated, treasured-beyond-measure, cherished, adored, and celebrated-over creation. They, as well as you, are His creation of immeasurable worth. Seeing people this way slows us down. C. S. Lewis wrote that if we saw the everyday people in their heavenly glory we would be tempted to bow down and worship them. That's true for the homeless beggar, the grocery store check-out clerk, and the guy who picks up the trash. People matter to God; therefore they ought to matter to us. So, treasure people of any kind and take the time to really listen to them in conversation. Listen for feelings, notice their body language and all their non-verbal communication. Your "treasuring" is letting them know that what they are saying matters to you.

One of the ways to do treasuring is practicing a short, little verse in Romans chapter 12, which urges us to be friends with ordinary people (vs. 16, NLT): "*Enjoy the company of ordinary people.*" One way to treasure the "ordinary treasures of God," is to learn the names of people you normally wouldn't. My dry-cleaning lady's name is Sunny. My mechanic's name is Carlos. Some of my favorite wedding coordinators are Stephanie, Brianne, and Krystell. The lady who pushes the cleaning cart around the strip mall I visit often is Manuela. Try it, they'll be surprised you asked.

3. At the beginning of each day, consciously pray,

"God, You will bring people and events my way to treasure today. Keep me on the alert to notice, pause, and treasure all of them. Remind me to assign them great value. Help me to recognize the whispers of Your Holy Spirit that encourage me to treasure what and who You put in my path today."

4. Keep the rules of treasuring in mind!

- We can't *skim relationships*.
- We can't fully appreciate *beauty* by blitzing by it.
- We can't *hurry* deep sharing of feelings, hurts, joys, and celebration.
- We can't speed up *reflection*.

5. Assign a deeper value to people, circumstances and God's provision.

The word "ordinary" is not in God's vocabulary. Every person is extra-ordinary. In His mind, no one is ordinary. In fact, no one is "normal." You and I are extraordinary in His eyes. All the time. Any person that comes across our path is someone worth treasuring because they are a miracle creation of God, just as we are: the child with Down Syndrome or Autism, the elderly man with dementia, the teenager who needs a drug intervention. They are all different versions of the people Jesus loves, and they are still treasures nonetheless.

Most things God brings our way to treasure are the everyday people, events, and circumstances that we find ourselves in most days. He brings us our spouses, parents, children, grandchildren, grandparents, and extended family and friends. We can treasure our health and our faults because we learn and grow through them. Depending on your tastes you can treasure

Coca-Cola, steaks, chocolate cake, and Caesar salad. We can treasure sunsets, waves, clouds and flowers, dogs and ducks, succulents and redwoods, lakes and rivers, mountains and deserts. We can treasure the truth of the fact that we can talk to God and that He loves to communicate with us. We can treasure any job we've had: as a policeman, a firefighter, a doctor, a Physicians Assistant, or a nurse. It's like we could put an imaginary sign on our children, our spouse, friends, anyone: "God's treasure." And it would be true.

Jesus' Story About Treasure

There's a story Jesus told about buried treasure. In His story, a gentleman is walking down a road and off to the side sees the corner of a chest sticking out of the ground. He goes over, digs it up and finds a Count-of-Monte-Cristo-type chest full of gold. He re-buries it, runs home, tells his wife, "Honey, we're selling the house, the land, everything." She says, "If so, get a new wife." (Actually, that's not in the text, I was just imagining that.) When they sell their belongings, they take the cash and buy the property with the treasure on it. After showing it to his wife, she says, "I am your slave for life." (That's not in the text either, but it should be.)

Jesus' point? Most interpretations name the treasure as Jesus who is worth everything we have. Thinking of it another way, I wonder if the treasure is Jesus' illustration of a person, of you and me. We are His treasure and we are worth selling everything He has to buy us back. Like that Elvis song, He "can't help falling in love with us over and over again." You and I are treasure to Him. In fact, He did give everything He had for us. We are worth giving His very life for.

The Secret to Mastering "Treasuring"

What's the secret to treasuring? Blaise Pascal lived from 1623–1662 and wrote a book named *Pensées*. In it, he wrote that all of our problems would be solved if we could learn to sit quietly in our room alone.

Why did he write that? Because treasuring is done when we stop, slow down, and do what I call *extreme noticing* on the *significance* of people, encounters, and experiences. Reflecting and extreme noticing can't happen without pausing, without an awareness of God's constant "with and within-ness," His "above and below-ness," His "to the left and right-ness," and His "in front and back-ness" to us. He desires to give us these experiences, but without an unhurried calmness of spirit, it won't happen. In other words, treasuring cannot be done if we are hurrying.

Exercises

- Whomever you lock eyes with this week, say to yourself, "That is one of God's precious treasures."
- When you look in the mirror at all, repeat to yourself, "I am God's precious treasure. He is very fond of me."

People are often driven to busyness because
they believe two pervasive lies:
It's all *up* to me.
It's all *about* me.

We can get trapped in the belief
that we are what we do.

Part 2: Too Much!

Enemy #2: Busyness

DO THESE WORDS SOUND FAMILIAR? *I have so much to do; I wish I could clone myself; You wouldn't believe how crazy my life is; I've got so much to do I can't think straight.*

These are the complaints of someone who has what I like to call "Busy Sickness."

Many of us only feel comfortable when we're doing something. We are trapped in the belief that we are what we do. Being still seems so strange to us, that something close to panic sets in when we try it. In *The Other Side of Silence,* Morton Kelsey writes, "The reason that most of us fill up our time and stay busy is that we are afraid to be alone. We do not want to deal with everything we find in ourselves. One thing I have learned from practically fifty years of listening to people is that *nearly all of us have our own inner monsters* (my emphasis). It seems that if we will just keep busy enough, we won't have to deal with them."[1]

Let's look at some symptoms of this modern illness.

- Do you rush around a lot?
- Do you get frustrated easily?
- Do you lose focus in the middle of a task or a conversation…even though you don't have ADD?
- Do you talk quickly…all the time?

91

- Do you forget where you're going—or why you're going there?
- Do you have too many projects going, but you're not making progress on any of them?

More seriously, does your busyness cause you to:
- Lose control of your emotions?
- Neglect your self-care?
- Get sick more easily?
- Be chronically late?
- Self-medicate with alcohol?
- Neglect important relationships?
- Neglect God?[2]

Busyness inflicts harm on our bodies, minds, and souls. What happens when we find ourselves trying to do more than we can? We feel *stressed* about everything. Here is a foundational truth: *God does not expect us to do more than we can.* God does not expect me to work 26 hours a day, or eight days a week.

"Busy sickness" is everywhere in modern society. But it's not inevitable. You don't have to live with this disease, and in this section of the book, I'll teach you some treatments that will bring you relief from this plague.

But before we get to the treatment, let's look at some of the reasons for this modern-day malady, and also at some of the harm it can cause.

Some Reasons for Busyness

Our fear of stillness—and the realizations stillness might bring—is the deep reason for our busyness. But there are some shallower reasons, too. Here are some surface reasons for our busyness—perhaps you'll recognize some of them in yourself.

1. The pursuit of *more!*

We buy larger and larger houses with larger and larger mortgages which leads to longer and longer hours at work.

2. The push for success.

We enroll our children in lessons and tutoring so they can be the brightest and best. But if a child is kept busy year-round, I can guarantee burn-out in high school or before. Having worked with teenagers for over a decade in my ministry life, I've heard firsthand how tired teenagers are of the packed schedules by the time they get to high school.

3. Busyness makes us feel important!

Being busy with work and family makes us feel like we're needed. Volunteering in our church makes us feel like we're needed by God.

4. We stay busy because we don't want to face relational problems.

When life's a whirlwind, we can push away thoughts of problems with our spouses or children because we don't want to deal with them. We think, "If we don't talk about these problems, maybe they'll just go away." (They don't.)

We know that busyness has replaced God as our top priority when it begins to cause harm to our bodies, our families, and our relationship with God. When we are pushed beyond our limits, *energy* is the main limitation. So why do I say "yes" to requests when I want to say "no"? Maybe I feel I need to prove myself. Maybe I don't want to let people down. Maybe I need the money. Maybe I want people to like me.

Maybe I am just scared of facing myself.

Parents and Busyness

Parents can take on a self-imposed pressure to give their children the perfect childhood. Parents fear that their failure to provide the right portfolio of experiences will ruin their children. As a result, parents enroll their children in music lessons, art instruction, language studies, extra tutoring, gymnastic classes, sports camps, summer camps, specialty camps, sports teams of any kind, and service projects.

Only a couple of decades ago, Sunday was "off limits" to youth sports practices and games. Not anymore. Whether it was baseball, football, basketball, soccer, lacrosse, or volleyball, the minds behind these club sports institutions figured out pretty quickly that church was rapidly becoming a non-factor in people's lives and that Sunday was a golden opportunity for practice, games, and tournaments.

But forget the "church factor" for a moment—when does a child or parent ever have just a "day off"? A day of rest or reflection, with this type of life? Parents think, *Well, we'll do this for a few years then get back to normal life. I guess this is just a season that all parents go through.*

That mindset is surrendering to the god of busyness.

What about unstructured play? Why the need to build a perfect resume for our children before they are 12? What about constructing snow forts, skipping rocks, building block cities, hosting tea parties with imaginary friends, and making forts under blankets? These play activities are often replaced with piano lessons, passing drills, and dawn-to-dusk activity. The danger of all this activity and constant motion is that it makes even the shortest amount of free time seem "boring" to children who don't know what to do with themselves. Then *on* goes the T.V.

The Myth of Multi-tasking

There is a myth that you can perform two tasks simultaneously as well as you can perform one alone. (Women often think they are better at this than men…at least according to my wife.) It's fine to believe that multitasking is a skill necessary in the modern world, *but to believe it is an equivalent substitute for single-minded focus on one task is incorrect.* Multitasking is like playing tennis with two balls (or three or four!). Some say they pay better attention when they multitask. But for a person to do better performing two tasks at once, it must mean that they can't fully engage with the first task and *need* two tasks to get their adrenaline flowing. In other words, *they lack the ability to focus.*[3]

94

Extreme, Necessary…Even Good Busyness

I have a friend named Scott. He married Becky, a brittle diabetic. While courting, she told him, "I don't think you want to get involved with me. I need a lot of care and I'll need more as the years go on."

Scott was not deterred. But Becky was quite prophetic. She has almost died at least five times. She's been hospitalized, at the minimum, ten times per year. She's often been found unconscious. She can go from "high" to "low," with regards to insulin or sugar, within a matter of five minutes. Managing her health could be a full-time job for a health care professional. But Scott does it himself.

He often carries Becky up to bed because she can't walk up on her own strength. Scott has given Becky countless glasses of orange juice and insulin shots when Becky is too "out of it" to know what's going on. Scott has managed working full-time while spending much of his "off time" sitting by a hospital bed. He has an application on his phone that reads Becky's blood sugar level from anywhere when he travels. When he's on the road, Scott will look at his phone, read the levels, then call Becky and say, "Honey, go grab a glass of orange juice right now."

After a few years of this, Scott and Becky talked about having a child. Becky couldn't (and shouldn't) conceive, so they each donated sperm and egg, and had the resulting embryo implanted in a close relative. Kelly was born nine months later, and she was born handicapped. She didn't walk until she was way past the age when other children were running. She had vision issues. Her legs, ankles, and feet were crooked…and on and on it went.

Here's one of many notes I've received from Scott over the years, telling me he couldn't be at our regular Monday evening men's group for a while:

My schedule is going to get a little hectic starting this week. Kelly goes in for surgery on Tuesday to re-align her ankles. The intent is to break her ankles and surgically re-position her legs and ankles over her feet. They will pin each ankle so she won't be able to bear weight for two months. After those two months, she should get the pins out and placed back in casts for another six months. She'll be using a walker for a while. In addition, we will be in Phoenix for five days of testing at the Mayo Clinic for Becky's active pursuit of a Pancreas Transplant. Right after that, we'll be in L.A. for four days of testing at the City of Hope. Once we complete the assessments at the two sites, we'll wait for the donor of a pancreas to die. Hopefully, we'll be near the top of the list.

"A little hectic"? Are you kidding me? I cannot tell you how many sleepless nights, ambulance rides, and seizures these two have gone through together. Scott's "being busy" with Becky is not a burden to him. It is not "busy sickness." It's his assignment from God. As if Becky's plight wasn't enough to manage, now Scott has Kelly too. Kelly is one of the most courageous children I know. And to me, Scott is a hero—a hero no one will ever hear about in the papers.

There are many of you out there doing this kind of thing day in and day out, year in and year out. You're journeying with your spouse's decline into Alzheimer's and all your time is spent with doctors, getting prescriptions filled, making sure your spouse doesn't wander away, or leave a stove burner on that would burn the house down. You're spending your life supporting, loving, and providing for a special needs child. You're holding up an entire household as a single mom. You're busy with a really hard situation.

In these situations and more, busyness with these good things can rob you of energy, happiness and hope. But you do not have "busy sickness." Once again, if this is you, you're a hero. Your assignment is going to be to find a way to experience God in a very tough situation where you don't have time or energy. It may be that your primary spiritual practice to major in is *rest*.

More Good Busyness

There are some other God-honoring reasons you might have a *season* of busyness:

- Financial setbacks that require you to take on two jobs, or to work more hours.
- Arrival of a newborn who claims some of your sleep hours.
- Needs of loved ones.
- A painful end to a marriage that requires you to be both mom and dad for your children.
- Your job may require sacrifices at times.
- Ministry or community service may ask more of you for a season.

Please note what these situations have in common: they are not permanent. They are *temporary.*

Everyday Busyness

These days, the standard answer to the question "Hi, how are you?" is "Busy!" (The answer used to be, "Fine!")

However, what if I answered the question like this? "Doing well. I have plenty of space in my life for simply thinking, reflecting, and being available to the people God brings my way. Sometimes I have gaps of time where I can do something I love or simply 'be.' How are you doing?"

It's possible I'd hear a response like, "Oh, ahhhh, wow!...that's...ahhhh... that's great!" But the other person's face will say, *I have no idea what you're talking about.* In their minds, they may secretly think I'm lazy. They may have a different look that says they can't remember the last time life gave them that opportunity.

"Free time" has become a foreign concept.

We have so many urgent things to do, so many people to meet, so many books to read and movies to go to. Our jobs demand time and overtime, or we're unemployed and spend much of our time looking for work or worrying about not finding it. Our families need lots of time and energy. Studying for exams, tests, or papers could fill every waking hour. Our houses or apartments or yards beg for our attention. We promise to do things for the church or for community organizations. Problems in many parts of the world concern us, especially because we can't really do anything about them. Our calendars are filled with appointments: doctors, dentists, music lessons, potlucks, concerts, sporting events, and meetings.

This is everyday busyness.

The Strategy of the Evil One

One of the many strategies of the devil is to get you to pack your blocks of time each day in such a way that there are no blank spots, no blocks of time where you simply have nothing planned. And we fall for it, because if we did have blocks of time like that, we might start to think we were unproductive, and that would be very bad. One author calls this a life with no "margin," no space for just nothing.[4]

If Satan can't make you evil, he'll make you busy.

(Old saying, author unknown.)

The inventions of the modern age (e.g., vacuum cleaner, laptop, iPad, washing machine) *have not* brought more down-time for people to relax in, but just more space to be "productive." St. Francis de Sales wrote, "While I am busy with little things, I am not required to do greater things" (*Introduction to the Devout Life*). He wrote that 500 years ago. And what he means is that I can talk myself into the fact that I've been a productive person with all my errands, emails, texts, postings, driving time, work time, and evenings out, but never really address the *significant* parts of my life that need attention: my soul, my heart, my mind, my body.

Jesus, the Man of Deepness

Our culture teaches and encourages us to hustle, chase, and cram. The world doesn't need more busy people. It needs *deep* people. To grow in deepness we need:

- *Silence*—if our words are going to mean anything
- *Reflection*—if our actions are going to have significance
- *Contemplation*—so we can see the world as it really is
- *Prayer*—if we're going to be conscious of God in every moment; if we want to know Him better and to enjoy Him.

Jesus knew how to use silence, reflection, contemplation, and prayer. In fact, Jesus was probably the most *un-hurried* person ever to walk this planet. He put *busyness* in its place often.

You might recall the rushed atmosphere of the synagogue leader Jairus, who begged Jesus to come quickly to heal his dying daughter. Talk about urgent! On the way to see Jairus' daughter, a woman who'd been ill for 12 years with a hemorrhaging problem, snuck up on Jesus and touched His cloak and got miraculously healed. Given the urgency of continuing His journey, how easy would it have been for Jesus to simply think to Himself, "I felt that, and I'm glad for whoever touched me, but I need to stay on task here, so I'm going to keep going." Instead, He stopped, found the woman, and had a discussion of some length regarding her history of health woes.

Jesus wasn't too busy to be interrupted, to stop and listen to someone's story, to take some time to make someone feel heard. He never neglected a person for an agenda. Jesus saw interruptions as divine appointments.

A Story About Busyness From Jesus

...a man sitting at the table with Jesus exclaimed, "What a blessing it will be to attend a banquet in the Kingdom of God!"

Jesus replied with this story: *"A man prepared a great feast and sent out many invitations. When the banquet was ready, he sent his servant to tell the guests, 'Come, the banquet is ready.' But they all began making excuses. One said, 'I have just bought a field and must inspect it. Please excuse me.' Another said, 'I have just bought five pairs of oxen, and I want to try them out. Please excuse me.' Another said, 'I just got married, so I can't come.'*

"The servant returned and told his master what they had said. His master was furious and said, 'Go quickly into the streets and alleys of the town and invite the poor, the crippled, the blind, and the lame.' After the servant had done this, he reported, 'There is still room for more.' So his master said, 'Go out into the country lanes and behind the hedges and urge anyone you find to come, so that the house will be full. For none of those I first invited will get even the smallest taste of my banquet.'" (Luke 14:15-24, NLT)

In this case, God isn't offended by a gross sin or a blatant moral failure, but by people being too busy to respond to an invitation of intimacy with Him. In the first century, when you were invited to a banquet, it was an act of deep friendship. Implied in that invitation was the hidden message, *You are a part of my inner circle. I enjoy your company deeply. Come and let's share some unrushed time together, because you matter to me.* Jesus desires our company always. He wants us to enjoy His company too. He'd like us to allow Him to teach us, assure us, comfort us, hold us, and lead us. In a constant state of busyness (as the people in this parable were), they blow right by the constant invitations of the Master (God) to provide for them, encourage them, and love them because they're so busy and preoccupied with their lives. Sound familiar?

So what do people get in this life for their hard work and anxiety? Their days of labor are filled with pain and grief; even at night their minds cannot rest.

- King Solomon, the smartest man in the Old Testament (Ecclesiastes 2:22-23a, NLT).

Giving God Our Best, Not Our Leftovers

When we're too busy, we give God our leftovers: the leftover time of our day, our leftover energy, and our leftover attentiveness. And, sometimes our days are so busy that we don't have anything leftover at all!

But I believe we can experience God in experiences many would call "busy." It takes practice. But it's not impossible, not at all. The chapters in this section are practices meant for "Everyday Joe and Joan." All of the practices in this book take time and repetition to work, so remember, *be gentle on yourself.* We must remember and live into how *gracious, patient,* and *loving* God is towards us. We have to embrace the truth that Jesus is *cheering for us, strengthening us,* and *valuing us.*

In whatever way you experiment with the following practices, picture God cheering you on with immense enthusiasm, kind of like we'd cheer on our child as they learn to stand, walk, run, throw a ball, spell, or write. Even an iota of success causes us to cheer for them.

God feels the same way about us when we attempt any practices to connect with Him.

The spiritual practices to combat busyness in everyday life are:

- NOTICING
- RECEIVING
- BEING USELESS
- BEING ALONE

As I mentioned before, these practices can be done by those with very busy lives, so read on and be encouraged that you can connect with God in rich ways in your normal days of life!

Lingering is a lost art.

Chapter 5: The Practice of NOTICING

I HAVE A GOLDEN RETRIEVER named Sadie. She's pathetically cute. She would lick a burglar to death. She hears a firecracker and runs for cover by jumping into the bathtub. She thinks that balloons are the face of Satan.

If you have a dog, your dog has little "quirks" that make them loveable. But why exactly do we love our dogs? They don't really do anything around the house. They just want to be pet all the time. They eat. They poop and then we have to...well, you know. *Noticing* my dog led to a few observations that tie into our life with Jesus:

First, *my dog is dedicated to closeness!* If I'm at home, Sadie is not far away. If I move from one room to another, she usually follows. If I'm upstairs in my office, she is no further than 15 feet away. I know of another dog that follows her owner when the owner gets up to go to the bathroom at 2:00 a.m., every night, just so that she can *stay close*. I wonder what Jesus' heart would be feeling if I made it my minute-by-minute agenda to simply *stay close* to Him.

I realize He's invisible to us, but bringing Him to mind, or asking Him a question, or asking for advice, or telling Him I appreciate something, or praising Him for something in creation, or simply resting in His presence, keeps me close to Him. My dog "practices the presence of me" constantly. I could learn from that with regards to my relationship with Jesus.

Second, *my dog is extremely ATTENTIVE to me!* Sadie watches me constantly, looking for who knows what (that I'll take her for a walk, or pet her, or give her a treat; I don't know). All I know is, when we're sitting around watching TV, if I make a move to get out of my La-Z-Boy to get some ice cream, she opens her eyes, perks up and pays attention. *Attentiveness* to God is really just a constant state of *alertness* to God's messages. Those messages might include direction, reminders of His love, urges to take action, or assurances of forgiveness—whatever the message may be, receiving them requires an *attentiveness* to the nudges and leadings from God. Sadie reminds me to practice my attentiveness to God throughout the day.

Third, *my dog has an UNWAVERING LOYALTY!* Sadie lives to please me. Dogs can sense when we're disappointed in them or angry at them, but it doesn't take long for them to turn that frown upside down when we let them know they are still loved. I can't help but love my dog, even when she poops on the carpet because she:

a) looks guilty when she does it, and,

b) has that look that says, "Don't be mad at me, I couldn't help it."

I've noticed that my dog's loyalty is much more about enjoying being in my presence rather than my behavior towards her. She may lick other people's hands and wag her tail for them, but she follows *me*. Likewise, I may be attracted to various things, but Jesus is always bringing me back to *Him*. And, once I stop to *notice* where I am, I'll always come back to my Master.

Fourth, *my dog is happy to BE, not really DO!* Does Sadie mow the lawn, do the dishes, earn a salary, vacuum the carpet, pick up her own poop, mop the floor, take a bath, get a haircut, or trim her toenails? No! She doesn't really *do* anything for me other than *be happy* whenever she sees me. She wags her tail when I scratch behind her ears and throw the ball to her. In other words, I'm the one doing the *doing*. She's just *being* with me. And she could be with me all day and be perfectly happy.

I struggle with feeling significant so I try to find things to "do for Jesus." I wonder, is Jesus perfectly happy to have me enjoy being in His presence without doing a single thing *for* Him? Sure, we are used by Him to forward His Kingdom, but not as a substitute for being with Him who loves you and me so richly and deeply.

Lastly, *my dog needs a leash!* When Sadie and I go out into the world on a walk, if I don't have her tethered to me in some way, all sorts of hurt, harm, chaos, and blunders can happen. You know what they are: running into the street where moving cars are, going into neighbors' yards and stepping on flowers, wandering away and getting lost.

I'm pretty sure I need various kinds of leashes (things that keep me tethered to my proximity to Jesus). I need Christ-loving friends, the Bible, the church, small groups, spiritual direction, prayer, service, and much more to keep me from wandering into the streets of sin and lostness where I could get hit by my own stupidity, or someone else's stupidity, or where I could hit them and hurt them.

The Monkees wrote a song called, "Gonna Buy Me a Dog." One of the lines in it is, "'Cause I need a friend now." I watch and observe Sadie (my friend) a little differently now that I've realized how much I can learn from her. By observing Sadie's behavior towards me, I see how I could follow Jesus more closely, enjoy His company more, be more attentive to Him, and keep my eye peeled for His guidance and direction. I'd like to grow to the point where I'm constantly in a state of "wagging my tail" at the sight and sound of Jesus in my life.

All of those insights came from *noticing*.

What Noticing Involves

Noticing involves:

- *Pausing* for at least 10 seconds. More like 30 minimum.
- *Staying* with a thought or impression and reflecting, *That could be God communicating with me.*
- *Lingering,* which battles the voice of Busyness, which is always screaming, "Move on!"

Before I share some "noticings" that I've had in the course of everyday, normal life, I want you to know the hard part of this practice is being attentive to what God wants to reveal to you without getting hung up on the questions, "What's significant about this, God?" or, "What are You trying to get me to understand?"

Don't put pressure on yourself to come up with something in this regard. Like anything, it takes practice. If you're confused, simply be honest about your confusion: tell God you're not sure why He brought this to your attention. Then stay calm and open and see if there's an inner prompting that comes your way. Sometimes a "nudge" or "a whisper in your spirit" from God may come that says:

- "This is how much I care for you."
- "I made what you're looking at, in part, for *you* to enjoy!"
- "See how much I'm into variety, different colors, and uniqueness… just like you are."
- "This is an illustration of how your life is right now."
- "That stop sign I'm bringing to your attention has to do with how busy you are. Do something about that."

Some of you might be wondering if a random thought or a strong impression in your mind or heart might be nothing. Ninety-nine times out of a hundred, it's something, not nothing. Trust that it's from God. Obey it, believing it's from Him. In certain situations, you might sense, "Be patient here." Consider it an order from Heaven. Just like it takes time to become perfect at understanding a second language, learning to sense God's leadings takes time and practice. Don't worry if you're not perfect in recognizing these leadings from God. Keep believing Jesus is communicating with you in every moment. So keep listening. Keep your sensors at maximum level.

Examples of Everyday Noticings

OCEAN WAVES

I live in San Diego and I surf. It hit me one day that waves are an image of God's grace, love, and forgiveness. Like different degrees of rainfall, there are different sizes of waves, some big, some medium, some small. Depending on our life situation, we may need to ride a big wave of grace. God gives us all kinds of waves to ride; maybe small waves at first, and then bigger ones. In other words, He might start us on experiencing His undeserved favor by smaller things like:

- opening a door for a job opportunity (experiencing His provision).
- getting into a specialized doctor quickly when it was supposed to take three weeks.
- providing a friend who sticks with you through a crisis.

Maybe a *medium-sized wave of grace might involve*:

- reconciliation between father and son, or mother and daughter, after a conflict.
- a peace in your heart when finances cause the selling of your home.
- forgiveness for a failure from your family and friends.

Maybe a *huge wave of grace, might involve*:

- experiencing God's tender care, comfort, and presence when your child dies of cancer.
- the providing of funds when health care skyrockets (and your spouse needs surgery).
- the looks, words, and touches of comfort and love that friends and family give when your spouse dies.

To catch an ocean wave I have to do two things:

1. Get in the right position
2. Do a couple of paddles…

…and then I'm riding it.

If I fall, there's another wave coming right behind it. Undeserved favor, the love of the Father, forgiveness, and new starts keep coming in, wave after wave, from Him. We simply need to get into position to ride the wave. He supplies the waves.

Like stepping out into the rain, I have to make a bit of effort to experience the wave (God's grace); positioning myself in the wave and then giving a couple of paddles. Remember, grace is always opposed to earning, not to effort. The effort in this practice of *noticing* is just getting into position and giving a couple of paddles. Meaning, we have to pause, gaze, and ask God to show us something. That's the paddling and positioning part. I call this ocean waves style of noticing, *learning to ride the waves of grace*. When you think of your life, there is no sin, failure, mistake, or lifestyle that cannot be covered by a wave of grace. There is no wave of grace that is uncatchable because of your past failures. And there's no limit to how much grace continues to come your way. Waves never stop. If we fall off our board, there's always another wave coming right behind the last one. If a fall happens, just a little effort on our part puts us into a position to own another wave of grace for ourselves.

THE MOON

My wife and I took a walk at night and we saw the moon. People often think of Jesus' words, "I am the light of the world," and apply it to the sun. But think of it, the moon shines *against DARKNESS* and, as Jesus said, nothing can stop the shining. I thought, *Jesus, my life sucks right now, and I'm in a dark place, but your love and grace are still shining on me. Help me to hold onto that.*

Practicing Noticing in Real Life: Let's Go on a Walk

Now that you've seen some examples of things you might *notice*, let's take a hypothetical walk—you and me and my dog, Sadie—so you can see what noticing might look like in real time.

I take Sadie for a walk most every morning. It takes about 25 minutes. Sometimes (not every time) I ask God, "Is there anything You want to show me, teach me, or remind me of on this walk with my dog? What do You want to bring to my attention at this time?" Then I simply remain *open* to anything I notice and I stay with what grabs my attention. Then I wait. I pause. I ponder. And I see if any Holy Spirit nudges come my way. (My dog can do the spiritual practice of waiting while I do this. She's old anyway.) Sometimes there's nothing, sometimes there're many things. When something grabs my attention; when there's something I *notice*, I always see it as an opportunity. God may be wanting to reassure me about His love or remind me of who He is, or remind me of His power and vastness, or remind me of His creativity in creation and that He made whatever I'm noticing, in part, specifically for me. Here are a few "Is there anything you want to tell me, God" *noticings* we might see as we walk with Sadie through my neighborhood:

A withering tree: The drooping-branched, shriveled-leaved tree reminded me of Jesus' parable about the fruitless fig tree (see Luke 13:6-9). The owner of the tree sees it isn't yielding any fruit. "Cut it down and chop it up," the owner says. The gardener replies, "Let me dig around it, use fertilizer and give it one more year." The owner says, "Okay. You talked me into it."

I thought, *The gardener will NOT give up on that tree.* And similarly, Jesus will never give up on me. He will bring to my days "fertilizer for my soul" in the form of experiences, people, situations, help, challenges, and encouragements that will have a life-giving effect; that will challenge me to *grow* further into Christ-likeness and not settle for a lukewarm relationship with Him.

Looking at that tree I prayed, "God, don't let me grow lazy in playing my part in *growing* further into a reflection of You. Help me to recognize opportunities that would stimulate my *growth* in You. And like that gardener, thank You that You won't give up on me."

Bushes that look good on the outside: If you stick your head inside most bushes, it's brown, unattractive and not too sexy. But those hidden branches carry the nutrition needed for leaves, flowers and beauty on the outside of the bush. That outside beauty draws people to smell the flowers. As I walked past these bushes, I reflected on my life.

Each of us has an inside life, our *private life,* the "inside of the bush" life. This is where the *real life formation* happens. It's unseen, out of the public eye, and not very sexy. It's *private.* It's our inner life. It's the life we live when no one is looking. But any private "formation-into-Christ-likeness" effort results in a healthy heart and mind on the inside (the hidden branches) and also yields loving action on the outside (i.e., greenery and flowers).

When you and I do *anything* to place ourselves in a position to learn from Jesus, when we take on *any spiritual practice* in private (Bible reading, study, prayer, confession, pondering, private worship, practicing Jesus' presence, any practices in this book, etc.) we are doing "*inside* the bush" work. The inner heart, mind, and soul work that results in an increased Christ-likeness *inside* eventually shows on the *outside* to people who God brings our way. When people smell the results (flowers) of our "hidden life with Christ," they are drawn to them and to you! That inner work results in an attractive life, one that draws people outside the faith to take a whiff. They might find the source of your beauty (Jesus) to be very attractive.

Succulents: California had been in drought conditions for almost a decade. People have designed entire yards with succulents. Why? Because they *store nutrients* for long periods of dry times. They store hidden nutrients and water. They don't require a lot of attention.

So, I thought, *What is stored in my heart for the dry times in my life with God, when God seems distant, when the Christian life seems to get boring or routine and not very exciting? What kind of spiritual nutrients do I have stored up in my life with God? What am I keeping in store for when hard times come?*

The only way to get a stored-up life with God—a life that's ready to endure the dry times—is to store up time with God in secret. We do those practices in private to store up *truths about God.*

What truths?

- God is *for* me, not against me.
- He is closer than the air I breathe.

- I am forgiven.
- I am loved with a passion so great, that it would knock me down if I saw it with my own eyes.
- There is *no condemnation* for those who walk with Jesus.
- I am safe in Jesus' hands. He's come through time and time again.
- His grace outdistances any sin I have.
- I will lean into the truth that He is present. I will continue with my private practices with Him even when I don't really sense His closeness, or see any results in my behavior or character.

This is the stuff inside a stored-up/succulent-type life that helps us endure in spiritual dry times or tragedy. What does practicing a stored-up life with God look like?

- Sometimes, it's a reviewing of times when God answered prayer for us.
- Sometimes, it's remembering the times when God came through for us. (E.g., opening a door for a job, having a youth worker come alongside and befriend your wayward daughter, or supplying a wise counselor when you came to a fork-in-the-road life decision. It's remembering when God was faithful. These stored up remembrances becomes invaluable when tragedy hits, when a spouse walks out, when betrayal happens, or when we fail.)

Noticings from Movies

One of my favorite all-time movies is *The Elephant Man*. It's the story of John Merrick, a severely deformed man who was a showpiece in a traveling circus. He shocked people with his appearance; a freak-show spectacle to paying customers. At one point in the movie, he is chased through the streets of England, and when cornered he yells, "I...AM...NOT...AN...ANIMAL!!!" Those were his first words spoken in the movie. No one knew he could talk. In fact, it was discovered he was a very sensitive, well-spoken gentleman.

"I am not an animal!" is the cry of the human soul. I am *not* an employee! I am *not* a maid! I am *not* a meal ticket! I am *not* a sex object! I am *not* an athlete! I am *not* an animal! I...AM...A...HUMAN...BEING!!! I have been created in such a way that I reflect what God is like. God knows my name. He hears my prayers. He loves me. He has hopes and dreams and feelings for me, too.

As the movie progresses, John Merrick becomes rather well-known in the area. Soon, one of the most beautiful and talented actresses in England comes to see him. Merrick is nervous about being in the company of such beauty when he is so ugly. Will she flinch? Will she look like she's seen a ghost? She enters the room, strolls right over to John and says, "Why Mr. Merrick, what a pleasure to meet you." Merrick is stunned and intimidated at the same time.

The actress notices that Merrick has been reading a play from Shakespeare. She asks him if he would like to do the dialogue with her. He starts to read his part. She responds with her part from memory. After a brief exchange of lines, she stops Merrick and says, "Why Mr. Merrick. You're not the Elephant Man. You're Romeo!"[1]

That actress captured the way God feels about us. Our sin does make us ugly through and through, but that's not the last word. In God's eyes, we are "Romeos." Beautiful, gifted, cherished, His masterpiece.

I meet people every day. On the surface, each person looks quite ordinary, but I'm training myself to see them as "Romeos and Juliets," God's precious treasures who matter deeply to Him. (Even the "hard to love" ones.)

Amy Adams stars in the movie, *Arrival*, a film about several egg-shaped alien vessels that park themselves around the world and just sit there. Unlike *Independence Day* and similar movies, these aliens are not here to conquer, destroy, or take over. However, the people of Earth don't know that. The military wants to know what the aliens' motives are. Then they plan to (violently) take matters into their own hands.

They commission Amy Adams, a famous linguist, to find a way to communicate with these alien invaders. The octopus-looking creatures communicate through a strange symbolic language. Each word looks like someone spilled an ink bottle over an upside-down cereal bowl with ink patterns formed around that blank circle. The aliens' language is difficult to decipher, to say the least. But over time, Adams and her colleagues figure it out.

In the meantime, there's a faction of the military that wants to blow the aliens away for no real rhyme nor reason, so it becomes a race for Adams and her team to find a way to communicate with the aliens before the world attempts to rid itself of this invasion. In the nick of time, she finds a way and bridges the gap between humans and aliens.

After seeing this flick, I was reminded of the dilemma God faced. "How can I best communicate with My valued treasures, men and women made in My image? What means would clearly reveal who I am and My motives? What's the language they will understand?" David Bowie wrote the lyrics to the movie *Starman*: "There's a starman waiting in the sky. He'd like to come and meet us, but he thinks he'll blow our minds." Good summary of God's dilemma.

Like the aliens in *Arrival*, God speaks a different language than fallen mankind.

- Mankind is all about behavior and performance. God's all about forgiveness.
- People can be all about payback and holding grudges. God's all about giving peace.

- Humans can be all about comparison and competition. God gave each person life as a gift.
- Humans think they know what's best for themselves, but Jesus actually knows how life works best.

So, how does God get Himself out in the open for all men and women to see? You all know: He came in person. And when He came, He didn't dazzle, impress, or demand homage. He didn't come to destroy or kill. But, in a real sense, He was an alien on the planet he made. And it took quite a while for people to understand His purpose for coming to Earth. His "language" was hard to figure out because it was very different from the way the people of the world spoke to one another. [2]

Jesus revealed that God is all about "undeserved favor" (grace), not good behavior balancing the scales against bad behavior. Jesus was all about forgiveness, not punishment; He showed us that love for God and other people is the ultimate goal for our lives here on earth. Life does not work well when achievement, accumulation of wealth, or looking eternally young is the ultimate goal. Jesus is all about transformation, not behavior modification. He's all about inviting oddballs, alcoholics, moral failures, the self-oriented, sex addicts, homosexuals, and everyday normal human beings to His party. He's all about a future in heaven for all, not about how many He can condemn to Hell.

Like the military in *Arrival* who wanted to get rid of the aliens, there were factions of people in real life who simply wanted to get rid of Jesus (see: Pharisees, Sadducees, religious types, and, ultimately, the Romans). They saw Jesus as a threat to their way of life, and schemed to kill Jesus.

Preconceived ideas about aliens moved some people in the movie to immediately say, "Get rid of them." Preconceived ideas about God moved some people in real life to get rid of the "alien," Jesus.

But soon, over time, many people began to understand Jesus' "language." Like Amy Adams' character in *Arrival*, people had to struggle with it. Jesus' parables weren't exactly clear when they were first spoken. At one point, Jesus' miraculous power was attributed to Satan. Like the aliens in *Arrival*, Jesus was grossly misunderstood. In the end, Jesus was arrested, tried, and crucified. The faction that wanted to get rid of Him seemingly won. Unlike the movie, there was no last ditch "save" with Jesus. Mankind killed the alien. Then, the surprise! The "revisit" of the alien: He rose from the dead. Even after His resurrection, it took a while for His followers to understand the reasons for God's "landing" on planet Earth. But with the coming of the Holy Spirit living with and within believers, there came an understanding of what God was up to, and grace was finally understood. Finally, men and women understood the purpose of God's visit to our planet. And the world has never been the same.

I've found that people are still surprised by grace when it's fleshed out in Christ-followers. People don't expect a loving, forgiving response to failure. People are caught off guard when they're not condemned and written off by Christians. We seem like aliens to people. I think I'd rather be an alien, showing up with a life and language that communicates what Jesus was all about—love and grace—and then allow people as much time as they need to "get it."

Noticings from Television

Some of you just leaped out of your chair with joy, "Does he mean I can increase my experiencing of God by watching more television? If so, I could watch it all day and get really super-spiritual." No, that's not what I mean. Television is here to stay, but like the cell phone, it cannot be what takes up a big chunk of your time. But, sometimes there are shows, commercials, and movies that speak to a biblical truth, a character trait, a decision that resulted for good, or a struggle that's worked through.

For example, before the 2016 Olympics, an interview was aired featuring the swimmer, Michael Phelps, the most decorated Olympic athlete in history. After his record-setting collection of gold medals in previous Olympics, he had some bumps in the road: a marijuana conviction and a six-month ban from US swimming.

But he came back a new person. He made a comeback from a mistake, a failure, a bad decision. And how did America respond? They rooted for him! *Everybody loves a comeback story!* Guess who's the author of *comebacks?* God is! You and I are "comebacks" from a life without God before we became Christ-followers. We're comebacks from all of the moral or lifestyle failures we've had during our journey with Jesus. Jesus is the author of all comeback stories. *We are all comeback stories!* Jesus' grace and love and sacrifice for us made the comeback possible, and all heaven is cheering for us. God's dream is for millions of comeback stories to be a part of His family. God *cheers* and *celebrates* our comebacks from leading a life without Him, from straying away from Him, from going on a moral vacation. He celebrates our returning home.

A cynical writer once said, *"The church is one of the few institutions that shoots its wounded."* It's true. Some Christ-followers and churches are not open to giving people second chances. But Jesus majored in wounded people, failures, people who'd screwed up. The Michael Phelps segment reminded me to celebrate regular, everyday-people-type comebacks. Like a couple whose marriage makes a comeback. Like someone who gets into recovery to address a self-destructive life pattern and comes back. Like a person who goes to therapy for a spending pattern that is out of control. These are the comebacks for which Jesus and heaven throw a party. That TV show reminded me to give people who've failed a second, third, fourth (and more!) comeback opportunities. Phelps reminded me that "as far as the east is from the west, so far does [God] remove our transgressions from us" (Ps. 103:12). I was reminded to *embrace and own that for myself.*

That image of Phelps triggered this prayer: "God thank you for making me one of your 'comeback stories.' Your grace, love, forgiveness, and Your presence never stopped when I failed. Now I'm restored and whole. Thanks for your patience while I was 'coming back.' Thanks for the people and programs that helped in my various comebacks. Thanks that You never stopped loving me through the whole thing."

Two Exercises to Practice Noticing

The 10 Minute Walk Exercise

Go outside and walk around for 10 minutes and ask, "God, would You bring to my attention one thing that You want me to notice and then guide me into understanding why You brought this to my attention?" If anything catches your eye, do the 30-second pause and listen quietly in your spirit. See if anything comes to mind. If so, that could be God communicating with you.

Please: be gentle on yourself. Maybe you *notice* something, and you ask God and you get *nada*. Don't beat yourself up. Don't think you're unspiritual. Don't think God is mad at you. Just remember noticing what caught your attention and linger on it through the day. Keep asking God if there was something He wanted to say to you about what caught your eye. Something may come to you later in the day as you "re-linger" on it.

Post-it Note Reminders to NOTICE

Get a Post-It pad and write the word "Notice" on several sticky notes. Throughout your day, paste them on noticings that come your way. Stick them on your bathroom mirror, in your car or on the door so you'll see it on the way outside. Tape one on your desk at work. Stick one on other places in your home or car that you frequent often. For a short time, make the word "Notice" a screen saver on your laptop, iPad or cell phone. (You can do this with any of the practices in this book.) Then, put an imaginary "Notice" sign on your spouse, children, friends, and anyone you lock eyes with. Notice what God might be saying to you in all your *noticings*.

May God bring you many *noticings* that let you know He's communicating who He is and His love for you all the time!

Digital culture is the new "background noise." It is the multitude I carry in my pocket. Rest is harder to find in a digital culture because technology has dissolved the two fundamental boundaries that are essential to rest: Being alone and Being Quiet.

- John Koessler, The Radical Pursuit of Rest

Chapter 6: The Practice of BEING ALONE

I was 15 when I went to my first Young Life camping experience. A group of adults that I had never met paid for four of us to go to a camp called Malibu. I thought, "I think that's in L.A. somewhere. I guess that will be okay." Then I found out it was in Canada. 47 high school teenagers and about eight Young Life staff members began a two-day bus ride to a dock in Vancouver where the *Malibu Princess* loaded another 250 students from all over the U.S. on an eight-hour boat ride to the camp.

The year was 1970. The Beatles had just broken up. The Vietnam War was still on the forefront of our minds. Flower children, long hair, and loud rock-and-roll music were the staples of our generation. It's no exaggeration to say that a large percentage of the students on that bus had experimented with marijuana and other drugs. Young Life specialized in "unchurched" teenagers. I was one of those unchurched teenagers.

Space on the page constrains me from telling you all the wonderful and fun activities that took place that week: water-skiing, canoeing, swimming in a pool blasted out of solid rock, team competitions with silly events that required no talent, and people who showed a genuine interest in me—even though they'd never met me before. There were the meetings at night with rowdy group singing followed by a speaker that explained who Jesus was and what He'd done for us in terms teenagers could understand. I wasn't raised in the church so this was all brand new to me.

Needless to say, I was overwhelmed with it all. I was bug-eyed the entire week. I listened, but I think my mind was too young to understand. It was all so *new* to me.

On the fifth night, the speaker asked us to do something weird. After he'd spoken about what Jesus had done for us on the cross, he asked everyone to go outside, in the dark, and find a place to be alone and silent for 15 minutes. I'd never done this before. Fifteen minutes of silence and aloneness? The way the 60's and 70's went, with the explosion of rock-and-roll music, there never was a quiet moment in a teenager's life. My friends and I always had record players blaring in our rooms. (Just like today, when students spend all their time with their earbuds in.) But, silence? Can you say uncomfortable?

I found out that the 15 minutes went really fast. I found I wanted more time, so I stayed there after the camp horn blew to signal the end of the silence. I didn't become a Christ-follower that day or week. My conversion came two years later with a second trip to Malibu, after my senior year. In that second "quiet time" I opened the door of my heart to Jesus and never looked back. I'll never forget that alone time. It gave a 15-year-old, gangly, insecure, and immature teenager the chance to reflect just a little bit.

That time of *being alone* changed my life.

God's dream: Interrupt the Busyness!

As we continue to examine how to put busyness in its place, here's a question for you:

Do you think it was God's intent that people never stop going, doing, running around, talking, texting, emailing, Twittering, Facebooking, posting, Instagramming, working, achieving, and moving?

No!

Alone time is something that *everyone* needs. But with tasks, assignments, deadlines, conversations, schedules, interruptions, and demands from little children, the first thing that usually gets sidelined is time to get alone to reflect, ponder, examine, and discern what is going on within us.

Being alone is depriving ourselves of the companionship of others in order to enjoy the company of God. It involves turning off the TV, computer, and cell-phone. It involves disconnecting.

Never being out of touch means never being able to get away. For true solitude and silence, we have to leave our electronic devices (phones and computers) behind. If we don't, we're merely relocating a State of Distraction from one location to another.
- David Brooks, Newsweek, April 2001.

Being alone and being quiet, when practiced, reminds us that God is fully capable of running the universe without our help. Being alone and quiet are countermeasures for a world that tries to persuade us that our worth is measured by our usefulness.

In this chapter, we'll talk about how to be alone, the benefits of being alone, and *what to do* with that solitary, refreshing time.

But first, let's talk about some of the roadblocks that might make *being alone* harder for you.

Bad "Being Aloneness" From Your Past

Some of you may have been punished in your childhood by being isolated from people for inappropriate amounts of time. The old "go to your room and stay there until I tell you" punishment may have gone on way too long for a child your age. Having these experiences might have created a nervousness about any extended time of being alone with God. For you, aloneness brings up negative feelings, not positive ones.

Maybe, as an adolescent, you had trouble making friends. Maybe a group of friends turned on you and shut you out. This is a very hurtful form of being alone because it involves rejection, meanness, and immaturity. It can brand you with feelings of, "What did I do wrong? Am I not pretty enough, 'cool' enough, or friendly enough?"

And, we can be "alone" while surrounded by friends and family who

121

genuinely care for us. We can be polite and courteous while inside we are dying for someone to listen to our struggles. We can feel a creeping separateness between ourselves and a spouse, or a boyfriend or girlfriend. It may be very difficult to open up to someone because we're afraid of how they'll respond.

Nervousness About Being Alone

The strategy of hell is to keep us from ever having time, space, or quietness to think through our lives, to think through what really matters and where our heart is with God and people. This opposition manifests as a relentless onslaught of people in every place we go.

If we are intentional about creating some spaces in our daily schedule for being alone, it can be a bit scary. It is very important to resist the urge to give up on it after five or ten minutes. That's not enough time to slow down and get comfortable with being alone. However, even if we can't stop our brain from being in overdrive, at least we took the time. (Remember, something is better than nothing.) Next time, you'll feel a bit more comfortable with it. You will start to feel less anxious with increasing the amount of alone time as well. Fight through the "nervous stage." Practice slowing your breathing down. Write down things you remembered you need to do, and then put that list aside. Keep returning to a place where, in your imagination, you are alone with God and He's smiling at you and He enjoys your effort at attentiveness to the love and grace that He's constantly sending your way!

Life Stages and Being Alone

Along with past experiences and the nervousness that comes with starting a new practice of alone time, where you are in your life-stages can have a major impact on how easy or hard you'll find the practice of being alone.

Life Stages Where Being Alone Is Easier:

A. You're single. Single people have the freedom to make their own schedules. They don't have to run their plans by a spouse or parents. They can schedule a walk on the beach, a mountain climb or some hours in their living space. They can drive to places where they can be alone and for any amount of time.

B. You're retired. Retired people have no employer telling them where and when to show up for work. Their children are grown up. Yes, there may be grandchildren, but in most cases they go home with their parents. Retired people can plan trips at any time of the year. They can take a day or even *days* to be alone with their thoughts, feelings, or concerns and to ponder all of that in God's presence with no interruption. Granted, many retired people choose to spend their energies in volunteer work or another vocational interest they've had for years but could not do when they worked. And that is wonderful. But for the most part, retired people have total command of their time. It would take very little effort to plan for some time alone with God.

C. Empty nesters. Currently, I'm in this stage. I have grandchildren, and I'm finding out I don't have the energy I used to, but I generally have control over my time. I can say "yes" or "no" to requests for my time and energy. Most empty-nesters still have five to fifteen years left of work. If that job requires an eight-hour day, that's a lot of time per week, but it's nothing that compares to the life stages below.

Life Stages Where Finding "Alone Time" Is Harder:

A. You're married. You might be thinking, *An understanding spouse would give their mate some 'alone time' if they wished for that. A spouse who knows their partner well, who knows they need that time to get emotionally re-charged, would gladly give them that time.* Would they really? Believing the best about couples, I'd like to think they would, but even the most understanding partner turns a one-person household into a two-person household, and that's double the people! (And if one of you likes having the TV always on, it can be like adding a *third* person—a very loud, distracting person—to your household!)

One more possible issue is the misunderstanding that comes when a spouse essentially says, "I need some time away from you for my own well-being." Sometimes that doesn't go well—an honest need for occasional silence can be perceived as rejection.

Let's just say, being married adds one more wonderful human being to your life who loves you. The partnership a good marriage brings can't be matched. But it's not as easy as singlehood when it comes to finding time to be alone.

B. You're married with children. When I mention the need for time alone to people in this life stage, I get laughed at. Busyness becomes a way of life for families, and it can last for over 20 years, depending on the spacing of your children. What does a parent do for alone time when they are transporting children to school, dance class, soccer practice, helping with homework, going to the store for food constantly, attending church, cleaning, cooking, and reading stories? And then you're also trying to fit in times with your adult friends and their families, time for your physical fitness, and your favorite TV shows. Oh, wait, both parents are working too. I'm exhausted just writing this. This life stage is, by far, the most difficult stage to carve out time to be alone with God. But there's one other life stage that is even harder.

C. Single with children. If there has been an amicable divorce and child-care is shared, there can be breaks for the single parent. If one of the parents lives far away, or is in jail, or has a drug habit, or lives in an unsafe environment for the children, then the responsibility falls on one parent to do all that I mentioned above, only without a partner to share the load. I feel the most for a single parent in these situations. In the majority of cases, the single parent is mom. Time for themselves? You can almost *fahget-a-bout-it*. The only benefit is if childcare is shared with the other spouse.

A Q&A About Practicing *Being Alone* in Various Life Stages

1. Does "being alone" only count if you go to a monastery and do a Silent Retreat for three days?

No. Very few have the time, space or desire for something like this. And many of you extroverts out there are thinking you'd last five minutes at a monastery. But if you can and you are drawn to this, by all means *do it!*

2. Does being alone only count if you're in a quiet place with no people around?

No, but it helps.

Still, your body could be surrounded by people and you can go to a "place in your spirit" where you are singularly attentive to God, asking Him a question, or listening for His prompting. You can be changing a diaper, mopping the floor, cleaning the garage, in a sales meeting, having lunch with friends, or walking on the beach and you can still experience God. Your mind and spirit, while in the presence of people, can be in a state of "having one ear turned to heaven." In a sense, you're intentionally reflecting on your feelings and thoughts and being aware of God's presence in the midst of all that. It takes practice, but it can be done.

It is also a perfectly fine practice to engage in a physical activity while being in a state of "aloneness" and quiet. I know many people whose time with God involves a walk on the beach or in nature somewhere. I know a very active retired teacher who puts on noise-reducing headphones in his workshop and has times of aloneness while doing woodwork. Several people I know experience "alone time listening for God's gentle nudges" while gardening, mowing the lawn, knitting, surfing, weight-lifting, vacuuming, jogging, doing the laundry, or driving. These are things you can do on "auto-pilot" so you can ponder, reflect and listen for God's nudgings while engaged in an activity you could "do in your sleep." This is perfectly legal. In fact, it is one of the ways God wired us up to experience Him.

3. Does it count if I can't spend any longer than a half hour or 15 minutes in some "being alone" time? Does it count if I did a bit of silence only two days per week or not all in one stretch because it's simply a terribly busy week?

Absolutely it counts! Always remember: *something is better than nothing*. Even 15 minutes in the course of a month can be 15 more minutes than you did last month. As I mentioned, for people in the busiest of life stages, these smaller *being alone* segments are the best you can do for a while. God is very, very pleased and proud of you in that. What "typical Joe and Joan" have to embrace is that there are many different ways to connect with God (which is what this book is about). And although "being alone" is one of them, it's not the only one, especially for people in a life stage where sections of free time are hard to find. (See the chapters on *Noticing, Slowing, Waiting, Treasuring,* and *Thinking Things Through*.)

I'm an introvert. I get recharged by being alone. Yet my entire working life has been people-oriented: youth work, teaching high school, and then ministering as a senior pastor. It took me a long time to realize that I must have a lot of absolute alone time to get my emotional batteries re-charged. Take the time to know where you are on the introvert-extrovert scale, because this will dictate how much you will need to lean into this "being alone" thing. And most of all, do *not* feel guilty about what you cannot do in this area because of a life situation or life stage.

Jesus and Alone Time

Now that we've looked at some of the challenges and blessings of practicing *being alone* at various stages of life, let's take some time to look at our model when it comes to practicing *being alone*: Jesus Himself.

> Interruptions were a problem before the digital age. Jesus was interrupted too. The crowd intruded on His privacy more than once. The difference between the crowd of Jesus' time and our age is that the crowd had to make a serious effort to interrupt Him. Today, the crowd can stay where they are and CLICK their way into our presence. Like Jesus, we occasionally need to withdraw from this kind of crowd...the VIRTUAL crowd."[1]

Though He poured out His time and His energy in loving others, a case could be made that Jesus was an introvert, and that He was re-energized by being alone. Let's look at five different times in the Bible where Jesus went away for some extended "alone time."

1. Jesus' cousin, John the Baptist, was beheaded by a narcissistic king. John was innocent of any wrongdoing. But he was a troublemaker, and troublemakers were killed if they bothered the people in charge. "When Jesus heard what had happened, He withdrew by boat privately to a solitary place" (Matt. 14:23, NIV).

Why did Jesus need this time? Isn't He the Son of God? Hasn't God seen millions of innocent people die? What was different about John's death?

The obvious answer is that Jesus was grieving. If John and Jesus were cousins, they grew up playing hide-and-seek together, sharing family meals, playing chase, sharing teenage struggles, and making friends in the neighborhood. John and Jesus shared a lot of life together. When the news came that John was gone, Jesus needed to grieve his loss. The Son of God was sad, hurting, and wounded emotionally. Never forget Jesus was 100 percent human as well as 100 percent God-in-the-flesh.

So, what's one reason to make some time alone for yourself a priority? *To sort through your emotions.* It doesn't matter if the emotions are sorrow, anger, discontentedness with your job, depression, feeling a chronic low-grade fatigue, feeling overwhelmed, or dealing with loss of any kind. Busyness can rob us of the needed time to process the "intense feelings" we have when life deals a blow, or life wears us down.

If Jesus was God in human form and He needed some alone-time to process what He was feeling, then we, as normal human beings, have to give ourselves permission to do this as well.

2. Another reference to Jesus taking alone time is Mark 1:35: "Very early in the morning, while it was still dark, Jesus got up, left the house and went off to a solitary place, where he prayed" (NIV). This reference occurs following a day where Jesus healed hundreds of sick people and exorcised demons. Jesus had a full day of people. He expended a lot of energy. He needed some time alone after a long day of helping and healing those people.

Many of you reading this are "giving out to others" most of your day. You may be supervising, encouraging, teaching, helping, guiding, correcting, listening, counseling, or shooting the breeze. Maybe you're energized by this. If so, that's the way you're wired up. But even an extrovert cherishes some "alone time" here and there.

It is essential for your own well-being to monitor whether your people time has crowded out your alone time. The truth is, if we don't do this, we "skim" in our relationships, never really going deep with someone because we're on to the next thing, or to the next person. There's no time to "depth" any relationships, nor time to think through how you were feeling in the experiences you had or that interaction with someone. And God usually gets the leftovers.

If we're too busy, there's no time to reflect alone on how the time with people went, to process what they were really saying, and to ask God, "Was there anything I need to respond to with that person, so they feel heard and understood?" And then to ask yourself, "What did those encounters or situations do to me? Were they life-giving or life-draining? Why? Do I need to adjust anything in my schedule, if I can, to give me more time to analyze what's going on inside me?"

3. "Immediately Jesus made his disciples get into the boat and go on ahead of him to Bethsaida, while he dismissed the crowd. After leaving them, he went up on a mountainside to pray" (Mark 6:45-46, NIV). This sentence

followed the miracle of feeding 10,000 people from five loaves of bread and two fish. After this miracle, many of the people wanted to crown Jesus as their king (see John 6:15). But instead of being swept away in the massive screams of, "We love you Jesus! Take charge of this messed-up country we live in! We know You can make things right!"....Jesus takes off.

In this situation, Jesus needed alone time to think through His singular purpose and assignment. His assignment was not what the crowd wanted. He was *not* on earth to become an earthly-type king, but a King of another kind: the type of King who would rule in people's hearts.

Be sure of this: being persecuted or minimized or insulted or demeaned is hard. It shakes us to our souls. It can make us doubt who we are and why we think we're here on earth. But applause and cheering is just as insidious a method to draw us away from our mission from God on earth.

Jesus faced this dangerous situation of being popular and well-liked. Believing this kind of hype can deceive us into thinking we're "all that." It can make us think "I'm the only one who can get this done right. I would be the perfect one to lead this thing."

Fanfare and popularity could have drawn Jesus off-mission. What was His solution? Get away, be alone with God, and talk things through with Him. Jesus asked God to re-enforce the task assigned specifically to Him. And what was Jesus' prime directive? *To solve the sin problem.* His assignment was: "Purchase forgiveness for fallen mankind by offering Yourself as a substitute sacrifice to pay for the debt of imperfection we could never achieve on our own."

It was definitely a task that deserved concentration and dedicated time for focus.

So, what is your prime directive? Why are you here on earth? The never-ending code we are to live by is: Love God and Love People. That's why you and I are here. Then there is a more specific assignment within that never-ending code that is the main expression of your love for God and people. Are you supposed to have all the spiritual gifts listed in the New and Old Testament? Of course not. Are you supposed to be passionate about every issue of screwed-up humanity? No! For example, am I supposed to have a high level of passion for the poor, recovering alcoholics, the mentally ill, gambling addicts, divorce recovery, housing the homeless, teenagers, children, and reaching the unchurched—all at once? Yes and no. Yes, all these matters should move our hearts to empathy and prayer, but Jesus is *not* expecting us to put our bodies, energy and checkbooks into *all* of them.

Jesus needed some time (after feeding the 10,000) of aloneness to get away from a wave of spontaneous popularity. In this time of retreat, Jesus was reminded that His ultimate assignment was much more than supplying food for hungry people. In the same way, we need to get away to stay focused on the major thing(s) God has assigned to us. Are you a teacher of the Bible? Major in that. Are you good at listening, asking good questions, and counseling? Grow into that. Are you passionate about preschoolers? Do you love to put systems in place so that things can run efficiently and in an orderly manner? Do you feel comfortable and "in your element" dialoguing with people who aren't interested in Jesus? Do you love working with your hands, building and fixing stuff to express your love for God and people? Do those things.

Don't feel guilty about not doing every single good thing in the world. Do the good that God has called you to do.

Jesus was not on earth to build houses in Mexico slums. He was here to take on the sin of the world and be raised from the dead, then to rule over our world and all that has ever been made.

So, what is God's dream for your life? It may take some "alone on a mountainside" time to think this through with God and get going on your specific assignment from God. When you know that, the possibility of getting pulled into something else that people say you're good at, but you know you're not the *best* at, lowers dramatically.

4. "But Jesus *often* withdrew to the wilderness for prayer" (Luke 5:16, NLT, emphasis mine). How many times and how often should I intentionally

grab "useless time?" We see the answer is in Jesus' example: OFTEN! That means on a regular basis.

This is where it's important to remember your life stage. If you're single, or an empty-nester, or retired, this might be easier for you because children aren't around demanding your time, energy, and attention. Other things will be shouting for your attention—the latest stock market news, volunteering, grandchildren, time with friends, preparing for retirement, or getting married—but you probably have a large amount of control over how you spend your time.

But if you are in that child-raising period of your life, the phrase "often withdrawing" may only be a source of guilt. Let me reassure you: God is with and within you, above and below you, in front and in back of you, to the right and left of you—He is with you in every moment you spend caring for your children. He is *not* disappointed in your lack of time for aloneness with Him. He knows you're almost never alone.

This key to *being alone* with Jesus during this life stage is having a "one ear to heaven" mindset. It requires doing the practice of *noticing* almost exclusively. In any situation with your baby or child or teenager, God will be revealing things about Himself to you. *Notice* them.

For example:

- When you are holding your baby, picture God holding you. He calls us His children. There will be times when you need to feel God's hold upon you, His tenderness and gaze upon you. You might pray, "Jesus, as I am holding my baby now, You are holding me in Your good hands. I am safe in Your hands."

- When you're at a park, watching your preschool children playing chase, climbing on the jungle gym, playing in the sand, or swinging on the swing. They are having fun. They're laughing, smiling and enjoying each moment. They aren't thinking about what's going to be happening in an hour. They are "fully present in that moment. As you realize this, you might think, *God, you love fun. You want me to have fun in this life. You made all sorts of things that can be fun. Like my*

131

child here, remind me that it's okay to have fun. Remind me that you love to see a smile on my face. Help me be here in this moment.

If you do that, in the middle of a park full of screaming children, you will have gone on a short "alone time" with God. This takes a little intentionality and practice.

One more example:

- Let's say your children are adolescents. By definition, they are "in-between." They are "tween-agers." They are transitioning from child to adulthood, but they aren't there yet. Sometimes they act like a mini-adult. Sometimes like a child again.

As mentioned before, this "one ear turned to heaven" mindset is a constant state of *being alone with God.* Practicing this really helps with our tempers. Rather than an explosion of anger resulting in words you wish you could take back, slow down a tense situation. A pregnant pause and a few moments of asking for God's help will result in coming up with good solutions (and consequences, if needed).

Looking back, I remember more of what I got wrong in my parenting than what I did right. In one case, I think we got it right. Our son was dabbling into the world of inappropriate teenage "fun" with some friends he didn't want us to meet. His grades held up for the most part, but he increasingly retreated from involvement in our family. He stopped communicating like he used to and there was some lying about where he was and what he was doing.

After my wife and I processed the sadness and anger over the situation, rather than going ballistic (one of my tendencies), we thought through what was most important to him. Answer: his independence to come and go in his car. So, we did the "contract" approach. We drew up a list of behaviors and requirements that he had to agree to, and came up with consequences (taking away some of his independence) if he violated the contract. We also built in rewards.

It took time, but to our son's credit, he began to respond to the contract, and to our increased attention, and his behavior changed.

The point in all this is that Karen and I sought out God's help as we asked, "What sort of consequences will reach our son? And what actions should we take that are appropriate for the behavior?" Contemplating this together while *being alone with God,* the idea came. When you're in the parent stage, you can experience *being alone with God* while in the company of your spouse and children, even in a situation where you have to do some tough love.

5. Prior to Jesus' arrest in the Garden of Gethsemane, he retreated to be alone with His Father in a very stressful situation (see Matt. 26 and Mark 14). Very soon, Jesus would be taken into custody. He would be punched in the face and body. He would be spit upon by multiple parties and have a crown of thorns shoved onto His head. Then He would be scourged by a nine-tailed leather whip with tips that had been sealed with tar and chips of bone. He was about to have His hands and feet nailed to the wooden posts of a cross. He was about to have that cross placed in the ground and raised, so that He could not lift up His torso to take a breath, slowly suffocating Him.

Who wouldn't be praying with the greatest intensity prior to facing this situation? It's recorded that Jesus was so stressed that His sweat started to turn red from blood oozing out of his pours (scientifically known as hematidrosis, caused by extreme anxiety).

What did Jesus pray for in this "alone time"? *He prayed "ASKS."* In the toughest circumstances of His life, Jesus asked if it would possible to find another way for humanity's sin problem to be solved. The Father's answer came back, "No, there isn't, but I'll be with You." Jesus made this desperate ask a total of three times. It was not answered in the way He wanted, three times.

The practice of being alone often involves ASKS of God. Being alone crystalizes what really matters to us. In the garden, Jesus' utmost concern was (possibly) the physical torture, but it also might have been that God the Father was going to "forsake" Jesus and allow the entire weight of mankind's moral failures to be absorbed into Jesus. Jesus would "become" sin, while having lived a life wherein He knew no sin.

So, what are your "asks" of God? It's easy to figure out what they are—

but only if you to get some slow, unrushed, unhurried, un-busy, *alone time* to figure them out. Once you're alone, ask yourself, "What do I find myself thinking about most of the time?" That's your prayer agenda. Usually, it's something that has you concerned, worried, or nervous. Is it finances? Your marriage? Your children? Your friend's situation? Your health? A hidden sin no one knows about? Whatever it is, *ask* as Jesus did. Yell at God. Express your raw, unedited feelings at God. That is what being alone with God is for.

Discovering Your Personalized *Being Alone* Preferences

Remember, experiencing God while being alone, or in a state of aloneness with people present, will take *practice*. So, what might *being alone* look like for you? You'll have to make a brutally honest assessment of how you are wired up to answer this for yourself. You'll have to come to grips with whether you've been forced to be an extrovert while really being an introvert (my story). You'll have to experiment with which *being alone* activities really recharge you. And you'll have to be brutally honest about how much time you really need or want to be alone, especially if you're extroverted and get recharged in a non-alone atmosphere.

What Do I Reflect on While *Being Alone*?

As I mentioned before, often the agenda for reflection is whatever is most on your mind. After processing that, you can move on to other matters. Here are some possible reflection topics that will change for you as life goes on:

But before reflecting, pray, "Lord Jesus, I am always in Your presence. But here and now, is there anything You want to say to me? Anything You want to point out to me?"

After listening for an answer, you can choose any of the topics below and ask any of these questions of God:

1. *YOU!* On the topic of *you*, here are some questions to bring before God and yourself:

God, show me what I'm feeling and why I'm feeling it. What's my strongest emotion? Where's that coming from? Depression? Unhappiness? Frustration? Trapped? Defeated? Hopeful? Encouraged? Forgiven? Understood? Loved? Cherished? Disappointed in myself? Failure? How would I describe my relationship with You currently? What might be three words that would describe it? What's *most* on my mind? What can't I stop thinking about? Why am I so tired all the time? Why am I not very happy?

2. *YOUR MARRIAGE!* On the topic of *your marriage*, here are some questions to bring before God and yourself:

How are my spouse and I really doing? What part am I playing or not playing in nurturing closeness with my spouse? Am I giving all my energy to my job and the kids and giving the leftovers to my spouse? Is there anything I need to own up to that may be causing a drift in our marriage?

Is there a continuing closeness in our marriage or a creeping separateness that has come about because of our busy lives? What are some things I could do to let my spouse know they matter more than any other human on earth? Have I gotten lazy with romance?

3. *YOUR SINGLEHOOD!* On the topic of *your singlehood*, here are some questions to bring before God and yourself:

Is there any area of my character or behavior that I want to address and change with God's help? How am I viewing the opposite sex these days?

What are the parameters I should have for a future spouse God? What's the best career path for the way I'm wired? What characteristics should I look for in lifelong friends?

4. *YOUR SITUATION AS A PARENT OR SINGLE PARENT!* On the topic of *your parenting*, here are some questions to bring before God and yourself:

What parenting style do I want to imitate or avoid from the parents I had? God, what style of parenting have You made in me? What am I most uncomfortable with in parenting? What areas of improvement could I begin to practice to become a better parent? Encouragement? Affirmation? Physical touch? In which situations do I get defensive with my spouse's critique of my parenting style? Why is that? How do we protect our marriage when our children constantly scream for attention? What adjustments need to be made in our schedules to create sections of quantity and quality of time for each other and also our family?

5. *YOUR STRUGGLES!* On the topic of *your struggles*, here are some questions to bring before God and yourself:

God, we're hurtin' for money these days. What should we do? God, I'm so tired, seemingly all the time. What's going on? Show me what's going on and what changes need to be made for my own well-being. God, I'm struggling with _____, and it's hurting my soul. What would you have me do? God, what steps do I need to take to get my anger under control? God, why do I feel the need to spend money to make me feel good?

Lord, is my schedule out of control? What is it about me that won't let me do something about it? Jesus, is there too much responsibility on my shoulders, both at work and home and at church? Show me what You'd have me do regarding that.

6. *YOUR CAREER SITUATION!* On the topic of *your career*, here are some "asks" and questions to bring before God and yourself:

God, I'm not happy in my career, and I feel paralyzed to change because any decision will affect my family, our lifestyle, and might mean we have to move. God, help me to discern what I'm most passionate about and let that guide my career path. Lord, what are my areas of giftedness? Guide me into a job where I use them and not just settle for something else.

7. *YOUR CHILDREN!* On the topic of *your children*, here are some questions to bring before God and yourself:

God, what form of affirmation and discipline is the right method for each of my children, who have different sensitivity levels and different personalities?

God, what methods would be best for each of my children to let them know they are loved? Words? Actions? Touches? Looks? All of the above? God, help me to study my children more diligently. How did You wire them up?

What communication skills do I need to employ to keep the communication lines open with each one?

8. *WHAT'S LIFE-GIVING and LIFE-DRAINING FOR ME?* On the topic of your energy, here are some questions to bring before God and yourself:

God, reveal to me the temperament You gave *me*. Show me where I'm trying to be someone else and not me. What is *fun* to me? What have I always wanted to do but haven't? Why haven't I? What situations, people, and events suck the life out of me? What situations, people, and events pump energy and life into me? What is my current energy level? (High or low?) What's causing that?

9. *HOW DO I THINK JESUS FEELS ABOUT ME RIGHT NOW?* On this topic, here are some different possibilities to bring before God and yourself:

Proud? Pleased? Disappointed? Mad? Indifferent? Offended? Unhappy? Grieved? Joyful? Thrilled? Passionate? Sympathetic? Delighted? Overjoyed? Ecstatic? Elated? Glad? Hopeful? Embarrassed? Ashamed?

What you think Jesus feels about you tells you a lot about how you view yourself.

Reflecting on the subjects represented by these categories usually only happens by *being alone* for significant segments of time. Give yourself permission to take some segments of time for *you* and *God*. Only take on one of these categories at any one time. Choose the one that moves you the most emotionally first. Embrace the life-stage you are in and be glad that God understands it and wants to live in it with you. And, embrace the one-and-only, unique, treasured by God...*you!* That's all God expects you to be!

Every heartbeat, every breath, every synapse function
in our brains, every sight and every sound that is
given to us every day is a gift from God.

Chapter 7: The Practice of RECEIVING

I know a single mom named Amy who has a very high paying job, but she lives in Silicon Valley. The average cost of renting a home there is a minimum of $7,500 per month. *And Silicon Valley landlords* only allow nine-month leases. Amy and her two children have moved three times in the last three years.

The time was coming up for another move and Amy was wondering if she should bite the bullet, move out of Silicon Valley, and just deal with a crazy-long commute.

The problem was, her son in junior high was the starting shortstop on his club baseball team, running for class president, and had lots of friends. Amy's ten-year-old daughter was a musically gifted child who was proficient on three different instruments and learning more all the time, with the support of the excellent music department at her school—where she also was a popular kid with many friends.

Amy hated the idea of moving her children out of their school district, but staying simply didn't make sense financially. Her mom and dad, knowing the value of a good adolescent experience, applied for a second mortgage on their condo so that they could help Amy and her kids stay in Silicon Valley. They were one day away from signing the papers.

On that day, Amy's son had a baseball game. A ground ball came at him, kicked up some dirt, and a rather large piece of dirt got in his eye.

It went into the back part of his eyeball. Amy took him to the ER, where he was successfully treated. Driving down an unfamiliar street on the way home, Amy saw a small Kleenex-box-sized sign on a telephone pole, "House for Rent." She yanked the wheel over and immediately called the number on this very small sign. She got a hold of the realtor coordinating rental applications.

Now, what you need to know is that when a house is put up for rent in Silicon Valley, it is rented in less than 24 hours. So, when Amy got the realtor on the phone, he said, "There are five people ahead of you, but I'll put your name in. C'mon down and fill out the paperwork."

She did, and she also told him about her family and job situation. Thinking she's out of the running, she drove home. Later that night, she got a call from the owners of the house. "We'd like to talk to you about renting our home. Do you have some time tomorrow?"

Amy said, "You betcha!"

The next day, Amy went over to their home and after Amy retold some of her story, the couple said, "You might find this strange, but when we looked at all the candidates, your story touched us deeply. We'd like to offer you our home to stay in."

Amy was shocked. *How did this happen? I was sixth on the list and LAST to apply.* Her gratitude factor went through the roof.

Then they said one more thing. "Now Amy, we have kind of a strange request for you."

Uh-oh, Amy thought.

"Rather than renting for the nine months that normal rentals go for, we were wondering if you could rent our home for two years."

Inside, Amy was doing backflips, but she calmly said, "Why, yes, I'd love to, no problem."

She signed the papers right there.

What *Receiving From God* Looks Like

Let's look at Amy's story: a ground ball to a shortstop results in a hospital visit, which results in a different route home, which results in Amy seeing a tiny sign, which results in her getting chosen out of a large group of applicants, and *then,* instead of the normal nine-month lease, she's given a generous lease of two years. You tell me, is God in the details or *what?* What a gift from God! What timing!

Amy's dad was able to cancel the second mortgage papers on the day he was driving to the bank to sign them. On the day Amy and her children moved out of their old house, the owners began knocking it down to build a bigger one. Her children were able to stay in their schools with all their friends and to continue to grow their blossoming gifts and talents.

All Amy could do was *receive,* and marvel at how God provided for her when she thought there was no hope but to move away. I think God sometimes does that kind of miraculous coordination of timing and circumstances to show us that He knows our situations; that there's no way this could have happened without it being *God-orchestrated and God-arranged.*

What's our role in incidents like this that come our way? *Receive* it! Be grateful. Give thanks. And stand in awe at the wonder of God's attentiveness to our lives and at the way He loves to give awesome gifts to us.

RECEIVING: The practice of increasing our DEPENDENCY on Jesus and others by not orchestrating anything ourselves. It's having a picture in our minds of open hands; it's *asking* of God and then waiting for His timing.

Receiving is categorically opposed to generating our agenda through activity and solving. Receiving is *anti-giving, anti-serving,* and *anti-producing.* Think of the things we can only receive; the things we can't possibly earn; things we don't deserve. The biggest thing we receive by far is…GRACE.

Justice is *getting* what we deserve.

Mercy is *not* getting what we *do* deserve.

Grace is getting what we *don't* deserve.

The Measuring Ruler

For several years, I was asked by a friend of mine who was a high school teacher to come in to his psychology class full of seniors and field questions about the Christian faith and about religion in general. The students were asked to write down any questions they wanted to, and I was asked to answer them in a way that non-churchgoing, cynical, and irreligious students might understand. The questions ranged from the role of women in the church, some churches' stance condemning homosexuals, and why Christ-followers seem to look down on nonbelievers and try to avoid them.

One of the questions that came up every year was: What's the basis for someone going to heaven? I always used a visual on the whiteboard to answer this question, guiding them through the following exercise.

I draw a vertical ruler. Then I say, "This is now a Morality Measuring Ruler." I put numbers going down the side with a "10" at the top and a "0" at the bottom. Then I ask, "Play along with me now. Who do Christ-followers say never sinned, never had an evil thought, word, or action? Who might be called 'morally perfect'?"

They say, "Okay, Jesus."

Then I write his name at the top of the ruler.

"Okay, if Jesus is up at the top, then what spiritual entity would be at the bottom, if we believed in this stuff?"

They answer, "Satan, the devil."

Okay. So now our ruler has Jesus at the top and Satan at the bottom.

Then I ask the students, "Who, in your opinion, was (or is) the most unselfish person, the most compassionate and loving person that has lived in the last 100 years?"

The students usually get around to one name, "Mother Teresa."

Then I tell them, "I've read a lot about her and some of her own writings, and she would not rank herself very high, but if you were to put her on this Morality Ruler, where would you put her?"

The students usually put her at about the 7 level.

Then I ask, "Who was the most evil person the world has seen in the last 100 years?"

The students sometimes suggest, "Saddam Hussein, Idi Amin, Osama bin Laden," but they usually land on Adolf Hitler.

So I ask them, "Where would you put Hitler on our Morality Ruler? Remember, Satan is at 0."

They usually give Adolf a 2 ranking.

So now we have this gap between Mother Teresa and Adolf Hitler, between a 7 and a 2. I ask the students, "Now, where would you put yourself on the Morality Scale?"

Every single year, it's the same. They always put themselves right in the middle between Mother Teresa and Adolf Hitler. So, I write the word "Us," at that in-between point.

Then I ask, "Now, where would you put the cut-off line for who goes to heaven and who goes to hell?"

Once again, every year it's the same answer. The students put the cut-off line just *below* themselves. In other words, they go to heaven, and anybody else below *them* doesn't.

Then I tell them, "This is how people think God operates. They think He does a moral rating system on everyone. They think God has a balancing scale in heaven that on one side has all our good behavior, good verbal responses, good thoughts and intentions. Then, on the other side of the scale is all our bad behavior, decisions, words, thoughts, and intentions."

Then I say, "We hope the good side of the balancing scale outweighs the bad behavior side and then we hope we'll get to heaven. But really, what kind of a God would never let us know where we stand in this system? That God sounds rather sadistic; keeping all of us in the dark about where we stand with Him."

Then I tell the students, "This is *not* how God operates." And I go on to tell them that we have two options for attaining heaven:

1. Be perfect

2. Receive grace

Using a baseball analogy, we can attain heaven by:

1. *Getting a hit every time we're up.* Meaning, whenever we have an opportunity to open our mouths, or respond with our facial expressions, or doing the right thing in any and every situation, we *always* do the right thing. We always "get a hit" in the behavior category… *and…*

2. *Never making an error.* We never drop a fly ball or make a throwing error. We never let a ground ball go through our legs. We play perfectly. Applying this analogy to our morality ruler, this means we never think a bad thought or say a demeaning word about anyone. We never lose our cool while driving. We never make a mistake with our words, thoughts, actions, and intentions…*ever!*

But here's the thing about baseball. As soon as you fly out, ground out, strike out, or get thrown out, you can never bat 1.000. As soon as you make one error, you are no longer perfect in that area either. The irony about baseball is that owners will pay millions of dollars to players who get a hit three out of every 10 times at bat. Basically, they're paying them more for their failures than their successes. But we think they are superstars for batting .300.

In the moral behavior world, we think God should be pretty pleased with us if we hit .300 in the "being a good man and good woman" scale. We think God should usher us into heaven for being between Mother Teresa and Adolf Hitler.

As soon as I explain this to the students, they know something's coming. Option #1 (be perfect) is out the window. They know God doesn't grade on the curve. Then what's the measuring tool for us morally depraved people?

The answer is *grace!* Then I explain how God provided a way to heaven through Jesus' life and death. I explain how the "gap" was wiped out by Jesus absorbing our errors and lousy "behavior batting average" upon Himself. He did it because He loves each of us and finds it a nightmare to think that we wouldn't be with Him in heaven. We did nothing to compel Jesus to do this. Nor do we deserve this. It's simply from His heart of wanting to give us *undeserved favor* (grace)...and then He leaves us to choose whether we want to receive His gift of getting reconciled with Him. (Or, as I said in the introduction, if we want to take His hand.)

GRACE CAN ONLY BE *RECEIVED, not EARNED!* This is the heart and soul of the Christian faith. It's what separates it from all other world religions. Religion is mankind reaching for God. Christianity is about God reaching His hand to us. We can only *receive* our initial salvation. *And,* we can only *receive* ongoing acts of grace from God through our lifetime, like Amy experienced—we can't demand them and we can't provoke them.

But we have all received them, you and me both.

My Experience with Receiving

The downward economy of the early 2000s forced us to sell our home.

I hate moving. I hate having to get your house in pristine condition, keep it that way till it sells, and then...the boxes. The sight of bubble wrap causes anxiety attacks in me. Buying a house is not fun for me. Doing the back-and-forth of the negotiations, signing endless reams of documents for the privilege (in our case) of moving all our stuff into a garage where it sat for two months while we renovated our "new" home (which had been built in 1955). What fun! The only thing worse than buying a house is buying a car.

Some of you are thinking, "Craig be grateful you have a house, a place to live." Yes, I should be grateful—and I am. In fact, as we were moving our stuff into the garage, my new next-door neighbor was walking away from his home, having lost it to the bank. I'm very fortunate and grateful.

We moved out of our old house on May 25. We moved into our renovated house on August 15. You may ask, "Where were you in the meantime?" The answer to that question triggered an experience that I would say was *one of the hardest experiences of my life*: I was in a place where I had to *receive!*

What did we receive?

We were guests in a friend's home for 2 ½ months. Another friend volunteered over 100 hours of labor at our new home, working on the baseboard and crown molding, and fixing our computers. Other friends helped paint. Another friend loaned us a trailer to take away trash. Yet another friend helped install window blinds. Some of my wife's friends helped decorate. One more friend helped reassemble a piano given to us by my wife's mother. In the middle of all this, I had back surgery. So, a month into this renovation, living with our friends, and our garage filled from floor to ceiling…I couldn't lift anything heavier than a milk carton. That meant I had to *receive* even more.

How Receiving Makes Us Feel

Receiving is hard. It's much harder than giving. I would much rather be a giver than a receiver. I am much more comfortable as a giver.

But getting older and breaking down physically has taught me to receive. Living in another person's home has taught me to receive. Being incompetent at many fix-it type things has taught me to receive.

Receiving makes me feel *uncomfortable, even nervous.* Why? Because I don't want to feel *needy!* I want to appear like I have my life all together. Receiving makes me feel like I need to balance the scales with the giver. "Oh we'll have you over soon." Or, "Let me help you when you move." Receiving makes me feel helpless. I can't *do something* to help. I just stand there.

Those are the uncomfortable feelings, but *other feelings emerged while practicing this gift.* Receiving made me feel *honored.* It was an honor that someone would value me enough to say, "Craig, you need help? It's a done deal."

Receiving made me feel *humbled.* When I receive, I have to face the fact that I'm not as all-competent as I thought. I'm not so all-knowing. I'm not so independent. Receiving makes me feel *dependent.* I had to lean on other people's giftedness, expertise, experience, generosity, graciousness, hospitality, and kindness.

Receiving *keeps my hands in the "open" position.* Tight-fisted people don't give or receive well. They think, "I don't need God or anyone." Giving is an open handed thing, *but so is receiving.*

In those two months of displacement and disability, God, through His people, filled my hands with gifts of their time, talents, and energy. Receiving *keeps me grateful and thankful.* Always a good thing. Finally, receiving *keeps me asking God, instead of telling God* what He should do. As C. S. Lewis said, through one of his characters in the Chronicles of Narnia who was describing Aslan (the Christ figure), "He likes to be asked." It is so very difficult for me to practice "the ASK", but age, injury, inexperience, incompetence, and fatigue amplify the truth that I am human and needy. Therefore I must *receive.*

Jesus and Receiving

There's a story in the New Testament of two sisters who invite Jesus, the 12 disciples, and most likely a rather large crew of other followers over for lunch (see Luke 10:38-42). One sister sits on the floor with the other visitors and listens in rapt attention to Jesus' teaching, while the other sister is making some detailed preparations for a lunch for 30-40 people. Martha (the kitchen sister) is growing steadily angry with the choice her sister Mary has made to be a "receiving bee" rather than a "worker bee." She's growing increasingly resentful with every cheese slice. Mary seems completely oblivious to Martha's situation in the kitchen. "There goes Mary again," Martha thinks, "just sitting there, having no clue about the amount of work I'm doing, the amount of responsibility I'm bearing; she's just listening to what Jesus is teaching. Well, I've about had it up to here and things are going to change *right now!"*

Martha walks to the doorway, interrupts Jesus in the middle of a parable, and with hands on hips and in front of everyone present, her irritated voice says, "Jesus, tell my sister to get off her lazy backside and get in the kitchen to help me. Can't you see what I'm *doing* in here? Obviously, *she can't.* So, you tell her. She'll listen to you!" (And all God's people said, "Awkward.").

I can see Mary's head lowering, embarrassed in front of everyone, starting to stand up to go help, but Jesus puts a hand on her shoulder to keep her seated. "Martha," Jesus says.

"Yes, Jesus," says Martha (arms folding across her chest).

"You are so busy in there *doing* so much. I wonder if all of it is necessary. You know, you could just lay out some cold-cuts or peanut butter and jelly and we can come through buffet style. Maybe only a couple of things might need to be prepared. Come to think of it Martha, really *only one thing is needed* (and it has nothing to do with lunch), and guess what, Mary's chosen that one thing (listening to me teach, which is food for her soul)...and she's staying right here to *receive* it."

A question that's always bothered me is, "What is Jesus getting at with 'the one thing needed'?" I'm not claiming to know absolutely, but maybe the *one thing needed* that Mary got right was that she chose to sit there and *receive*: receive Jesus' wisdom, Jesus' teaching, Jesus' explanation of God's love. It's like Martha was the *do-er* and Mary was the *re-ceiver!* There's nothing wrong with what Martha's doing, but Jesus protects Mary from being called out for being a *be-er.* Maybe Jesus is saying that in this particular situation, where people are *receiving* teaching and encouragement from Him, what's most needed is *being.* There will be other times for majoring in *doing.*

I have wondered if those hard moving months of mine were a lesson from Jesus, directed at me, saying: "It's okay to be Mary for a while, Craig."

It's as if Jesus were saying, "Craig, I already know you have a Martha mindset." (I'll bet many of you reading this have a "Martha" mindset.) "Craig, you see the needs of others and you strive to meet them in love and in my name." (And by the way, dear readers, so do so many of you.) "But, Craig," Jesus says, "If you look closely, *most of your life has been and continues to be about receiving.* I gave you your life, your spiritual gifts, your abilities, your friends, your employment opportunities, your smarts, and your health. Your next breath is a gift from me. I open doors of opportunity for you to minister. And in addition to all that, all the beauty you see around you or travel to, that's a gift too. Your wife, children, family, and church are all gifts from Me.

What you learn about Me, I reveal it to you. That's a gift. So Craig, I'm not asking you to *do* a lot; some things, yes; but I am asking you to *receive* even more. So please, *practice receiving* the gifts I give: the whispers I give, the fun that I bring, and receive what I bring your way ministry-wise, so that My Kingdom will keep advancing. Just stay open and keep on receiving. That would bring me joy."

Practice Receiving From the People God Brings into Your Life.

Often God provides several categories of help from people. They can come in different forms depending on our life situation. When they come your way, reflect on the truth that God brought them to you. Let's look at some things that we receive from people that we need to receive *as if they were coming to us directly from God.*

Receiving the *Comfort* that Others Offer

As a pastor, officiating funerals is part of my life. The worst memorial services are for children who die before their parents. In these circumstances, it is difficult to know what or how to give comfort to the bereaved. One thing I do know: your presence with them is a source of comfort. You become Jesus in the flesh for them and your "withness" communicates Jesus' sorrow, tears, and grief for them personally. And when it happens to you, you can *receive* Jesus' presence, empathy and comfort from the people who have simply showed up.

Receiving the *Assurance* that Others Offer

Often we doubt whether we are very good Christ-followers. We think we're not very effective volunteers or ministry leaders. Maybe you beat yourself up regarding behavior or emotions that are not very "Christ-like." Some of these doubts come from a past where a parent never communicated your value as a treasure that God delights in. Rather, you were beaten, abused, demeaned, minimized, ignored, punished unreasonably, and told that you were ugly, a problem not a person, and that you'd never amount to anything

Some of you have lost jobs, homes, marriages, and friends to a variety of circumstances: betrayal, downsizing, economy downturn, and lack of commitment to a relationship. You need assurance that you are loved, cherished, valued, and significant in spite of the circumstances. You need affirmation and encouragement.

In all of these situations and more, we need to be assured that we are loved by God. Most of the time, God provides assurance to us through a *person* acting as Jesus in His place. Sometimes *we* are the person doing the assuring. Hopefully, our looks, words, touches, and actions will be a reflection of what Jesus would do if He were in our place. If we are the one in crisis or in need, we must see the person Jesus has sent (often time, it's a family member or close friend) as Jesus in the flesh. And any form of assurance they give that you are loved; that God is aware and attentive to you, working overtime behind the scenes to help, provide, resolve, and give strength to endure… that assurance is coming directly from heaven through that person. Practice *receiving assurance* when it comes your way. It's a real spiritual practice that reminds us that we are loved by God.

Receiving the *Affirmation* that Others Offer

I was a public school teacher for five years. I can assure you that "atta-boys" and "atta-girls" are almost non-existent in the school system. Occasionally, when being periodically evaluated, the evaluator might take the time to compliment me on what I was doing well, rather than only pointing out what could be improved. But in my experience through my years in ministry and in the school system, being affirmed by a boss, co-worker or supervisor is something that is simply not done. It's not in the culture of the workplace. *And people are dying for it!* It can even happen in the church.

The church is volunteer-driven. If the volunteers go on strike, the church is finished. The *most valuable resource* of the church is volunteers. The same could be said about Little League managers, soccer coaches, team moms, volunteers to feed the homeless, volunteer youth workers, in-class tutors, and leaders of recovery groups. I learned this truth early on in my ministry career with Young Life and as a pastor: volunteers make the church possible.

So, each year in my time as a senior pastor, I'd take one Sunday for a Volunteer Recognition Day. We'd celebrate our volunteers, name them, praise them, thank them, and recognize their contribution to the ministry of our church. Then we'd feed them a wonderful lunch. Personally, I made a vow to write eight thank-you notes each month (two per week) to thank people for what they did voluntarily.

I especially noticed the "behind the scenes" people: people who prepared snacks for after the service, people who closed the building up after Sunday services were over, the volunteer Sunday school teachers, the greeters, and the ones who counted the money from the offering. Verbally pointing out that the church would come to a grinding halt without them; giving a small gift here and there; writing a note; creating a culture of affirmation for anything small or big *pays off,* because people are not regularly given compliments like: "You're doing a good job," "we appreciate your efforts," "you're really helping out," "you're really doing well," or "we simply appreciate *you* for who you are."

Now, *there's only one proper, appropriate, good response when affirmation comes your way: RECEIVE IT!* Don't deflect it. Don't minimize it. Don't think that what you do is not very much. *Receive it!*

Picture the compliment as coming straight from heaven, affirming *what* you have done, but also *who* you are. So please, anyone reading this book, find things to affirm in your young children and your old children, your spouse, your friends, your coworkers, your boss, and your extended family; the janitor, the grocery store clerk, your secretary, or the people under you. Anyone whom God brings across your path. *Thank them* for what they do or how they've served you or just who they are.

And then, practice receiving affirmation when it comes your way as well. You matter to God and you matter to God's treasures: people. So when someone affirms you, allow it in to your heart, soul, and mind. Allow their words to be the human form of God affirming you saying, "Well done my daughter, my son! *Well done!"* By receiving this you are practicing your faith in Jesus.

Receiving the *Protection* that Others Offer

Picture this as "shielding." What sort of protection have we received? What have we been protected from by God? How have people protected us in our lives when we could never repay them for it?

We may have been protected and we never knew it. I've heard stories of people being spared in car accidents by the smallest of margins. Someone ran into the perfect person to help them with an abusive spouse. Someone came to the rescue of a child or teenager whose home-life was a train wreck. Someone became an advocate for a person being attacked verbally or professionally. Someone stepped in to help someone who lost their job. All of them *received* some form of familial, relational, occupational or marital protection.

I can think of two roles that people (as God's representatives) play in protecting:

1. *Defender:* This person is an advocate, someone who steps in front of someone to shield them and protect them.

People tend to form opinions about others without knowing the whole story. We don't know the whole story behind a divorce. We don't know the whole story on why someone can't seem to hold down a job or why someone acts so insecure, immature, petty, and, critical. We don't know the whole story on why someone morally failed, why they became an alcoholic, or why they don't have any friends.

Christ-followers should never be the accusers in these situations. Christ-followers, when confronted with any form of tragedy, failure, or difficulty, should be the ones who think, *That could be me. Who am I to throw them under the bus?*

Instead, Christ-followers can *protect* people by pointing out what is called "the other side of the story." We never know the whole story of someone's life, so our motto should be, *"We don't know the whole story."* Or, *"We haven't heard the other side of the story."* Maybe we've only heard one side, one version of someone's story, and we jump to accuse, judge, and condemn. Christ-followers should be the ones to stop the gossip, the prejudices, and the jumping to conclusions by protecting others from these kinds of things. In other words, coming to their defense by becoming their advocate.

And again, if we are defended by a friend in this way, there is not much to do but *receive* it. In those people who defend us, we can imagine that they are a "Jesus in the flesh" person who is expressing His loving protection for us. It's the spiritual practice of *receiving* and it automatically draws our hearts to God in gratitude and thanksgiving.

2. *Supporter:* This person is the one who comes alongside you when you're running out of gas or hit a quitting point. Rebuilding a marriage takes time. Working through an admission of needing a recovery program takes time. Being hit by a tragedy may be a "for the rest of your life" thing. If you're any sort of leader, quitting can seem like a good option almost weekly.

When we are pondering things like quitting our job, getting engaged, selling our home, getting divorced, or placing our child in a program to get help, we need the support of a person alongside us. When we go through grief, confront someone, or serve as a volunteer, we need some support. It may be that, at any one time, you need emotional support, relational support, in-crisis support, financial support or parental support. These supporters are people who will challenge you to "Hang in there," "stay the course," "endure," "don't give up," "it would be easy to quit, but don't," "you are not alone in this; I'm with you and I will stay with you."

Support from the group members to one another is why AA works. It's why any recovery group works. A volunteer group or small group works because the group develops relational bonds that lead to supporting one another and carrying one another at times while they are serving or learning. Developing the courage to take a risk often comes through the support from a real, live human being.

Once again, *supporting* is something we can only *receive*. It is something

153

we practice. Being supported by people is a reflection of God's supporting us, something we can't really pay back, but only welcome with open hands.

Receiving the *Provision* that Others Offer

God provides. Jesus promises He'll give us what we need: food, clothes, and more. He assures us that He knows we need this kind of stuff.

When I resigned as the senior pastor of my church, I had no job waiting for me. And I was scared. I gathered some people around me and asked, "Any ideas of what I could do for the rest of my working life?" Eventually, two vocations emerged: officiating weddings and becoming a minister-at-large. In the first vocation, a friend formed a website, launched it and then I had to wait to see if anyone would ask for my services. This business was not targeted at church people, but to people outside the church. I was in a position of total dependency on God to provide for paying bills, food, shelter, and clothing. I was scared. "Is this going to work?" I thought.

As each lead came in and was booked, my appreciation for being on the receiving end of God's provision skyrocketed. After taking my pastor's salary a bit for granted through the years, suddenly I was in a position of total dependence on God's bringing couples my way to get married. It was, and continues to be, a very humbling experience in receiving.

The same could be said for the minister-at-large endeavor. I know it sounds kind of shady, like, "What is a minister-at-large?" It's forming a legal, charitable, one-man ministry in which I serve and help in whatever God brings my way. Again, the *provision* part of this is that I rely on charitable giving from individual donors to fund this ministry. I rely on God moving in people's hearts to give to my ministry in addition to their church and other ministries. I was scared, again. Will God provide? He has. And once again, with every donated gift, I am deeply humbled by the hearts of the givers, and I'm humbled even more by God saying, "Craig, trust Me. I will provide." I'm not getting rich, but I've never missed a meal, a house payment, or been unable to fill up my car.

Receiving God's provision is humbling. As I received His provision, my heart automatically turned to Him in gratitude. I knew I was in His presence yet again, like always. God is in the business of forming humility in us. Receiving from Him does the job pretty well and it counts as a spiritual practice.

Receiving the *Guidance* that Others Offer

No matter what we're contemplating, God is available and ready to give guidance. Again, it's a gift that we can only receive. "Guidance" is another way of saying "giving direction." Leadings from the Holy Spirit is one way God gives guidance. Many of you have experienced a leading from God that helps with a new direction to take: starting or stopping something, taking action or waiting. Guidance from God is something we can only receive.

Receiving the *Confrontation* that Others Offer

There may be something in our lives that is eroding our relationship with God and others. Soon, it becomes noticed by others. At some point, a trusted friend musters their courage and says the last 10% to us. It is a gentle, "I've noticed something: a pattern in your life. Am I reading this right?" It comes from someone who's willing to be a part of the solution as well as the confrontation. Someone may need to be confronted about their workaholism, about ignoring their spouse or children, about their health and well-being. Some may need to be confronted about having no "fun-factor" in their life.

No matter what the circumstances are that need confronting, it takes a lot of forethought, research, and prayer to do the confronting. *But*, it also requires the one being confronted to have a *receiving heart*. Defensiveness is easy. It's the usual knee-jerk reaction to being confronted. Denial can be another response. But receiving hard truth helps us grow into a greater reflection of Jesus.

I've been confronted many times about many things. I do *not* like it. I get *very* defensive. I tend to go to the "poor me" place: "I'm trying my best. I'm working so hard. My plate is so full and now you're going to tell me how I don't measure up?"

The key to receiving (good) confrontation is to realize the confronter is *not attacking you as a person* (i.e.: "you suck!"), but addressing a behavior, a pattern of responding, or a growing attitude that's causing concern in others. A good confrontation elicits a response of, "Yes, you could be right." Depending on what the confrontation is, a *receiving* response might be:

- "You're right, I have been ignoring my spouse."
- "You're right. I need to spend more time with my children."
- "You're right. I spend more time looking at my phone than paying attention to my children."
- "You're right. My spending is out of control. I'm deep in debt and I need help."
- "You're right. I'm exhausted and I don't know how to get my schedule under control."

Those responses are doing the practice of *receiving*. This is just as valuable in God's eyes as reading the Bible, because when we're aware that God gives all these things to us, our character is changed. We grow increasingly humble. Our gratitude factor skyrockets. We are more aware that every good gift comes from God, even confrontation. We become aware of His attentiveness and His shaping influence forming us into increasing reflections of Jesus.

Receiving: The Practice for Everyone

Receiving is a spiritual practice we can all do. But here's the *key*: We have to *admit we have needs, identify our needs, and then verbalize our needs to Jesus and those around us.* Don't be a hero. The Day of Uselessness (the 7th day, or Sabbath day) is a great time to practice receiving. It will take repeating in your mind the truth that God loves you even when you're not *doing* for Him.

As we practice receiving from God (from whom all things ultimately come), and from the people who love us, I pray the eyes of our hearts would be opened to the generosity of the *constant Gift-Giver*: Jesus. And as we receive, I pray we'd see, behind all the people who rush to help us when we are in need, the face, the eyes, the smile, the eagerness, the hands, and the feet of Jesus, the One so eager to give to us.

Some More Ideas for Practicing Receiving

1. Practice one line RECEIVING prayers:
- "God, you love me when I'm not *doing* for You."
- "God, I did nothing to orchestrate or generate the solution to that situation. Thank you for giving it to me."

2. Reflect on all that has been given to you in the categories of:
- physical health
- housing/clothing/cars/toys/luxuries
- food, water
- your passions, desires, likes
- your particular spiritual giftedness
- people: spouse, children, friends, family
- church
- purpose and meaning
- forgiveness, salvation, adoption, sanctification, the Holy Spirit, the promise of heaven...

...and thank God for any reminders of these that come your way.

3. Ponder the promises Jesus gives:
Depending on what life situations you find yourself in, have a few of these passages memorized so that you can receive them and allow them to be true for you. Or, you could tape some of them in places where you'll see them each day: the bathroom mirror, the refrigerator door, the dashboard of your car, or your screensaver. (I have shortened and paraphrased these promises from the Bible.)
- You will see the Kingdom of God (John 3:3).
- You have eternal life (John 3:16).

- Your sins are forgiven (Matthew 9:2).
- You have reward and treasures in heaven (Matthew 6:20).
- I (Jesus) will answer your requests (John 15:16).
- You are *not guilty* (John 8:11).
- I will never send you away (John 6:37).
- You will live forever (John 6:51).
- I do *not* condemn you (John 8:11).
- You will hear My voice (John 10:16).
- I will comfort you (Luke 16:25).
- You will be rewarded for your service (Luke 6:35).
- You have treasures in heaven (Matthew 6:20).
- I will be with and within you always (Matthew 28:20).
- You will experience strong resistance (John 16:33).
- You are Jesus' friend (John 15:15).
- You will be with Jesus in Paradise (Luke 23:43).
- You will receive power to do ministry (Acts 1:8).
- The Holy Spirit will teach you what to say (John 14:26).
- I will raise you up on the last day (John 6:39).

So, practice receiving for a while. Look for anything mentioned in this chapter that is a gift from God. Reflect on your entire life, asking God to reveal to you the times and incidents that were "God-things" that could only be received. In your mind, you could assemble a portfolio of these gifts from God. Then be humbled by His attentiveness to your life as you realize that these are things that could only be received from the loving hand of our Heavenly Father.

158

Final Questions for Reflection

What do you feel like you've *received* from Jesus lately? Where do you have need currently? What do you need help with? What do you wish to receive from God right now? What do you want God to do for you?

We have become a society that has fallen in love with noise.

- George Prochnik, In Pursuit of Silence

Part 3: Too Loud!

Enemy #3: Noise

Noise! It's Everywhere!

HERE'S A NUMBER TO REMEMBER: *85 decibels*. Above this number, it is recommended that hearing protection be used in order to prevent the cumulative effects of hearing loss.

What sorts of noises do *not* cause hearing loss of any kind?

- 75 decibels: dishwasher
- 60 decibels: normal conversation
- 40 decibels: refrigerator
- 30 decibels: whisper

What kinds of things make noise from 85–100 decibels?

- an alarm clock
- a vacuum cleaner
- heavy city traffic
- a garbage disposal[1]

Here's a quick test to tell if the noise level is above 85 decibels: if you have to raise your voice to talk to someone who is an arm's length away, you are most likely in an environment where the noise level is above 85. Remember, prolonged exposure to just the 85 decibel noise causes gradual hearing loss.

Ever notice that the noise factor in bars and restaurants is high. At most restaurants I have to raise my voice to be heard. That means the noise is above 85 decibels. Zagat, the restaurant review company, reports that *noise* is consistently customer's #2 complaint nationwide, ahead of high prices (#3) and second only to poor service (#1).[2]

Moving further into the red zone, at 95–105 decibels, we find:

- table saws
- a jackhammer
- an emergency vehicle siren
- a portable personal stereo with ear buds at maximum volume.

No more than 15 minutes of unprotected exposure at or above 95 is recommended. Some experts now suggest that 45,000 fatal heart attacks per year may be attributed to noise-related cardiovascular strain.

And, if you want to go deaf really quick, place yourself around the following, which are above 105 decibels:

- peak stadium crowd noise
- jet engines on take-off
- firecrackers
- cap guns, shotguns, a .357 Magnum revolver.

At least 15% of adults have permanent hearing damage due to noise exposure (and this is an "old" statistic).[3]

Now that's just the noise "out there." What about pumping the sound directly into our ears with earphones and earbuds?

John Hopkins University, in July 2008, released results of a study that indicated the incidence of hearing loss in the U.S. is approaching epidemic proportions. According to the study, a staggering one out of three Americans now suffer from some sort of hearing loss, much of it *noise induced*. The study went on to say that personal sound devices were more harmful than jet noise. "Anytime you can hear someone else's music leaking through their headphones or earbuds, that person is causing hearing damage."[4]

Noise and Violent Behavior

Author George Prochnik did a ride-along with a policeman one night. The topic turned to domestic violence. The officer said, "The majority of domestic disputes these days are actually noise complaints. We go into these houses where the couple or roommates or the whole family is fighting and yelling. The television is blaring so loud you can't think. The stereo is on high. And on top of that, someone just got home from work who just wants to relax and sleep. It becomes obvious what they are fighting about. They're fighting about noise. They don't know it, but that's the problem. So the first thing I say to them is, 'Don't tell me what you're fighting about. First, turn off the TV, the stereo and the video games.' Then I just let them sit there for a couple of minutes. Then I say, 'Now, doesn't that feel different? Maybe the real reason you were fighting is how *loud* it was inside your apartment. Now, do you have anything to tell me? Do you?' You'd be surprised how often that's the end of it."

Nervousness Without Noise

I don't know if there's any place to go where there isn't some sort of sound (background music or television) going on. It doesn't matter if it's Starbucks, a dry-cleaning store, McDonalds, a doctor's waiting room, a pharmacy, or the grocery store.

It's almost as if our culture has been conditioned to be very uncomfortable without some sort of noise going on. People get nervous and even agitated when it's completely silent. Why? Because noise is everywhere and without it, people feel like something abnormal is going on. They are not used to it at all. People become agitated because they are finally alone with their thoughts. In silence, there are no lyrics to sing along to. When there is quiet we have to think about the hard things: our rocky marriages, our "fly by" parenting or a moral struggle, or the fact that we really don't have a close friend...or whether we matter to God.

Always remember, most of the time evil comes at us sideways, at our flanks, where we can't see it coming. Noise is something we have become so accustomed to that we don't even think about it. When we eliminate quiet in our lives, evil wins. Our heads are filled with news stories, the weather, fashion, traffic, movie stars, politics, housing renovations, and sports because the TV is on at least four hours a day in most homes. Or, our heads are filled talk radio, sports talk, and opinion shows. We could spend all day watching CNN, Fox News, or ESPN. There are cable cooking shows, women's channels, reality shows, game shows, movie channels, jewelry channels, porn channels, and channels that show old TV series. They run all day and night so we can have access to them anytime we want. In some cases, we spend more time with the television than we do with people.

It will take a monumental effort to escape noise in our world.

But it will be worth it. Because when we are quiet, then we will be able to hear more from the One who matters most.

Jesus and Silence

Up against this onslaught of our culture of noise is a sentence describing Jesus that we've already read:

> **...Jesus often withdrew to lonely places and prayed...**
> *- Luke 5:16, NIV.*

In other words, it was a regular practice of the Son of God, the incarnate Deity, the fullest expression of God on earth, the One who was and is and is to come to get away from noise so He could think things through, listen to His Father, commune with Him, and order His mind and heart so He could head back into the demands, questions, confrontations, noise, and the hustle and bustle of His culture.

If Jesus needed it, so do we! There is simply no way around this. If we want to hear from God on a regular basis, regarding pressing issues we have or just everyday life, we must have regular infusions of *silence!* That means, no background music, no earbuds, no TV in the background; we need a *noiseless* environment! It seems that God speaks most clearly to us in *that* setting—more so than in any other. Time after time, throughout the Bible, God speaks to prophets, teachers, disciples, regular people, and Jesus in the atmosphere of *quietness!*

A Biblical Story About Hearing from God While Silent

For the better part of their history, Israel was ruled by kings. The first king was Saul, followed by David, then Solomon. After Solomon, things went downhill. Until Israel was conquered by the Assyrians and then the Babylonians, ruling kings were kept in check by special messengers called by God: prophets. These men and women were commanded to get in the king's face by confronting despicable behavior. If any prophet really ticked the king off, the royal decree became, "Off with their heads!" Kings and queens could be very unstable.

One such king was Ahab. His wife was Jezebel—and Jezebel ruled the roost. Ahab did whatever she wanted.

Israel was in bad shape because of these two. They did not allow people to worship the true God of Israel, but instead, promoted pagan gods—who were no gods at all—sacrificing to them to try to manipulate them into providing good crops, fertile people, and military success.

Things were bad and getting worse until God sent a prophet named Elijah to pay the king and queen a little visit. Elijah had been a thorn in Ahab's and Jezebel's sides for quite a while now, so when Elijah showed up, Ahab said essentially, "What now, you troublemaker?" Elijah told them that God was none too happy with their leadership and their influence over the people. God wasn't happy that they'd pushed Him out of the picture.

So, Elijah was told by God to issue a challenge to Ahab and Jezebel. "You bring all your fertility prophets out to Mount Carmel and I'll meet you there. You bring a big old bull to sacrifice and I'll bring one too. Then, you will prepare a huge wood pile for a giant bull barbecue. Kill the beast, cut it up, and then place the animal pieces on the wood. Now here's the challenge, Ahab and Jezebel: the god who brings fire from heaven to burn the sacrificial bull will be the God of Israel. You can go first, then I'll go second, and we'll see who brings the heat."

The arrangements were made. Lots of people came out to witness the event. The fertility prophets went first. They danced around the wood and the carcass and even cut themselves to show how devoted they were, but no fire comes. Elijah let them go on for several hours, giving their god plenty of time to light the fire. But nothing happened.

Then Elijah stepped forward and essentially said, "Now watch this!" He called for several large jars of water to be poured on the bull and the wood, not once, not twice, but *three times*. It was a "just to be sure I'm not pulling any trick" gesture for Ahab, the prophets, and the people. Then Elijah looked heavenward and said, "God, show them who You are and the power you have." And God did. Fire from heaven burned the bull, the sopping-wet wood, and the ground around it.

Now Jezebel, who was back at the castle, heard what happened and was enraged. She promised that she would have Elijah's head on a platter if it was the last thing she ever did. Elijah was frightened and ran to the desert wilderness and hid in a cave. It was here that Elijah had a really good pity party for himself. Soon, God showed up. God asked Elijah, "What are you doing here?" (not because He didn't know, but because He was inviting Elijah to share openly). Elijah told God, "I've done everything You asked and this is what I get: a cave in the desert with no food or water. I'm being hunted by a psychopathic, narcissistic queen who wants my head and all I've ever done is what You asked me to do."

I empathize with Elijah. It was supposed to be a victory parade after Mount Carmel, but it turned into a full retreat because of the wrath of Jezebel. Elijah needed to hear from God—instruction, reassurance, and a what-do-I-do-now conversation. Elijah wondered if God was really going to come through with restoring the country, even after the fiery miracle on the mount.

God listened. Then He told Elijah to go to the entrance of the cave he was staying in because God was going to pass by. Standing there, Elijah felt a breeze hit him, then some real wind, then a gale-force wind. Then there was a not-of-this-world wind, which tore the rocks apart, shattering them to bits. But the Bible records, "God was *not* in the wind." In other words, He wasn't in this very loud, noisy, even deafening display of power and destruction.

Then, the ground started rumbling under Elijah's feet, and the rumbling built to a mighty roar as a 10.9 earthquake hit the mountain, throwing Elijah down to the ground. But text said again, "God was *not* in the earthquake." I've been through several earthquakes living in California. Besides the earth shaking so violently that you can't even walk, the deafening wave of "loud" is ear-drum shattering. In Elijah's case, God doesn't show up in this noise-filled display of an earthquake.

After the earthquake came a fire. Elijah patted out his singed robe and beard, took a deep breath, and thought, "What next?"

But there was nothing. Just silence. God let that pregnant pause go on for a bit, and then Elijah heard "a gentle whisper" (see 1 Kings 19). He knew this was it—the time when God was going to "pass by." So he did what any sane person would do. He grabbed his robe and pulled it over his head so he wouldn't die from seeing God's beauty and majesty. Then, as he was standing at the entrance to the cave, with his robe pulled over his head, God whispered the same question He had asked before: "Elijah, what are you doing here?"

You see, God was *not* in the *noise!*

You'd think Elijah would have a different answer to the question this time, but he repeats his story of being hunted by Jezebel. God listens, then whispers to Elijah what he is to do next. God didn't speak in the wind, earthquake, or fire, but in a "gentle whisper." That's usually how God speaks to our spirits today. It's a gentle nudge; an impression, prompting, or leading that is whispered or "impressed" to our minds and spirits. If we surround ourselves with constant noise, there's a 99% chance we won't hear Him. That's why we have to fight noise.

People sometimes tell me that they have a hard time hearing from God on a certain matter (or any matter). Chances are, they are in a rush (hurry), have a packed schedule (busyness) and they have surrounded themselves with sound all day and night (noise.) God is *always* communicating with us, or at least trying to. We just can't hear Him. I believe it is possible to maintain a type of communion with God that enables us to hear His gentle whispers, promptings, impressions, and nudgings even in the midst of the loud, the busy and the rushed world we live in, but it takes a *quieted soul* to do this. It means we must begin to practice *being quiet* for varying segments of time in various atmospheres, depending on our temperaments and schedules.

> **"We need to find God, and He cannot be found in noise and restlessness. God is the friend of silence."**[5]
>
> *- Mother Theresa*

Three Forms of Constant Noise

There are at least three forms of media that bring noise to our lives. Often, television and music are going on at the same time in any given location (any bar, waiting rooms for car repairs, restaurants, doctor's waiting rooms):

1. Television (and video games played over the TV's sound system)

2. Radio (and podcasts)

3. Music

Jesus commanded us to be kind to strangers, *but we don't have to allow them to move in and overrun our homes.* Noise is an unwelcome stranger in our homes. Yet we invite this stranger into our lives constantly. These three sources of noise clutter our minds and drown our ability to think reflectively. Noise drowns out common sense. Let's look at all three...

Television

> **With the exception of sleeping, children spend more time in front of television and electronic screens than they do in any other activity. As a result, more than 60% of obesity cases can be linked to excess TV viewing. TV noise has certain dominant themes. Studies indicate that, by the time a child graduates from high school, he or she will have witnessed more than 200,000 violent acts on television, including 16,000 simulated murders.**
> *- Teresa Tomeo, Noise.*

Sometimes parents use the "noise box" to help them cope with daily life. The parents reason that they have to work hard at their job, then work hard at home with children, so they rely on TV to help make their lives more manageable. TV can keep the peace and facilitate family routines such as eating, relaxing, and falling asleep.

> **In a recent study, it was found that one in three children had a TV in their bedroom, in which it was on all or most of the time. Tired and stressed out parents use the TV to keep their kids occupied, calm them down, avoid family arguments and teach their children the things parents are afraid they don't have the time teach themselves.**
> *- Teresa Tomeo, Noise.*

Radio

Radio noise has decreased with the invention of the cell phone, iPod, CD, Satellite Radio, sports talk radio, and the Internet. Radio is losing the battle for the ears of humanity. What's been one solution? Shocking the audience with blatant sexual banter or yelling at each other over an issue. "Shock jocks" can get away with an alarming amount of sexual content and unfiltered opinions. In recent years, three of the most infamous shock jocks were banished to satellite radio where they can say most anything (e.g., Howard Stern). Even with its eroding popularity, radio can still be a source of constant sound in cars, and in work cubicles, auto repair shops, and other work environments.

Remember, if you begin to practice being quiet in short bursts, you'll feel uncomfortable, even a bit nervous at first, but hang in there and crash through that "quitting point" and the rewards of quietness will have a soothing effect. And you'll hear from God more regularly as well. Years ago, I adopted a personal code: no music in the car until noon (except on weekends while I'm driving to weddings). There's nothing noble about that, and many of you reading this know you'd go crazy with that long of a time. But, remember, *something is better than nothing.* Maybe on your commute to work for one day a week, you drive in silence and simply invite God to speak into your mind and heart. It can increase from there.

Music and Music Videos

The battleground for this type of noise is in headsets, laptops, cell phones, earbuds, car stereos, and Bluetooth. It almost seems that our culture is frightened by quiet, because there never really is a time or place where we are not surrounded by music. Music is played in Target, drug stores, Walmart, tire repair stores, and doctor's waiting rooms. In many places, piped-in music has been replaced with high definition television.

I took my car in to get a routine check done that I knew would only take about 35 minutes. I took a couple of books to read. The waiting room had three large screen TVs and the sound was up on all of them. I couldn't concentrate at all. That's why I carry those orange-colored foam ear plugs wherever I go. Libraries used to be a quiet place to go. Not anymore. Students and adults just talk away. It is very hard to escape TV, radio, human dialogue, or recorded music. They're everywhere.

How Do We Hear from God?

What sort of practices might increase our chances of hearing from God like Elijah did? In our day and age, some people claim they have heard an audible voice. Who am I to question that? But, if the voice told them to kill someone, rob a bank, hurt their spouse, or blow up a building, you can be sure that's not "hearing from God."

Most of us "hear" from God in the form of a *strong impression*, or a *nudge* to say or do something. We may be hearing God if we sense an *inward pull* to speak, listen, comfort, or be silent. He might give us a direction to go with our careers, or ideas on how to love our spouses better, or insight into one of our other relationships. But if we are going to sense His gentle nudgings, we will *have to spend some time being quiet*. There's just no way around it. Why? Because, like with Elijah, God mostly communicates in gentle promptings. We have to be quiet to hear them or sense them. The devil does *not* want us to hear God. Therefore, the devil has developed the strategy of *noise* to surround people throughout the entire world.

The three practices I'm going to encourage you to take up in the fight against noise are:

1. Being quiet (silence)
2. Listening for leadings from God
3. Thinking stuff through (reflection)

Try This Out...

Exercise #1: Go on a "Noise Hunt." Take a week to do intense *noticing* of the noise factor in your normal everyday routines. Notice what you hear in every store, waiting room, and any other place you visit, and see if there's any place where you escape noise.

Exercise #2: Do extreme noticing of what effect noise has on you (if any). How does constant noise (or lack of it) make you feel? Write down some feelings you have as you do this.

A few moments of relaxed silence, alone, every day are desperately important.

- Thomas Kelly

Chapter 8: The Practice of BEING QUIET

A Starbucks Story

I OFTEN MEET COUPLES I'M marrying at a local Starbucks. I love Starbucks. But I usually try to meet couples outside, not inside, for reasons I hope will become clear. On a recent visit, weather forced us to meet inside. While waiting, I found my agitation level rising. I knew why. You Starbucks visitors know how close they place the tables and chairs. Eavesdropping isn't hard. In front of me was a group of five men and a woman. Behind me and a little to the right, a group of four female friends were enjoying swapping stories, laughing, having a great time. As the background noise increased and more people crowded the room, the conversational volume rose.

The speaker that was pumping background music was just over my head. The volume level was just over the softer volume of normal background music, so it was a bit agitating (to me anyway). A constant beeping of the microwave oven made me want to stand up and yell, "THE PASTRY WARMING PROCESS IS FINISHED! TAKE IT OUT OF THE OVEN PLEASE!" The grinding of the mixers, the sound of the steamers, and the cell phone text alerts all added to the noise factor.

I felt like I couldn't think. My senses felt overstimulated, especially my hearing. The noise was sucking the life right out of me. Seemingly, the noise wasn't bothering anyone but me. I felt like I was weird. I had some moments where I could block out the noise…somewhat…but I was also very distracted.

This is an introvert writing, so many of you extroverts reading this are thinking, "Craig, you're too sensitive to this stuff!" You'd be right, but you're most likely an extrovert talking. You would be right at home in that Starbucks. There's no need for you to apologize for that, nor feel less "deep" than any introvert. And I'm not apologizing either. It's simply how God made each of us different. But I was a distracted, agitated mess when that couple arrived.

Examining the spiritual practices of BEING ALONE and BEING QUIET should ALWAYS be done through the lens of YOUR GOD-GIVEN PERSONALITY! So, don't feel like you're not a good Christ-follower if you can't do large sections of time being quiet. Quiet time is still essential for you, but your proper segments of time will be naturally smaller.

Finding Quiet Is Hard!

Rather than thinking of the noise surrounding most of us as a pollution issue, we might think of it as a dietary problem. Our aural diet is miserable. It's full of over-rich, non-nutritious sounds served in inflated portions. Conversely, we don't consume enough silence. A poor diet can kill us. It kills us because of what it contains and what it doesn't contain. When we educate children about diet, we not only talk about the hazards of fast food, but also about the benefit of healthy nutrients. Why can't we do the same with quietness? Our culture is silent on the benefits of silence. Why can't educators introduce what scientists and researchers already know about the benefits of silence into public education, and teach on its desirable effects?[1]

A few moments of relaxed silence, alone, every day are desperately important. Being quiet is not only necessary but critically needed to deepen our intimacy with God. Why? The importance of intentional listening, or learning to quiet ourselves, is that it is needed to hear and sense what the Bible calls "the still, small voice of God" and to experience His presence (that He is with and within us, in front and behind, to the right and left, above and below).

Here's the problem: Being quiet is very, very difficult to practice. But, of all the dance steps (spiritual practices) we do with Jesus, getting alone and being quiet are the beginning of doing life with Jesus on a moment-by-moment basis. And we have to return to them again and again.

Today, noise has become normal and silence has become the disturbance. We have become accustomed to noise. Children and teenagers literally don't know what it means to be quiet. Why can't churches, many of whose services are an hour long "wall of noise" teach about the benefits of silence, of being quiet and intentionally listening for God? In Quaker church services, people enter in silence and remain silent for 30 minutes. New York is building "pocket parks" using unused land so people can have a quieter, more peaceful place for silence and solitude.

Usually, when we take any amount of time to be quiet, we begin to realize our thoughts are everywhere else but where we really are. We have constant divided attention regarding what is right in front of us, whether it is our spouse, a flower, our children, a place in creation, a friend, or a situation. Sometimes, I can't get a song out of my head…for hours, so there's a constant state of un-quietness in my brain. The song becomes a looping tape that plays over and over again. It's hard to stop it.

Noise separates us from Jesus. Noise divides us from ourselves. Our biggest objection to being quiet is that it smacks of non-productivity. The continual noise from our world and inside us prevents us from hearing what is going on deep within us. As Socrates put it, we live "unexamined lives," lives that are a mile wide and one inch deep.

Bad Silence

It is possible that being quiet was a means of punishment in your childhood. People can be hurt by silence. Perhaps a parent gave you "the silent treatment." I have listened to several stories of adults who recount things like, "My mother didn't talk to me for two weeks." Or, "My friend completely shut me down and shunned me for days." Maybe quietness is something you're afraid of for some reason. There's nothing to feel guilty about in these situations. It's part of your story. Maybe you're extremely extroverted and the idea of being silent for any length of time conjures up feelings of dread. You feel like it would be a complete waste of time and you know you'd hate it. After 10 minutes you'd be looking for the door.

If any of these scenarios apply to you, it would be helpful to identify your feelings about quietness and where they might have come from. You can use these questions to help:

- When you think of being silent for a time, what feelings, thoughts, and images arise within you?
- What has been your experience of silence as a child, an adolescent, and an adult?
- Have you ever been punished by silence? What was that like?
- Do you long for more silence? (Be honest about this one.)
- If not, why are you resistant to being quiet?
- If you long for silence, where and when do you long for more of it in your life?
- What do you think might be the benefits of being quiet with God?

If you have some deeply ingrained negative feelings towards silence, it is very beneficial to talk to God about them, working it through with Him together. Then, it is helpful to talk about it with a trusted friend, a spiritual director, a pastor, or a Christ-follower you know will be gentle with you. Even then, you might still have some resistance toward this practice. That's okay. God isn't mad at you. Instead, He's very pleased and proud that you're on the journey to discover how being quiet might benefit you and your relationship with Him.

Nervousness About Silence

Even if you are someone who enjoys periods of not talking or enjoys settings where there is no music or television on, or who enjoys putting Home

Depot foam earplugs in your ears or turning off your cell phone, it doesn't necessarily mean that silence will be a welcome friend to you. *Being quiet is difficult for most people!*

When we are quiet for short, medium or extended periods of time, we may feel vulnerable, fearful, or nervous. Our culture relies so heavily on words and noise to manage, control, manipulate, and protect ourselves from facing what needs to be faced about ourselves.

Being quiet is for "bumping into yourself." That's why people avoid it. It's why people can't get into a car without turning the stereo on, or walk into a room without switching on the T.V. They seek to avoid the confrontation of "bumping into yourself."[2]

In addition, our culture is dead-set against quietness. Wherever we go there is noise. When I was a pastor, we experimented with having the sanctuary in silence when people entered, and what happened was that the vast majority stayed in the lobby because chatter and noise was much more comforting. We gave up on that quickly. We have been trained to be comfortable with noise and nervous with silence.

Why are we so nervous about being quiet? Because when we slow down, and place ourselves in a position where we're alone and quiet, we might begin to hear those inner voices. Some of those voices may involve feelings of guilt, regret, or anger at ourselves, or feelings of inadequacy. When we start feeling this way about quietness, we might think, *Hey, anything is better than facing this stuff about myself.* So we watch a movie, surf the net, call someone, play solitaire, grab something to eat, or play with our phones.

Nervousness about intentionally listening for God's quiet promptings can come from the need to face a tough issue in our lives. It's possible your *marriage* has some major issue(s) and getting alone with those issues and realizing your part in that can make you nervous, because you have to face the question: what parts of our marital discord do I need to own? It's possible that there's something that needs to change in you with regard to your

177

parenting. Facing up to that means you may need to apologize in some way. There may be some hidden "somethings" going on that nobody knows about and in silence, they scream out to be addressed. It could be *financial* issues or *relational* issues with a friend or family member.

Having some time of quietness can make us nervous about what "addressing it" might mean. Being quiet usually results in self-examination. As a result, people may conclude that they need to own the truth that they might be an alcoholic, shopaholic, a gambling addict, a porn user, a flirt with the opposite sex (while married), a workaholic, an absent father or mother, or "way into" money, or not really serious about following Jesus. These things are not easy to own or admit. Often, owning and admitting these "last 10% truths" about ourselves leads to openness, healing, and hope. But they won't be faced or owned if we don't make an intentional effort to be quiet for a time.

Correcting False Ideas About Ourselves and God

Quiet, intentional listening is an excellent practice for correcting false notions of God and yourself. Most people perceive God as being mildly disappointed in them most of the time. But, place yourself in situations where you open yourself to Him by asking, "God, is there anything You want to impress upon me right now?" Then intentionally listen for a while, and you might sense Him impressing your mind with nudges like, "I am your Forgiver. I am the gracious One, Your loving Savior. I am kind and gentle. I am patient and caring, and not disappointed in you. In fact, you're My treasure. I want to restore and bring health to your heart and soul."

Sensing these messages of God come in times of quietness. Remember the analogy of taking God's hand to dance? Intentionally listening for any length of time, is our part—the "taking His hand" part that we do. Out of these time segments of quietness can come some very godly actions, like confession to a real person or coming out in the open about something we've kept hidden from everyone. And here's the great thing that happens: we end up experiencing the forgiveness, grace, and love of God in the form of the person you're confessing to. Hopefully, after confessing to them, they will say, "You know, this doesn't change a thing between us. You are still loved and forgiven." All of these scenarios are triggered as a result of intentionally carving out quietness for ourselves.

What the Bible Calls *Being Quiet*

In the Bible, intentionally listening for God is often referred to as "stillness." Stillness is associated with wisdom (Psalm 4:4, Proverbs 17:27-28). Stillness is the prescription for the recovery of physical and emotional strength and deeper experiences with God (Isaiah 40:31).

If you can get through those initial "nervousness points" and stay with quietness for a bit, you'll experience an inner relaxedness. The inner noise factor in your head will fade and you'll begin to sense the presence of God. When we practice periods of time to be quiet, we are essentially making room for our heart, soul, and mind to listen for Jesus…something we rarely make room for.

Good Times to Practice Any Form of Intentional Listening for God

1. *Before deciding to get married.* When something major is coming your way, it's always smart to get alone and get quiet, inviting Jesus to help you discern your way through a decision that will affect the rest of your life. *Getting married* is a really big life change. Suddenly, you go from doing whatever you want with whomever you want, to having to check in with someone else about how your decisions will affect them. Your future spouse may have an opinion about what you want to do, how you want to do it, and when you want to do it. A life partner is probably the second most important decision you will ever make on planet earth; the most important is deciding to become a Christ-follower.

I mentioned earlier that one of my occupations is officiating marriages, and you need to know I officiate second, third, and fourth etc., weddings for couples. Why? Because I believe in a God who gives us second, third, fourth, and "seven times seven" chances when we fail in any area of life. Forgiveness is the umbrella over everything, so I enjoy being a part of giving couples another chance at marriage. But it doesn't mean that I don't challenge them to think it through carefully since they have already had a marital situation that didn't work out. I encourage them to get alone, get quiet, and take a long time to intentionally think it through.

Here's an interesting fact:

The men who drafted the U.S. Constitution had a giant mound of dirt built on the street outside Independence Hall so that their deliberations would not be disturbed by passing traffic.
- Supreme Court Justice Felix Frankfurter[3]

2. *Before other major decisions, like switching careers, taking a new job, or moving.* It is a rare person or couple that takes the time to really think through a career move when it involves more money. It is a rare person who turns down a higher-paying job because the effect on their children, their marriage, their friendship circle, and their church outweighs the financial benefits. More money usually trumps everything.

When I was pastoring a church, I would listen to stories of pastors who would say, "I'm really praying through this issue of moving to a bigger church, with more salary, a bigger staff, that has a building and has better housing."

I'd think, *What's to pray about? I know you're going. Who wouldn't? I would!* It would take a serious amount of intentionally listening for God's still small voice about staying where they were. And if they felt God leading them to stay where they were, I'd look at that and say, "Wow!"

I know a man, Jake, with a huge heart for urban ministry. He worked in a very poor, depressed, crime-ridden part of town. Many of the teenagers he worked with slept on the floor of empty apartments which weren't being rented at the time. He not only was their youth minister, but he became the local high school basketball coach. He would need to pick them up from school in a van and keep them with him until game time because if they walked home, they probably wouldn't make it back to the game. In addition, Jake had to buy them food before the game because most didn't have food at home.

Jake has a family of two biological children and one adopted child of drug-addicted parents from the neighborhood. Over the years, Jake turned down many job offers because he felt so strongly that God had assigned him the task of transforming inner-city San Diego, one life at a time, with the love of Jesus.

But soon the pressure of raising money for an increasing staff, and the situation of his family and the grind of the endlessness of poverty, shattered lives, and hopelessness led to him responding to an "ask" from a church, in inner-city Oakland, for Jake to become their pastor. He would still have to raise funds, work in a similar poverty-depressed area, recruit leaders, train them, nurture them, and still find ways to reach those outside the church. But he was able to get into a larger home and a more stable salary situation.

Jake agonized about leaving his dream, the vision that God had given him of building Jesus-followers in an area that is the poorest of the poor. He went to a retreat center for a couple of days to take extended time alone with God in silence, seeking out the "should I stay or go" question. He took the job. I'm happy for Jake and his family.

Some leaders are "starters." Others are "enrichers" for the starters. Others are "maintainers," forming systems for a smoothly-running church or company. All three are needed in the Kingdom of God. Jake is a starter. After starters get things started they get bored, fatigued, and unchallenged. Jake figured that out in a long period of intentional silence and listening for God's leading. He was energized by moving to a dying church to start something new.

These are the kinds of decisions that need aloneness and quietness in God's presence to "slow the train down" and really think things through with God. If you're facing this kind of decision, seriously consider being alone and being quiet in an undisturbed place. Slow yourself down and ask God,

"What do You think? Is this opportunity from You? Speak to my spirit about this. I'm really listening and needing to hear from You." Of course, talking it through with close friends, spouses and family can sometimes be God's voice speaking through them, but pay most attention to that strong, gut feeling that is most likely God talking.

Another reason to seek out quietness with God is...

3. *Simply because you want to have uninterrupted time with God!* There may come a point in your life where you're burned out; when you want to take a break from hurry, busyness, noise, and distraction. You might have a serious inner need to slow down your pace of life and unplug the electronic tethers of your cell phone. Maybe you might sense a real "pulling" to want to listen to God; to let Him be your Teacher, Counselor, or Comforter. Maybe you need some reassurance that you still matter to God. It really doesn't matter what the reason is. But, if you find yourself wanting time to sort through any of this stuff and you want to hear from God in some way, find a place where you won't be interrupted. Make intentional listening for God a priority, not an afterthought.

I recently dialogued with a woman I'll call Joy who was actively serving and participating in her church. Joy was serving in a class by helping people gain tools to experience Jesus deeply. She was serving at the thrift store and food bank. She was serving as a weekly small group leader. In this small group was a woman with a narcissistic personality who constantly demeaned Joy and told her how she should run her life. This woman did this to everyone else in the group, too. She is what I call a "small-group killer."

As Joy spoke, her frustration was obvious. Her decreasing energy level was palpable. After sharing all this, I said to her, "And how much time do you spend taking care of yourself? Do you have time in your week to do something that you enjoy and that pours life back into you? How's it going with having enough relaxed, unrushed time for intentionally listening for God to whisper to you that you are His beloved, whether you serve Him or not?" I suggested she take some time to ask God, "How would you make changes and adjustments in my life, God? What would you suggest I take away?" I was able to communicate to her that it's okay to do things for your own well-being, along with serving. I hope she will take the time to be alone, have some intentional time of silence, and do some intentional listening for God's gracious, tender, and loving whispers for her life.

When It Comes to Quietness, Your Personality Type Matters

Introverts are reading this chapter and cheering. Extroverts are reading this and thinking, "Really?" Remember, introverts get emotionally recharged by being alone. Extroverts get recharged by being with people. So, in the case of *being alone* and *being quiet*, introverts most likely already have found times and places to do this. The introverts have to be careful of not cutting themselves off from relationships. Extroverts need to be careful of being constantly with people and never stopping to think through what's going on inside them.

There is nothing wrong or right about being somewhere on the spectrum between introvert and extrovert. It's just the way God created you. So, embrace that. God delights in you because of that. But I have found, being an introvert myself, that we are often misread and misunderstood. When reality TV shows promote people saying whatever they want whenever they want, when interruption is the norm, and when yelling and screaming at each other makes for good entertainment, our lives are full of anti-introvert examples. The more brash, outrageous, loud, and obnoxious you are, the more entertaining you are. Who's entertained or interested in watching an introvert study people and situations and then ask thoughtful questions that *depth* the current conversation? That doesn't make for good television.

It is very important that you learn how God wired you up in this *being alone* and *silent intentional listening* thing. Extroverts may need to experiment with quietness and aloneness in shorter bites of time, because long periods of time prove to be counterproductive. Please know, I have several extroverted friends and they help draw me out when my natural tendency is to watch and observe. I think I help them to think things through, and encourage them to respond with their second thoughts, rather than just impulsively sharing their first thoughts. We benefit from one another's differences. Embrace your differentness and adjust the amount and degree of quietness and aloneness you practice accordingly. For everyone, start small and grow bigger with practicing these two dance steps with Jesus.

Can I "Do Quietness" When There Are People and Noise All Around?

Absolutely! I know that getting to a place that is completely quiet is next to impossible. In addition, it would take going to a faraway place to be completely alone. Physically, it takes a lot of effort to find places of solitude and silence, *but there is a state of mind and spirit in which you can be in the vicinity of people and have a quietness of soul (our inward self)!* While being in the midst of people, we can still hear or sense God's gentle nudges, but doing so requires a choice of doing intentional listening in our hearts and souls. If our inner spirit, our emotions, and our mind are in that "one ear tuned to heaven" position, we are doing "inner silence." Inner silence can slowly become a constant reality that we carry around with us all the time. This inner quietness enables us to be fully present in the moments God brings our way. The truth is, God is always present, but we are not always present to God. Silence enables us to be present to God. A constant intentional listening awareness allows us to hear promptings of what to do or say in any given situation you find yourself in.

Remember, God is the friend of silence. One of the surprises of these alone and quiet sessions is that we become increasingly present to the people God brings our way. We're more attentive, actively listening, really thinking through what would be a helpful question to further *depth* what someone is saying and what we might say to encourage them. In other words, we become Jesus to others.

As we practice getting alone, being quiet, and intentionally listening

184

for Him, gradually listening for God ceases to become about a geographical place, but instead becomes about an inner readiness of our hearts. Quietness and aloneness become a quality we carry with us regardless of the circumstances or location or even the noise factor. But, in order to develop this inner quietness while being surrounded by noise and people, it is necessary to make "going away" physically a regular practice. Physically going away is extremely important at the initial stages but also through the rest of our lives with Christ.

Several Ways to Do Silence

1. Stop talking!

When I was in transition from being a pastor to a minister-at-large/wedding officiant, a friend of mine, Bill, suggested we do a Quaker practice called a Clearness Committee. I was to gather some close friends who knew me well and really wanted to help me move forward after leaving my almost 20-year-long pastoral career. The rules were simple:

- No one was allowed to comment, pontificate, give an opinion, or say what they thought or felt. The only thing the group could do was *ask questions.*
- They took notes on my answers to their questions. They probed deeply into any feelings they sensed behind my answers. No conclusions were drawn. No subtle "in my opinion" type questions, that were really intended to be a comment, were allowed.
- A week later, we reconvened and they shared what they had observed in my answers and what they felt God might be doing in my life.
- Periods of silence were encouraged between questions and people were instructed to constantly be listening for promptings from God for what to ask. (With this said, silence felt very comfortable.)

I felt so valued and cared for. For once, I was the one talking, not listening pastorally. I felt really heard. I felt this way because no one was allowed to interject a story of theirs that was triggered by one of my responses. There

185

were no, "Oh yeah, that happened to me and boy it was bad…" There were no, "That reminds me of something God is teaching me right now," or "Man, I feel you; I've been where you are and it wasn't fun." No interruptions, just questions. And then people stopped talking.

In everyday life, you might want to experiment with refraining from speech. Just tell your spouse in advance. Most of what passes for listening today is not listening at all. It is merely a pause between sentences. We are busy formulating our next sentence while the other person goes on talking. Genuine quietness is different. When we are intentionally listening, we *yield the floor*. Someone else takes control of the conversation. If you are a verbal processor or a habitual interrupter, you probably often can't wait to interject or you *over-participate*. Silently listening trains you to do focused listening.

One other way to practice being quiet is to engage in a *modified fast from speech*. Go for a day speaking only when someone else speaks first. Keep your responses to a minimum. Let others have the last word. Combine this with a complete fast from email, social media, and your cell phone and see how you feel.

2. Practice physical and mental stillness!

It's perfectly legal to get yourself into a comfortable physical position. It's a great idea to have a comfortable chair. Physical discomfort is a big distraction to entering into a time of silence. But once you're comfortable, practice actual physical stillness, to the extent that you can.

Mental stillness is even harder. Random thoughts are like mosquitos buzzing about. Rather than beating yourself up because of your mind wanderings, have a piece of paper nearby so you can write down whatever distracts you and then mentally "lay it aside." God understands what our culture has done to us, but we must make some effort to enter into mental stillness. When other thoughts come into your mind that are not worthy of the list nearby, say to yourself, "Lord, I had that thought, I'd like to lay it aside now and continue to focus on being with You." Over and over again, I had to practice this. When you have short periods of time, you can simply ask God, "Is there anything

You want to say to me in this time I have?" Then, stay alert.

Mental Stillness and Using the Bible

Sometimes, mental stillness comes more easily when we repeat a phrase or verse from the Bible. Here are a couple of examples to experiment with:
- "Be still, and know that I am God" (Ps. 46:10, NLT).
- "Be still before the Lord and wait patiently for Him" (Ps. 37:7, NIV).
- "I find my rest in God alone" (Ps. 62:1, NIRV).
- "Search me, O God, and know my heart" (Ps. 139:23, NLT).

You can make up your own:
- "Jesus, you are with me always."
- "God, you are the lover of my soul."
- "You are for me, not against me."
- "Lord, You embrace me in Your presence."

Sometimes you can focus on one of God's attributes:
- "God, you made me, you know me, you bought me back."
- "You do not condemn me."
- "Lord, you are my Provider." (Substitute: *Strength, Guide, Hope, Comforter, Help in time of need*...and others)
- "Jesus, you are my Wonderful Counselor." (Substitute: *Mighty God, Everlasting Father, Prince of Peace.*)
- "Lord, You are present to me, always."
- "God, You are all-powerful and all-knowing."

A Few More Specific Ways to Practice *Being Quiet*

1. Start by looking for opportunities to be silent and intentionally listen.

Start with normal everyday life situations. You might think there are not any real-life situations where you can practice quietness and being alone, but there are. I find that a car can be a monastery retreat center if used wisely. So, when driving, I have a quiet atmosphere in which to intentionally listen for Jesus' still, small voice.

2. Use natural breaks in your normal day to do a mini-silent retreat.

This can be done when you have a 10-15 minute window of time: waiting for your children to exit school, waiting for someone to arrive for an appointment, waiting for your car to be repaired (this might be longer than 15 minutes!), waiting in line to check out with your groceries.

Begin by taking advantage of *being alone* situations that already exist in your regular routine: your drive to work and back, your exercise routine, your daily walk (with a dog or without), time in the shower, time spent vacuuming or dusting. Of course, in any of these situations, you could have music piped into your earbuds or have the radio on in the car, but this is where we can practice replacing that constant sound with quietness. (Please know that the exception to this rule is people who connect with God through listening to worship music. They hear Him in those words. But remember, sometimes, even with that, occasional silence is still needed.)

3. Finding time with a little more intentionality…

Experiment with intentional listening for God when you:

- take a drive
- get up early
- rent a boat
- stay up late
- soak in the tub or Jacuzzi
- do yardwork
- use a work break or lunch break for the purpose of being alone and quiet with God.

And with some of those under your belt, try these:

- Remember to practice *slowing*. Walk slower. Drive slower. Eat slower. While doing this practice, do some noticing and listening for inner leadings from God. In this way, your body becomes a sanctuary for God's living presence.
- Set an appointment with God in your calendar each day or week.

People won't question you if you have an appointment. They won't ask who you have it with.

- Book some time at a retreat center for a day or overnight.
- If you can, find a place for quietness and aloneness. Convert a place in your home. Find a specific place in a park, or by a stream, the ocean or a lake—a place where you can be quiet and alone. Designate a certain chair as a place where you meet God and think of it as your sanctuary.

4. A Technology "fast!"

A "fast" is going without something in order to pay attention to God and His presence. Fasting is usually associated with food, but what about fasting from TV, music, cell phones, movies, iPads, and laptops? Eventually, this "fast" can turn into a habit, then a routine, then something very easy and commonplace.

It is so hard to be silent, silent not only with my mouth, but even more, silent with my heart. There is so much talking going on within me. It seems that I am always involved in some inner debate with my friends, my enemies, my supporters, my opponents, my rivals and myself. These inner debates pull my heart far from God.

- Henri Nouwen

Silence and *prayer* seemed to go together in Jesus' life on earth. Most people define prayer as "talking to God." That's true…but it's also *intentionally listening to God*. Sometimes we feel guilty that we don't articulate our prayers very well, especially compared to some who sound so good when they pray. Let me assure you all, moving throughout your day and intentionally listening for God *is* prayer. It's not the volume or beauty of the words, necessarily. I've gone many a day simply asking God questions like:

- "What do you want me to do in this situation?"
- "Is there anything you want me to say or not say to this person I'm

talking to? What do they need from me? A look? A word? A touch? An action?"

- "What's going on in them that You can see, Lord, but I can't?"
- "Is there anyone you want me to write to/call/visit/do something with today…or someday soon?"

Then I wait…quieting myself…and more often than not, something, someone, an idea, a reminder comes my way. But it happened in an arena of *not* being surrounded by *noise*. The devil is all about noise, so pursue time slots, moments, and then a few scattered longer periods of quietness. Remember, start small. Something is better than nothing. And I guarantee you will increasingly sense that your Father in heaven is with you and within you; in front and back; on the left and right; above and below…and that He's whispering to you always.

We need to find God, and He cannot be found in noise and restlessness. God is the friend of silence. Trees, flowers and grass grow in silence. The stars, moon and sun move in silence. We need silence to touch souls, especially our own.
- Mother Teresa of Calcutta, A Gift for God.

Exercise:

Do a "Noise Noticing Day." Pick one day and do intensive noticing of the sounds around you wherever you are. Notice not only the obvious sound but the background sound and the constant sounds. How does all that make you feel? Have you found you've grown used to it? How does silence make you feel?

Pam Guyer
Laurie Bjord-Jane
Culps
✓*Jerry Olsen*
✓*Karen*

People are meant to live in an ongoing conversation with God, speaking and being spoken to.

- Dallas Willard, Hearing God

Chapter 9: The Practice of SENSING LEADINGS FROM GOD

God's Ordinary Whispers to Ordinary People

SOME OF YOU READING THIS have trouble believing that God really wants to communicate with you constantly. You might think, *He has a universe to run. Why would He be so involved with me?* That is a lie from Hell.

Ordinary people can sense God's leadings. If you have a packed schedule, you can discern a leading from God. If your life is full of hauling children around everywhere and working part-time, you can receive inner promptings from God. If you're retired, single, divorced, or a teenager, you can receive strong impressions from God. We just need to develop an awareness that Jesus is speaking to us—always and through most everything that comes our way.

Sometimes, God speaks to us through a new idea. Other times, He speaks to us through His creation. He whispers to us in conversations, fictional characters in books, plays, movies, works of art, backpacking, running, and dancing. He speaks to us when we face a physical challenge that causes fear, like rock-climbing or flying. He prompts and nudges us to overcome challenges that build confidence. God speaks through church services, small group meetings, TV commercials, programs, and news reports. God spoke to Adam and Eve, Enoch, Moses and Elijah. We tend to see these biblical conversations with God as exceptional moments in the history of mankind. However, they were not meant to be exceptional at all. Rather, they are examples of the typical human life God intended for us: *God's indwelling His people through His personal presence.*

What Leadings May Seem Like

Here's what people say when they sense a leading or prompting from God:

- "It was strange; I just felt this urge to go over there."
- "I was talking with them and I sensed a nudge to put my hand on their shoulder."
- "She was talking and I wanted to insert myself to tell her I understood, but I sensed an inner leading that said, 'Just let her talk. Ask her questions about what she's saying. Deepen the conversation.'"
- "I was listening to him talk and suddenly something came in my head. I didn't know where it came from, but I shared it with him and he said, 'That's so helpful.'"
- "I was meeting a fellow worker for lunch. I noticed he seemed a bit down. And out of the blue, two words came in my head, 'ENCOURAGE HIM!'"

These are examples of a phenomenon that is easily mistaken for coincidence. It's not weird for Christ-followers to have many:

- strong impressions
- sudden promptings
- inner suggestions, even commands (not necessarily from an audible voice)
- gut feelings.

These can be brushed off as "random thoughts," or "inconsequential feelings," when in fact they are the whispers of God specifically to you. You may think, "Doesn't this stuff come naturally?" It's possible, but if you live with a constant awareness that God is *with* and *within* you, you will experience more and more of these God-messages if you obey them. No matter how weird they might seem at first, if you begin to practice this and grow in your ability to live in this "one ear tuned to heaven" mode, I guarantee you will experience the *thrill of being used by God!* And you'll experience what it's like to be constantly aware that you are always in God's presence.

A Leading I Didn't Want to Obey

If noise is reduced or eliminated in your life, and you're open to hear the promptings and leadings of God, here's what will happen...

One day, I was doing yard work in my front yard. It was 95 degrees. I had just finished about 2 ½ hours of work and I was tired and ready to go inside. Then, my next-door neighbor turned the corner pulling a trailer. It's filled with wet concrete. He was putting in a pathway in his back yard. I sensed a prompting that had to be from God because I personally was not "feelin' it." The leading I sensed was, *Go over and help him.*

My godly, inner response was "Really? NO, come on! I'm hot. I'm tired. My back is killing me. Give me a break, God."

Silence.

So I walked over to my neighbor and asked, "Hey, is your son going to help you with this? It looks like a huge project."

He says, "No, he's gone somewhere."

I'm thinking, *Wonderful, God. Thanks a lot.* But I say, "Listen, I don't know how to lay concrete. What if I load the wheelbarrow and run it back and forth to you, and you can do the smoothing and all that?"

He said, "Would you do that?"

I said, "Sure, no problem." But inside I'm thinking, *What have I gotten myself into? I'm going to die here.*

Three hours later, we were mostly done. I don't know how many wheelbarrows I filled and dumped. I did it with a lousy inner attitude, but I still did it.

Did I obey the leading of God? Yes. Did I do it with a whiny, "poor me" attitude? Yes. (My neighbor wasn't aware of my bad attitude, but it was there.) Did it count that I obeyed but did it with a lousy attitude? *Yes!* It helps to be ready and prepared for these surprise divine interruptions, but, like me, sometimes we're not ready. Still, obeying them, even with a less than stellar attitude, is still *obeying* the leading from God. So take heart!

Do I know why God wanted me to help my neighbor that day? No, I don't. And some of you reading this might say, "Ah, you were just triggered to do the right thing." You could be right. But when I sense those strong leadings, I've learned to obey no matter how simple they may be, because when a Christ-follower obeys what they think is a leading, God will give them more and more.

The Right Leading for the Right Person at the Right Time

It's a good idea to earnestly seek God's guidance in these situations. But God's dream for us; His desire and wish, is that we would have one ear tuned to heaven 365/24/7. His dream is that we'd constantly live as if He were with and within us. Because the truth is that He is communicating with us all the time. Prayer is not only talking to God: *a major part of one's prayer life is listening for God.* As I've aged, I've begun to do more of the latter because I figure that what God has to say really matters and I need to listen even more intently than I speak. Maybe that's why we have two ears and one mouth.

It is critical that we believe and buy into wholeheartedly, that God's plan is to have the *right* person in the *right* place at the *right* time for His *right* purposes. I'm often amazed at who ends up talking to who when there's someone that needs to be heard. A mother who wonders if she's parenting her two-year-old properly ends up talking to another mother who has children in junior high and high school. The older mother has been through this stage and can empathize thoroughly. She can reassure the young mom that she's not the worst mother on the planet and maybe can give some examples of how she herself screwed up—but also can talk about what worked, so that the young mom has new methods to try.

Why didn't that mom get led to me? Because I'm not the best person for her situation.

Even if someone comes to me for advice on something, my first instinct is to ask myself, "Is there anyone else who has more experience and training on their issue?" God often arranges a struggling alcoholic to meet someone who's in AA. People who struggle with spending or gambling are often led to someone who knows their plight and can offer to come alongside to help. Think back over your life. Were there any incidents where you were concerned, worried, or preoccupied with something in your life? Your career, your marriage, your children, your finances, your life with God, a hidden self-destructive habit? When you brought it out in the open, did God give you the right person in the right place at the right time for His right purposes? If so, you experienced God's plan, which is the rescuing and forgiving and restoring of your life.

Remember when Jesus said to His followers, "It's better that I go away," i.e., be crucified, resurrected, and return to Heaven, "…because I'm sending the Third Person of the Trinity, the Holy Spirit, to live in you. Essentially, I will be *with* and *within* you, above and below, to the right and the left, in front and back. And everyone can have full access to Me, at any time and place, if they've taken that step of faith to *trust Me*. If you practice this 'I am with and within you' truth, I will continue to:

- lead you
- comfort you
- teach you
- empower you
- confront you
- warn you
- transform you."

This is an exciting way to live life!

Leadings from God vs. Leadings from Ourselves

I was standing outside after a church service and an acquaintance was telling me about a class he'd attended that morning. He told me that there were a couple of new young women in the group who had shared their "less-than-Christ-like" mind on the class topic, and he'd felt it was his duty to "straighten them out on the matter."

I asked him, "Have they been coming to this church for long?"

He said, "No, this class was their first experience at a church."

I was fuming. Here were two women who came to discuss an issue in an open, accepting, and supposedly loving environment of a church, and they were blasted for having a secular mindset.

I asked the guy if he'd recognize them. He said, "Yes, they're walking away right over there."

A very strong impression came to me, *Go over to them and apologize.*

I ran over to them. One of them was crying, and the other one had her arm around her shoulder to comfort her. As I got in front of them I said, "I heard what happened in that class you attended and I'm so sorry that happened. You were treated badly, and we are at fault. I know it may not make any difference, but please allow me to apologize deeply for how you were treated. I am *so sorry.*"

I added that they had a lot of courage to come into a church setting, and I apologized again that they hadn't been treated kindly, letting them know that they mattered to God, and that we'd failed in reflecting God's love for them.

Then I went back to the guy who'd said the harsh words to these two women. I was livid. I didn't sense any leading from God to shred this guy but I couldn't help myself.

And the lesson to learn here is: don't think that whenever you have some "righteous anger" that it's from God.

I was so ticked off that I let this guy have it. I have the spiritual gift of sarcasm, so I said, "Hey, man, thanks for being the kind of example to those two women of a genuine, loving-hearted Christ-follower. Your callous words and actions resulted in two brand new people, people who've never been to this church before, high-tailing it out of here because they were hurt so badly by *your* actions and *your* words. Well done. Way to be an example of Jesus."

I was hot. Maybe too hot. Too harsh, too sarcastic. But I had spent 13 years working with unchurched teenagers and knew how to approach and handle teenagers who were investigating this Jesus-thing. I could have corrected any number of behaviors or opinions teenagers had, but I needed to wait and invest in their lives until I had won the right to be heard. And I knew these women had just experienced everything you don't want to have happen in a "Christian" environment.

There were two leadings in this incident. The first was, *Go talk to them.* That one was from God. And the second one (which could be argued wasn't really a leading, but just me being ticked off) was, *Go confront that guy so he doesn't hurt others.*

I followed both of them, but I'll never know the results of what I did.

How Do You Know You Are Sensing a "Leading" and It's Not Indigestion?[1]

1. *Ask God, "Is this message truly from You?"* Much of the time you'll sense a confirmation that it is or isn't.

2. *Ask yourself, "Does this leading line up with biblical truth?"* God won't lead you to steal, kill, insult, demean, or minimize someone. (I could be blamed for minimizing that guy in the example above, for sure). He won't lead you to lie on a resume or cheat on your income taxes. However, if you read the Bible carefully, several people were sent by God to confront kings, leaders and people in general. Their language was harsh. Some might interpret their words as insulting and demeaning. What do we do with that? I tend to trust that the harsh language used was the only way to get through to some hard-hearted people. Sometimes, the only wake-up call that works is raw, unedited words. At these times, a leading to use anger-filled words is not only appropriate but the godly thing to do.

3. *Ask yourself, "Does this leading seem intelligent?"* God gave us a brain for a reason; to think things through. As we increase in understanding who God is and what His commands for life are, we can line up this leading with that truth. God often speaks to us in our "second thoughts" so I'd recommend taking a step back, and thinking things through.

4. *Ask yourself, "Is this leading in tune with my character; how God has wired me up?* This is a tough one for people who like to give advice or tell people what they should do. I would strongly caution against giving advice…period. We might be leading someone away from what God wants them to experience and discover for themselves. If you have been wired up to have a quick "giving advice" trigger, ask God to prompt you to ask more questions first. Then listen. You may sense the person in front of you is asking about something outside of your experience. Refer them to someone who has a similar history.

5. *Ask someone you trust, "Do you think this is a leading from God? And if so, how do you think I should handle it?"* The "training process" with God is ongoing, and He may speak through a trusted friend or someone more experienced in receiving the whispers from God. They may have handled a similar situation in their past. In those conversations, often some of their words will "ping" with you. That's usually the Holy Spirit prompting you to stay with that truth and run with it. Make sure that anyone you ask for advice knows the previous four questions and walks through them with you.

The answers to these five questions will help you determine whether the leadings you sense you're experiencing are actually from God.

Life-Changing Leadings

Sometimes, in the midst of confusing times, insecure times, and "not-knowing-the-future" times, God can send some really *big*, life-altering leadings. These types of leadings usually involve some major life shifts and are sometimes high risk.

I've had what I would call two major life-changing leadings in the past ten years:

1. "Trust Me."

After resigning my position as a pastor (a job I'd held for 20 years), I was working three jobs to try and make ends meet.

I tend to do internal worrying. I have a mild form of depression. So I can get a bit down and negative. So, after a year of doing these three jobs, I was beginning to wonder what I was doing with my life. One day, I was doing some errands and I sensed a strong, inner nudging, *Pull over!*

I pulled over to the side of the road. I waited and said, "I'm here listening, Lord." I sensed the phrase, *Trust me!*

That was it. No, "I've got this job lined up for you." It was simply, "Trust Me!" Part of me wanted some more details on that. The other part of me was very comforted and assured. God knew my situation. He'd heard my worries. He knew I was frightened. "Trust Me" changed my entire demeanor. I calmed down. That inner calm lasted until some new directions came my way: officiating weddings and forming my own charitable organization called, "Craig Knudsen: Minister at Large." Both of these have been going for many years now. God came through.

2. "Write!"

This leading had been one that kept getting repeated in my spirit for several years. In addition, my friends had been saying, "You need to write more, maybe even a book." My first response was, "What could I possibly write about that someone more famous hasn't already written about? What do I know? I'm just a regular guy."

Still, the leading kept getting repeated in my heart. So, I started writing two short, monthly essays. Writing two essays a month has been great practice. I have been doing it for seven years now. In addition, I'm one of those people who writes cards, letters, and emails to people to encourage, instruct, or comfort. I've always been writing in some way, shape or form.

Still, people kept saying, "You need to write a book."

Finally, I said, "Okay, I'll give it a shot."

If you've read this far into this book, you now know that, as best I could, I obeyed the leading to "write." Whether this book makes any money or not doesn't matter. The point is to obey the leading. Money isn't the reason for writing. It's to encourage, help, and reassure normal, hurried, busy people that they can experience God in the midst of their normal lives. If it helps anyone, God wins!

Big Leadings You Might Receive

Those are the two big leadings I've had over the last decade. What might be some other "BIG" leadings that you might sense from God?

- *Quit your job!*
- *Move to another city.*
- *Ask her to marry you.*
- *Do an intervention with your child.*
- *For your safety, get away from him and his domestic violence.*

These types of leadings take a massive amount of courage to act upon, but I believe God will open doors for you if you're willing to take one courageous step of faith that God is behind them.

Following a Wild and Crazy Leading

This one was weird. I was in a seminary class called, "The Holy Spirit." The professor brought in several guests from a variety of church backgrounds who articulated how they experience the Holy Spirit. One week, he brought in a man who was a part of The Vineyard church. This church practices what scholars call "The Ecstatic Gifts of the Holy Spirit." Meaning, they make *healing* and *speaking in tongues* (different languages; some of them very weird) and *miracles* a regular part of their prayer life and church services.

This man was not on the staff of the church. He was a volunteer. He told us a story of a young man he knew who was involved in a terrible car accident. He had major head trauma as well as other injuries. His head had swollen significantly. He was near the point of death. This man, I'll call him Mike, felt a strong prompting that said, "Go visit him and pray for his healing."

Mike was very hesitant. *I'm not a pastor,* he thought. *I've never done this before. I don't know what I'm doing.* But he went to the hospital. As he prayed for the boy, he said he felt a strange warmth going through him, so he lingered with his hand on the boy's chest in silence. Soon, he left. The next day, doctors were stunned that the boy's vitals had stabilized. In a couple of days, he opened his eyes from the induced coma. Within a couple of weeks, that young man walked out of the hospital. The doctors had no explanation. Mike, following a silent whisper from the Holy Spirit, was a part of healing that boy who was at death's door.

As Mike explained this to our class, I could sense some enthusiasm from some of my classmates and some skepticism. Mike went on to tell another story. Soon after the healing of this boy, there was another car accident and another young person was in dire straits. Mike thought, *Well, I'm the man for this situation. I'll get down there and God and I will do our thing.* He arrived. He prayed. The boy died. Mike was stunned, dumbfounded, confused. "Why didn't it work this time, God? One boy lives, the next one dies. What's up with that? I prayed just like last time." He told the class that he assumed he would partner with God in healing any and every one that came his way. Was there no leading from God on this second boy? Even if there wasn't, why should it matter? He was supposed to pray for him anyway, right?

Mike told the class that that experience humbled him and from then on, he spoke of God's mystery. Sometimes He heals. Lots of times (it seems) He doesn't. Mike went on to lead the class in asking for God's healing presence. Several students went up and were prayed for.

Then, one of my seminary friends went up front to ask for prayer. He whispered to Mike, and then Mike said aloud, "Glenn has a degenerative heart condition. The doctors say he won't live more than five years from now."

Now, Glenn's wife and newborn son were in the room with us. I'm thinking, *Oh, man this is awful.*

Mike put his hand on Glenn's chest and started silently praying. As he did this, I started to sense that I was being called to go up front, but I stayed seated. Then Mike stopped praying and said, "There's someone here who is supposed to pray for Glenn."

I thought, *Oh crap, it's me!* But I didn't immediately say anything. No one spoke up.

Mike said, "I think someone here is supposed to pray for Glenn."

I sheepishly raise my hand and said, "It might be me."

"C'mon up," Mike said. I walked up front and Mike gently said, "Just place your hand on Glenn's chest and pray whatever comes to you."

I had no idea what to ask. I placed my hand on Glenn's chest and silently asked God if He would please heal Glenn's heart. I thought of the heartache of never seeing his son grow up. I didn't pray anything profound. In fact, words seemed hard to come by.

As this is going on, I started to feel warm...then hot. Not because of the temperature in the room, but something coming from within. I wasn't sweating. I thought, *What is going on?* But I kept my hand on Glenn, and he felt the warmth too. It lasted for a minute or two and then it was over. Glenn and I looked at each other, knowing something had passed between us.

As you might imagine, from then on, I was *very* interested in Glenn's heart condition. In three months, the doctors told him his condition hadn't progressed any further. At six months, the doctors were astounded by what looked like a progressive healing of his heart condition. At the one year mark, there was no sign of his life-threatening heart disease.

From that point on, I was much more open to stories of the ecstatic gifts. But I've never felt something like that since, and it's been thirty years.

To finish the story, I saw Glenn about ten years later and he said, "You know Craig, it started at that class." I asked how his son and wife were doing.

He said, "Well, my wife tragically died of cancer about three years after that class, but my son is fine. I'm remarried and have another child. I'm doing well."

I thought, *Oh my gosh! Your wife died?* God healed Glenn. He didn't heal his wife.

Here's my point again. In that class, at that moment, I felt that strong nudge to raise my hand. And I was quite skeptical of this whole thing. I wasn't in the charismatic camp at all, and yet God used me in Glenn's life. That was a very dramatic leading from God. Most of the ones that have come my way aren't even close to that kind of life-or-death scenario. But regardless, leadings, promptings, and nudges from the Holy Spirit are God's means of being present to us in our normal everyday lives. The question is, "Will we practice listening? And then, will we obey what we sense is coming from God?"

Five Main Categories of Leadings from God

Many teachers and pastors have written about the following five categories of leadings. I learned about these five categories from Bill Hybel's book, *Whispers.* They will help you increase your awareness of God-type promptings.

Leading Word #1: "GO"

After leaving my Senior pastor position, the time came to find a church to attend. We landed at a larger church and visited for a few months. Over the weeks, I noticed a man about five rows up from us. He wore board shorts, flip-flops, and cool surfer t-shirts. My kind of guy. One morning, during the greeting time, I sensed a leading of, *Go and introduce yourself,* so I walked up to him and said, "Hey, I'm Craig and you are?"

"John" he said.

"Hey, great to meet you. I see you every week and I'm jealous of your hair, so I just had to say hi." (John has that full head of gray hair that my bald dome would kill for.)

He laughed and then we started chatting after church. Then we went on a bike ride. Then more bike rides. Then lunch, smoothies, dinners. There came a time when the church was forming small groups. John said he was going so I went with him. We signed up for the same group. We've been meeting for four years. Over this time, I met his wife, family, and friends. We have become close friends. John is one of God's wonderful gifts to me.

It all came from obeying the leading that I now know was from God, "Go say hi to that guy." You never know.

What other "GO's" might we receive?
- "GO help that person."
- "GO get involved."
- "GO serve in that opportunity."
- "GO volunteer for that."
- "GO attend that class or small group."
- "GO see a marriage counselor; a family therapist."
- "Go take a meal over to a grieving family."
- "GO write an encouraging email or text."
- "GO apologize."

Leading Word #2: "NO"

Pastors can be lightning rods for criticism. People don't like one thing or another and they decide to let you know about it. In our day and age, confrontation happens mostly through emails and texting. This is the worst form of conflict resolution. It *always* needs to be done face-to-face, or at least over the phone, so you can hear voice inflections, sense the person's tone of voice, and get a feel for their emotions. Also, you have a chance to tell the other person that they don't know the whole story.

I received one of those "criticism" emails once. I crafted a well-worded "attack response" that demeaned the person's intelligence, their judgmental-ism, and arrogance. It felt good to write it. When I was finished, I re-read it and deleted it, because I felt a strong Holy-Spirit prompting saying, "NO, Craig. Do *not* send that e-mail. It will only escalate the issue." God was right, as usual. There are too many ways for the written word to be misinterpreted. So, my standard response to a confrontational e-mail now is to write back, "Sounds like you're disappointed. Let's set up a time to meet and we can talk this through." 99% of the time, I never hear back.

That "NO" leading saved me a lot of hassle and grief.

Some "No's" you might hear from God:

- "Do NOT confront that person unless you're going to be a part of the solution."
- "Do NOT lob that verbal grenade of sarcasm, demeaning, or minimizing a person." Don't say words you'll regret later.
- "Do NOT hold a moral failure against someone forever." Remember, as *you* have been forgiven, so you and I must forgive others.
- "Do NOT take that job!"
- "Do NOT marry that person. Call off the wedding."
- "Do NOT spend that money."
- "Do NOT get that credit card."
- "Do NOT buy that home. The mortgage will kill you."
- "Do NOT click that mouse."
- "Do NOT call someone that name."
- "Do NOT label that person."

What if your friends are saying "NO" and God's saying "GO"?

There might be a situation where everyone around you is saying "NO" because you brought them in on it to help you discern, but you sense the Holy Spirit is still giving you a strong leading to "GO."

At one point in his travels, Paul the apostle was about to board a ship from Ephesus that was bound for the Jerusalem area, where there was a warrant out for his arrest. All the Ephesian church leaders were begging him not to go. They knew how much he was hated in Israel. They wept tears of sadness and pleaded with anguished voices, "Paul, *don't go!"*

Paul said, "You're breaking my heart. Please, I know this is where God is leading me to go, so send me on my way with glad faces."

Interesting, no one on that dock said to Paul, "You know, Paul, you've been led by God to go to places and not go to places in your travels. You've been led to say things and do things. Who am I to say that this leading from God isn't from Him, just because it will lead to hardship, maybe arrest and trial, maybe even imprisonment? Who said that God's leadings are always easy? So, I'm trusting that this path you're taking is a God-led thing." If anyone had said that, I think Paul would have hugged that guy to death.

Everyone was saying "NO" but God was still saying "GO!" That's the toughest "obey the Holy Spirit" thing to do.

Ok, so "GO" and "NO" and now...

Leading Word #3: "SLOW"

You might sense from God, *This is going too fast. SLOW this thing down. Think it through for some more time. Bring others in to help you discern if this is from God.*

Another word for "slow" is *"wait."* Take some more time to stay open to the Holy Spirit to give additional guidance through direct promptings or the friends around you who might bring wise counsel.

Most often, "SLOW" messages from God revolve around major life issues. God may nudge you with a "slow" if you find yourself rushing to give advice to someone who's not asking for it.

What types of things might prompt the Holy Spirit to send a "SLOW DOWN" message to you?

- "SLOW DOWN those radical steps you want to take with your child."
- "SLOW DOWN the decision to get divorced."
- "SLOW DOWN regarding taking that job offer."
- "SLOW DOWN the decision to marry this person."

Slow down the speed of following a lead that affects your family, the church you're involved in, the friends you've grown up with, or the ministry you have going. It's not necessarily a "NO" from God but it's definitely worth a *slow!*

Leading Word #4: "GROW"   *Love God + people*

When Jesus was asked what the entire message of the Old Testament could be condensed into, He replied, "Increase your capacity to *love God* and *love people!*"(See Luke 10:27.) Since that is the prime directive of God for the people He made, it should be the prime directive we follow. We are given help and strength to grow in this endeavor by the Holy Spirit (God Himself), who lives with and within us. Therefore, if you are wondering what God's primary agenda is for you, it's that you would increasingly grow into a clearer reflection of Jesus' heart of love towards people. His dream is that Jesus' words, actions, looks, and touches would be done through us.

Loving people is doing what Jesus would do if He were in our place. This directive from God is something we are always *growing* into. Any and every spiritual practice that we engage in joins us with God in His ongoing process of developing a "Jesus-type" heart, mind, attitude, and readiness for action within us.

The good news in all this is that our everyday world is God's classroom designed for us to experience His presence, guidance, comforting, teaching, and encouragement. Therefore, everything is a "grow" opportunity. Every encounter with people is an opportunity to grow us into further Christ-like-ness, to develop our character, and to sense His loving presence.

God wants us to grow in our knowledge that He is more concerned about *who we are* than about *what we do.* It is a tough concept for most American Christ-followers to really believe that God's primary stance towards us is that He enjoys us regardless of whether or not we're productive for Him.

Moses was a shepherd *for 40 years* before he was asked to go back to Egypt and lead the Israelites out of slavery to a land God promised. What did Moses "do" for God in those years? Watched over sheep.

These silent, unproductive years of Moses were the character formation years of his life. In fact, those "silent years" re-formed many of the Old Testament heroes into men and women they never would have been without those years.

God also wants us to grow in our desire for Him—He wants us to desire *Him* more than we desire *His answers for our lives.*

God is not about being our personal Google map. His dream is that we'd be content knowing Him; worshipping Him and enjoying His presence in everyday life, not just in crisis or turning points in our lives. It's the difference between wanting God to solve our problems versus learning to live with problems, knowing that He is good, kind, loving and gracious. This truth is very hard to live out, especially in situations where everything changes.

In tough situations where we aren't getting any answers from God, the question becomes, "Is God really *enough?* Just Him, not His provision or answers or explanations? Is He Himself enough for me?"

When it's really bad, am I going to hold onto the truth that God is *for* me? (See Romans 8: 31.)

The bottom line is that "God is *for* us, not against us" when things don't go our way. He's for us when our house is foreclosed upon. He's for us when we find out our child has special needs. He's for us when our spouse walks out on us…and doesn't come back. He's for us when your child dies before you. God being *for* us (i.e. on our side, closer-than-ever, comforting-helping-assuring us that He's not gone anywhere, that this is not a punishment for your sin)…and *not against* us, is the truth about Him that we have to hold on tight to when we don't get the answers from Him we want, or any answer at all.

His dream for us is that we'd follow Him whether life goes well or not. He has spoken most clearly through Jesus' life and teaching. Therefore, learning Jesus' story, imitating His example and following His teachings is our prime directive. My job is to follow Him. My job is to obey His leadings. Will I continue to follow Him when life deals hardship, sorrow and loss? When any of us do this, we have reached the varsity level of doing life with God.

As sensitively as I can write this, when hardship comes your way, don't spend a lot of time trying to discern what aspects of the event is "God's plan" or not. Instead, know that you are now on the tough road of following God when life gets tough. He's with and within you there too.

Leading Word #5: "KNOW"

What will the Holy Spirit be constantly whispering for you to know and count on? These things:

- "Know that you are my beloved child. I will never stop loving, forgiving, and assuring you that you are Mine."
- "Know that I am *closer* than the air you breathe."
- "Know that you are *safe in My hands.*"
- "Know that I know *you* and *your* current situation and I am working behind the scenes on it always, no matter what the outcome may be."
- "Know that you are cherished, of extreme value, my treasure, my one-of-a-kind masterpiece."
- "Know that you are *not alone.*"
- "Know that there's no need to worry."
- "Know that I will walk with you through pain, sorrow, tragedy, loss… *nothing* can separate you from My love."
- "Know that there is *no condemnation* for you. There is only the future of heaven for you."

The Role of the Bible in Receiving Leadings

God's whispers often come when we are reading and pondering His story in the Bible. Therefore, it is critical to *read, know,* and *retain* truth from the *Bible*. I'm often asked, "Where should I read?"

- Major in the records of Jesus' life: the gospels; Matthew, Mark, Luke and John.
- Memorize the promises God gives to us in the Bible:

    a) "[Jesus] saved us, not because of righteous things we had done, but because of his mercy" (Titus 3:5a, NIV).

211

b) "There is no condemnation for those who belong to Christ Jesus" (Romans 8:1, NLT).

c) "The temptations in your life are no different from what others experience. And God is faithful. He will not allow the temptation to be more than you can stand. When you are tempted, he will show you a way out so that you can endure" (I Corinthians 10:13, NLT.)

There are three places people are in at any given time:

1. Before pain

2. In pain

3. After pain

So it helps to have these two verses in our heads:

a) "And I am convinced that nothing can ever separate us from God's love. Neither death nor life, neither angels nor demons, neither our fears for today nor our worries about tomorrow—not even the powers of hell can separate us from God's love. No power in the sky above or in the earth below—indeed, nothing in all creation will ever be able to separate us from the love of God that is revealed in Christ Jesus our Lord" (Romans 8:38-39, NLT).

b) "'For I know the plans I have for you,' says the LORD. 'They are plans for good and not for disaster, to give you a future and a hope'" (Jeremiah 29:11, NLT).

Remember, the more leadings, promptings, internal whispers, and nudges we sense and then *obey*, the more and more will come your way.

We must make it our primary goal not just to hear the voice of God, but to be mature people *in a loving relationship with Him*.[2]

Try This:

Take the next week to practice being attentive to the Holy Spirit. Practice the "one ear turned to heaven" image. Start small. Maybe practice this while you are with your spouse, roommate, close friend, or one of your children. See what God nudges you with.

The reflective life is a way of living that prepares the heart for receiving something of eternal significance that can come our way in an ordinary day, at any moment, when we least expect it.

- Ken Gire, *Seeing What is Sacred*

Chapter 10: The Practice of THINKING THINGS THROUGH

REFLECTION, OR THINKING THINGS THROUGH, is an exercise in being attentive to our feelings about our relationships, past experiences, and other events, while listening for God's thoughts and impressions.

How *Thinking Things Through* Matters in the Business World

Consider the term "think tanks." It exists because large companies have found that it is useful and profitable to set aside time for their creative people to think up new ways of doing things: new ideas, new angles, and new methods to organize their management structure. They ponder staff cuts and additions, changes in job descriptions; they dream up new products to sell or improve on existing ones.

Apple Inc. has a code they live by: "Stay two years ahead of the competition." This pushes Apple employees to spend days in think tanks devising ways to improve existing products and inventing new ones.

Google has their "eight pillars of innovation." Number 3 is, "Strive for continual innovation, not instant perfection." Number 8 is, "Never fail to fail."

Apple and Google are two of many companies in the world that separate themselves from the rest because they never settle. "Status quo" is a swear word to them. These companies don't coast; they are the leaders of innovation because they are *thinking through* every product and every way they do things constantly.

Several years ago, I heard a speaker named Jim Collins. He had done years of research on 20 unique companies. He studied the differences between the top 10 companies and the companies that ranked #11-20. The title of his book is *Good to Great*. He found that one of the big differences between a top 10 business and a business in the second 10 is that the top 10 companies were constantly thinking through how they could improve service and production. They included more employees' input on how things ran and created an atmosphere where no idea was a stupid one.

Thinking things through *really matters* in the business world.

How Thinking Things Through Matters in Sports

Why is it that certain sports and sports teams constantly succeed? They never settle on their laurels. The New England Patriots of the NFL, the San Antonio Spurs of the NBA, and the St. Louis Cardinals of MLB are consistent winners year after year because they think through their organizations top to bottom all the time.

For years, baseball was "America's game." Executives thought, "We are the king of the hill. Football, basketball, and hockey will never catch us." And they sat back at their desks, put their feet up, and puffed on a victory cigar... until all those sports caught and passed them like they were standing still. They weren't thinking through how to improve the game, improve player-management relationships. Baseball is the one sport that has had multiple player strikes while the NBA has had none. The NFL is a multi-billion dollar organization, far and away the most popular sport in America. (Soccer still owns the world).

Thinking things through *really matters* in the sports world.

How Thinking Things Through Matters in the Church

How about churches?

I met with a pastor from England a few years ago. I listened to him describe the miniscule involvement of people in any sort of church in England. Statistics say that less than 1.4% of the population of England attends church. As older worshippers are dying off and younger people don't even have church on their radar, we may see the near end of the church in England in our lifetime. They are holding on for dear life.

In America, 40% of people say they attend church, but in reality it is less than 20%. This means that more than 80% of America's population finds something else to do whenever churches gather. At the current rate of decline, the church in America will match the current rates of church attendance in England within 20-25 years.

Unless churches start *thinking things through* and reinvent themselves in some way, they will continue to decline. Soon, America's churches may be more irrelevant to the secular population than they already are.

Authorities on church trends state that one of the reasons for the continued decline is the church's *slow response to change as change is accelerating all around them.* The church grew tremendously with church innovators like Willow Creek, Saddleback, and other mega-churches in the 1980's and 90's. They continue to pass on their wisdom at church conferences. Thank God for them. They revitalized the church in America at that time. They are currently working hard to find out how they can reach the generations beyond the Baby Boomers.

I struggled with this phenomenon in the church I pastored. We couldn't come up with new ways to attract young married couples, single people, and even families with young children. Our church demographics consisted largely of Boomers, along with a small group of young families. We had no minorities. Single people would come in and realize, "There's no one like me here." Many single divorcees felt the same. I didn't know what to do to address this. If we opted for some sort of radical change in our worship

217

service, our Boomers might have left and I don't think altering a worship service would have attracted young people anyway. As I mentioned, attending a church service isn't on their radar. And churches have no time or space to think through new ways of doing church because churches are busy just trying to hang on for dear life.

Thinking things through in the church *really matters!*

How Thinking Things Through *Really Matters* for *Ourselves*!

Thinking things through is a genuine spiritual practice. It can be called *reflection, pondering, extensive consideration, mulling over, quiet noticing, or reviewing.* It is creating space for taking some extended time to process things with God. It is an exercise in attentiveness to your thoughts and feelings over past or present situations, over experiences and relationships, while being attentive for God's impressions and promptings. Thinking matters through may be what keeps you from making a dumb decision. When we purposefully reflect on our feelings, our careers, our friends and direction in life, we open ourselves to being guided by God in whatever area we are pondering.

What if we never reflect on anything? What if we are so desirous of being entertained or so accustomed to responding to stimuli, that we never take the time to reflect about ourselves and where we're headed in life?[1]

Thinking things through takes time.

Where to Do Reflection?

Much of what is sacred is hidden in the ordinary, everyday moments of life. To *see* something in those moments takes slowing down so we can live our lives with more reflection. It means taking a closer look at people, ourselves, what's in front of us, and what God might want to say to us while reflecting. To see these things, we have to slow down and notice. To take them in, we have to *stop* and linger!

218

My wife's family has a condo in Aspen, Colorado. One of activities we like to do there is hike the Hunter Creek Trail. All along the trail, Hunter Creek is cascading down the steep incline. The most recent summer hike we took followed a winter with lots of snowfall. The creek was roaring like a river. Sometimes we couldn't hear each other talk while standing next to each other. Occasionally, we'd stop to rest and then move on. At a few spots, I asked if we could linger a bit. I wanted to ponder what I was seeing just a bit longer.

At one point, my friend Rick asked me what I was seeing on the hike. Sheepishly, I told him a few things:

- *Water rolling over the rocks, both big and small.* These remind me of God's undeserved favor (grace) and love because the water rolls over all those rocks, covers them, and it never stops. Those rocks are us. God's love and grace never stop covering us, washing over us, getting everywhere (like water does) in our lives. And whatever the size and number of our moral failures (big rocks, little rocks, and tons of rocks)…grace can get to them. How do we receive this grace? We have to step into the water and let it cover us.

- *Aspen trees.* Hundreds of Aspen trees originate from one tree. The one tree's root system spreads and small saplings spring up from it. One tree can be the source of over 200 other trees. I thought of the first tree being Jesus and each individual tree springing from it as individual people touched by Him, now growing into His likeness, one life at a time.

- *One step in front of the other.* When we reached the top, we followed a narrow trail in a meadow. We couldn't walk side by side. While we were walking in single file, my wife started singing an old chorus by Rich Mullins, "And step by step You'll lead me, and I will follow You all of my days." Our walking formation reminded me that Jesus is leading me into good experiences and surprises when I follow His commands and teachings.

- *The rocky part of the trail.* Again, my wife noticed that we had to carefully step over rocks of all sizes and shapes. Some were loose and some were firmly embedded, and we had to watch our step. But there was no other trail by which to get home. It reminded me of the life of a Christ-follower. It's the "both/and" phenomenon again. The pathway of life will have events, failures, successes, relationships, tragedies, and more. Like hiking over the rocks, we'll have to navigate all of it somehow. But that trail of life, which is full of those obstacles, is still the way home to heaven and it's the only trail. There is no easier trail out there. Life's road will always have rocks in it.

After sharing some of these things with Rick, he asked, "How did you come up with that stuff?"

I answered, "Do you know those times where I asked the group for a bit more time to stop? It wasn't because I was tired (well, maybe I was); I just wanted to *stop* and take a bit longer to reflect on what I was seeing and ask God, 'Is there anything You want to show me in what I'm seeing?' And this stuff came. But, Rick, it took what I call the '30 second pause.'"

Folks, 30 seconds is a minimum amount of time to stop. It usually takes at least a minute of pausing in order for true reflection to kick in. So, for the rest of the hike, we all practiced the at-least-30-seconds pause. It ended up being fun.

Jesus and the 30 Second Pause

Jesus was teaching in a courtyard when a group of religious men dragged a half-naked woman to Him and threw her on the ground in front of Him. They had done this because she was caught having sex with someone else's husband (see John 8:2-11). They must have known this woman's reputation or "known" her, in the biblical sense, themselves. They'd followed her, waited until she was in the middle of sex with the guy, barged in, and grabbed her. (I wonder how long they watched the sex act happening).

After dragging her before Jesus and the large crowd gathered to hear Him, the religious men pointed out that the penalty for adultery in the Old Testament is stoning, a penalty that had not been practiced for centuries in the Jewish culture, but it was still written there. The crowd started to pick up some stray rocks on the ground. They said to Jesus, "If this is what's written in the Law, what do You say we should do with her?"

And this is where it gets weird. Instead of answering right away, Jesus bent down and started writing in the sand. For how long? Who knows? But I bet it was at least 30 seconds; enough to make them uncomfortable. Why did He do that? He wanted to slow the momentum down and make people reflect on what they were about to do. After the pause, Jesus straightened Himself up and, as if they hadn't gotten it already, said, "If you've never had a moral failure. If you've never thought, said, or done anything that was wrong, go ahead and chuck those rocks." Then He bent down and started writing again, giving them some more reflection time.

Soon, the sound of "whumps" filled the air. It was the sound of rocks dropping to the ground. The oldest people there led the way in the rock-drop. It's as if the older people knew right away, "My life? No sin? I'm out." Then everyone else followed.

Jesus gave the people two reflection times just to let *their own* words sink in ("We want to kill this woman; not the guy sleeping with her…just her"). The second reflection time came after they were confronted with their own human condition.

In each instance, Jesus forced reflection onto people, and it saved a precious, one-of-a-kind treasure of God, in the form of this woman who slept around with married men. Go figure.

In What Types of Situations Can I Practice Reflection?

If our lives are packed (which they usually are), it will take some intentionality to grab times of reflection. But remember our code: *Anything is better than nothing!* Reflection comes naturally when you're in a setting where your heart and mind is drawn to listening for God or talking to Him. As we've mentioned, you can find time for reflection while you're performing routine activities.

For example:

- *Brushing your teeth* offers 1–2 minutes where you can reflect on the day ahead and picture the people you're meeting with, or the appointments you have, the children you're caring for, even seemingly meaningless errands. While doing these things, you could pray, "God, in each thing I do today, remind me to be thinking through what's going on, knowing You are present with and within me in all of that. Remind me that I am an expression of Your love and grace."

- *Taking a shower* gives you anywhere from 3–7 minutes for thinking things through. You could reflect on the truth that washing yourself physically is a repeated symbol of being morally and spiritually cleansed by Jesus' blood and sacrifice on your behalf. In light of that, every person you lock eyes with today either has had that experience, or is someone to whom God is giving multiple messages encouraging them to discover that truth. Any person you encounter is God's beloved treasure (as are you). Pondering that in the shower can prepare you for seeing people washed clean like a white robe because of Jesus' work.

- *Driving* can offer a private, quiet environment to reflect, ponder, and think about things. Depending on the length of the drive, you might ask God, "What issues would you like me to do some thinking on during my drive?" And whatever comes in your head, don't dismiss it as a prompting you generated yourself. Act as if it's from Him. Then think through all that's involved with it. In a sense, you are having a counseling session with Him as He listens to you ponder. (Just keep your eyes on the road while doing this!)

- *Space your appointments with a larger time cushion in between them.* Instead of scheduling appointments so close together that there's no time to think through how the conversation went, plan in some space to ponder what just went on. Maybe jot down a few notes. Reflect back on how you felt at certain times or what God might be prompting you to do for follow-up. When I do this, I sometimes ask God, "Is there anything I could do further to encourage or empathize with the person I just met with? Would an email or hand-written note or text be appropriate? What's behind some of the things I was feeling? Let me know, God."

- *Schedule time in your calendar for "thinking things through."* Most people think that giving themselves a half hour or an hour for reflection in their schedule is wasting time. If someone were to ask you what you did in the last hour, there's a tendency to say, "Nothing." The other person is thinking, *What a non-productive way to use time!*

The next time someone asks you this, why not say, "I was cultivating some thoughts on what next steps I should be taking with some very important matters—steps that will increase my effectiveness as a person in the everyday world." Who could criticize that?

- *Doing household tasks.* I put on noise-cancelling earphones when I work in my yard. Some women do household chores and errands with no self-inflicted noise in the background. Many men and women can do vacuuming, dusting, scrubbing, trimming, raking, or sweeping while their minds are pondering other matters. Often, when I'm doing yard work, I practice being open to God. I think of my wife, son, or daughters, and their spouses, and ponder, *What's going on in their life right now? Is there any way I can be a support and cheerleader without being intrusive?* Often a prompting comes to me while I'm riding my bike: *Call him/her,* or, *text an encouraging word to them, or do something for them that would mean a lot to them.* I've had some ideas for this book while mowing my lawn. But it takes some intentionality to not listen to music all the time, and to use the time for reflection instead.

- *While doing something you love!* Having *fun* often triggers the reflection process, because we realize that fun is a gift from God. We become aware that the particular kind of fun we enjoy is the unique way God wired us up. *Fun* can draw us to God. Running, walking, surfing, knitting, cooking, swimming, hiking, reading, watching a movie, snowboarding, skiing, canoeing, travelling, windsurfing, mountain climbing, or roller-blading. These activities (and many more) can stimulate thinking of another kind. Usually, we are happy and smiling and totally "into it" while doing them. Often times, these experiences take us out of normal everyday life and give us space to think things through with God. And you can have fun while doing this!

- *Going to bed at night.* Before dosing off, at the end of an ordinary day, reflection is asking ourselves, "Have I loved well? Has love been heard in all my conversations? Has it been seen in my eyes and face? Have others felt loved when they were in my presence? Was any truth I spoke today spoken in love? Were the decisions I made today based on love? Were my reactions loving? Have I loved well today?"[2]

Creating space for yourself to ponder, reflect, and think things through can have a game-like quality to it. Be creative with this. Look for time slots where you can intentionally give yourself the gift of pondering, even while you're doing something else that you can do on autopilot. You will find that God will meet you there by offering guidance, prompting you with assurances that you are loved, and giving you suggestions regarding the area of life that is on your mind.

Catholic psychologist Dr. Gregory Popcak wrote, *"All significant human development— psychological, intellectual, emotional and spiritual—comes through reflection. The highest faculty as a human person is our mind because it is where we discern, reflect, choose and decide to act. Through reflection, we determine how we will respond to life, others and to the promptings and leadings that God gives."*[3]

The Bible and Reflection

The Bible is full of people who nurtured a reflective life:
- Isaac reflected in a field in the early evening (Gen. 24:63).
- David reflected on his bed during the night (Psalm 63:6).
- Solomon reflected in a field during the day (Proverbs 24:30-32).
- The Psalmist reflected on God's law (Ps. 1:2), on creation (Ps. 19:3), on God's wonders (Ps. 119:27), and on God's attributes (Ps. 139:1-17).

- Mary reflected on the greeting spoken by the angel (Luke 1:29), on the story the shepherds told about angels telling them to come (Luke 2:19), and on the statement Jesus made when He was twelve (Luke 2:51).

- Peter reflected on a perplexing image revealed to him in a vision (Acts 10:19).

- Paul reflected on the events in Israel's history (I Corinthians 10:1-11).

- The entire book of Hebrews is essentially reflections on the meaning behind the Old Testament symbols and practices.[4]

How Long Do I Reflect on Things?

The short answer is: whatever length you feel is needed. With very important matters, the reflection process can go on in any and all of the spaces I mentioned above. It can go on for days. The more pressing the concern, the longer you're likely to ponder. When that issue gets resolved in some way, the amount of time you spend reflecting on it will go way down. That's normal. Don't beat yourself up for *not* thinking about some other matters when you are preoccupied with a personal matter of great importance to you. God understands. In fact, what you are reflecting on *is* the prayer agenda for now.

When Jesus was pondering how He could communicate who God really was, He went off for 40 days in the wilderness. When He was about to be arrested, He had two to three hours to seek the Father out with questions and doubts, and to ask for courageous strength. Once again, if Jesus regularly needed *thinking things through* time, we must need it even more.

Can I Think Things Through with Others?

Of course. When a sense of indecisiveness is still present inside you, reflect even more. There's no need to hurry anything. God is the author of perfect timing, so He may be whispering, "Wait," because the issue you are thinking through is big. In this case, you might feel better thinking these things through with someone you trust, someone who will value what you are pondering, who will listen intently, and who will ask good questions and say the last 10% that no one else might say. This should be someone who feels like a wise counselor to you.

What types of questions might you ask of this person? Below are some courageous questions that will help the reflection process.

- What do you notice about me?
- What emotions do you see?
- What's your read on my zest for life?
- What seems to be my energy level?
- What does my "happiness factor" look like to you?

Some Lists to Help You in Your Practice of Reflection

You will find that the agenda for reflection comes naturally. It's simply whatever is most on your mind! But if you need a little help, below are some "thinking stimulators," set apart in several different categories, that you can use to inspire deeper reflection.

Pondering Yourself

- What are my predominant feelings? Why might I be feeling them?
- Are there any areas of my life I keep hidden? Who could I come clean with?
- Is my capacity to love increasing?
- Is Jesus' influence growing larger in my life?
- Is my awareness of Jesus' constant presence increasing in frequency? What's a new practice I could do to shake things up and make that happen more?
- What do I do for fun? What *is* fun for me? If I don't take time for fun, why not?
- Are there any relationships that need my attention in some way? Do I need to encourage someone? Affirm someone? Thank someone? Assure someone? Confront someone?

- What sorts of things make me happy?
- What sorts of things are life-giving to me? Life-draining?
- Is there anyone I need to do conflict resolution with?
- In what situations might God be asking me to *wait?*
- What sorts of things distract me the most from being attentive to God?

Pondering Your Career

- Which danger to my life with God (hurry, busyness, noise, distraction) am I battling most now? What steps could I take to disarm its grip on me?
- How happy am I in my current career?
- How strong are my feelings about moving or staying in my current geographic location?
- What is it that I'm really good at? What do I really enjoy?
- What steps would I need to take to move on to a career I would like better? More education? More training?
- What do friends, family, and colleagues say I do well? Don't do well?
- Who could I trust to speak into my life with career advice?
- What sorts of tasks and assignments suck the life out of me? (Administration? Working alone? Working with people?)
- What sorts of tasks and assignments get me really pumped up?
- What sorts of people groups do I really enjoy? Children? Infants? Adults? The elderly? Single people? Teenagers? College Students? Divorcees? Those married with children? Empty nesters? Successful people? Depressed people? Business people? People who are gifted in leadership?
- Am I a "starter" or an "enricher" or a "maintainer"?
- Do I need to take some career assessment tests?

Pondering Your Marriage

Before the wedding:

- Should I marry this person?
- What's on my "non-negotiables" list for a potential spouse? Are there any areas I will compromise in?
- What are the 2–3 character traits I won't settle for in my potential spouse?
- What part of my parents' model of marriage am I bringing to my marriage? (Either good or bad?)
- Do I (we) need professional counseling before we get married? Is there one real major concern I have?
- What do I admire about my potential spouse?
- Is my future spouse in a solid faith journey with God?

After the wedding:

- Are our careers getting in the way of our marriage? How are they affecting us?
- Am I expecting too much from my spouse? Am I trying to change him/her? If so, why am I doing that?
- How are we handling disagreements and resolving conflict? Am I the one settling every time? Do I feel resentful that I'm not heard or valued?
- What part do I play in escalating a disagreement?
- What do we repeatedly have conflict about? Where is that coming from?
- How did my parents resolve conflict? Am I bringing that to my spouse and I don't realize it?

Pondering Parenting

Before marriage:

- What are my feelings about being a parent? Am I scared? Confident? How do I think having a child will affect our marriage intimacy?

- How does my spouse feel about having children? Are we both on the same page?

When children are on the way or already here:

- What part of my parents' parenting do I want to imitate or not imitate?
- Do my spouse and I agree on discipline? Or, is one of us going to be undoing the discipline of the other? Am I too severe with issues of minor importance?
- Which issues are non-negotiable discipline matters?
- Have I taken the time to *study* my children's temperaments and which encouragement styles and discipline styles would be best for them?
- How would those discoveries change the way I interact with them?
- What are our rules/guidelines on technology use? TV, phones, iPads, screen games? How are we going to enforce these?

Pondering Your Relationship with God

- How would I describe my relationship with God right now? Close? Creeping separateness? Distant? Intimate? What's causing any of these?
- Do I sense God communicating anything to me repeatedly?
- "God, what's the *major issue* in my life right now? How do You want me to deal with it?"
- How is God feeling about me currently? Joyful about me? Disappointed in me? Anything in between? Why am I thinking this about Him?
- What am I praying about the most? Why is that?
- What characteristics of God is He assuring me about these days? That He is strong? Wise? Powerful? My provider?
- Am I increasingly allowing, adopting, and appropriating God's messages of love and grace for me? If I'm not, why not?
- In what areas do I doubt God? That He won't provide? That He doesn't hear? That He doesn't care?
- Which spiritual practices have a high "I want to" factor to them?

- If I imagined meeting Jesus one-on-one, with Him sitting on a chair across from me, what do I think He'd say to me? What words do I imagine Him using with me?
- In what areas of my life can I imagine God cheering for me?
- Where am I at with forgiving myself? Am I allowing God's grace and love to apply to me, as well as to the general public?
- Currently, how would I describe how I feel about myself?
- In what settings do I really feel connected and close to God? In His creation? While I'm alone? While I'm with people? Doing service for others? Using my spiritual gifts? In corporate worship? Private worship? On a beach? Being active?
- What adjectives (see list below) would I use to describe my relationship with God? Why do I feel this way?

List of feelings (maybe just circle 5 or so):

Confident, sympathetic, satisfied, receptive, accepting, great, fortunate, delighted, overjoyed, thankful, important, ecstatic, satisfied, glad, elated, energetic, optimistic, liberated, thrilled, peaceful, comfortable, pleased, encouraged, relaxed, certain, blessed, reassured, sensitive, passionate, sympathetic, comforted, loved, intrigued, engrossed, curious, anxious, excited, enthusiastic, optimistic, hopeful, certain, secure, angry, irritated, annoyed, upset, resentful, worked-up, lousy, disappointed, powerless, discouraged, ashamed, guilty, dissatisfied, terrible, bad, uncertain, sense of loss, embarrassed, unbelieving, lost, unsure, pessimistic, alone, incapable, fatigued, inferior, vulnerable, empty, frustrated, dominated, neutral, weary, bored, pre-occupied, disinterested, fearful, anxious, nervous, scared, worried, frightened, restless, timid, threatened, crushed, deprived, painful, dejected, injured, offended, inflicted on, heartbroken, aching, humiliated, wronged, alienated, sorrowful, pained, pessimistic, unhappy, lonely, grieved.

Reflection and Growing Intimacy with God

Reflection counts as a spiritual practice. It is one of the "dance steps" Jesus teaches us. While doing any *thinking things through,* it is not only permissible but encouraged to ask the question, "Will I give myself permission to have time and space to pay attention to my own well-being?" If you're not involved in serving in some capacity, take some reflection time to go through what your giftedness is and what you're passionate about, and once you receive some answers from God, get involved in it. If you're serving too much and doing little self-care, will you give yourself permission to take a sabbatical so you can think through why you feel the need to be so over-involved with ministry? All of these topics and more demand pondering and thinking things through over time. Repeat whatever *thinking things through* method you feel most comfortable with: walking on the beach, swinging in the hammock, doing yardwork—repeat these over and over because God's timing on solutions from reflection are His alone.

May your reflections yield a closer, more intimate experience of God's *withness* to you.

Try this:

What's *most* on your mind? Take some extended time to think it through, meticulously, and then ask God to whisper to you about it and take notes on what comes your way.

The human race is allowing itself to fall under the mysterious, addicting spell of the screen.

- Edward Hollowell, Crazy Busy

Part 4: Too Many!

Enemy #4: Distraction

what distracts me?
KINDLE?

IN THE PIXAR MOVIE *Up*, there is a memorable scene with a dog who has just received a collar that enables his thoughts to be spoken out loud. The dog has his front paws up on a man's chest, looking right into his eyes, wagging his tail. The voice collar speaks, saying "Hello, my master made me this collar. He is a good and smart master. He made me this collar so I could talk... SQUIRREL! ..." Then there's a pause, and then, "My master made me this collar. He is a good and smart..."

Too often, we are like that dog: so distracted by the many things around us that we fail to notice God's presence in our everyday moments. We essentially have "spiritual attention deficit."

What Are the Biggest and *Most Alluring* Distractions in Our Culture Today?

After reading several resources, I would say The Top Seven Distractions today are:

7. *Listening to music.* The average amount of time each of us listens to music each day is 45 minutes.

6. *Texting and updating social media*
   - The average person checks their Facebook account, Twitter, and other

233

sources 17 times a day, which comes out to 1 hour per day, 7 hours per week, 30 hours a month, 365 hours a year, or 15 days per year checking their social media.[1]

5. *Watching TV!*
   • Children 2–11 years old watch TV an average of 24 hours per week.
   • Adults 35–49 years old watch TV an average of 33 hours per week.
   • The average child sees 40,000 TV commercials each year. Children as young as 3 years old recognize brand logos.[2]

4. *Playing video games!*
   • According to Nielsen, the average U.S. gamer age 13 or older spent 6.3 hours a week playing video games during 2013. That's up from 5.6 hours in 2012, which was up from 5.1 hours in 2011.

3. *Surf the net!* Average number of hours on the Internet per day by age:
   • 16–19 year olds: 7.2 hours per week
   • 18 –32 year olds: 7.4 hours per week
   • 33–52 year olds: 5.89 hours per week
   • 53–64 year olds: 4.41 hours per week

2. *Online distractions* like: YouTube, Twitter, Amazon, Netflix, Flicker, Hulu, Blogger, and Reddit)
   • Latest statistics: the average person uses these for 45 minutes per day.

   And the number one distraction in our culture…drumroll please…

1. *YOU GUESSED IT! YOUR CELL PHONE!* Talking on it, texting on it, fiddling with it, and looking up information, directions, and more.
   • The average amount of time spent on our cell phones:
      a) 90 minutes a day
      b) 23 days a year
      c) 3.9 years in a lifetime…staring at a phone screen.
   • Americans check their cell phones 150 times a day. That's every 6

minutes, and it's only getting worse. We spend more time with our electronics than we do with each other. One third of all teenagers send more than 100 texts a day, or 3,000 a month.

Have any of you noticed that when you're out at a restaurant, whether the people you see there are couples or families, all heads are down, doing "whatever" on their cell phones, and no one's talking to anyone? Here they are, supposedly spending quality time with one another, and they not only aren't talking to one another, but they're not even looking at one another.

Research shows that less than half of U.S. families eat together on a regular basis, and when they do sit down, distractions abound: The TV is on, someone's playing solitaire on their iPad, someone has earbuds in, someone's texting. "Pizzled"[3] (pissed off and puzzled) denotes how you feel when a person, without either asking permission or providing an explanation, brings out his or her cell phone to make or answer a call while you are walking together, eating together, meeting together, riding together, or doing anything else together.

Don't get me wrong. Our world is digital and it's not going back. Books made of paper are disappearing. You can read them on your iPad. College lectures, post graduate seminars, and medical school resources are all online. Research in any field these days is all done through our laptops. Doctors, dentists, financial institutions, hospitals, schools, and businesses are going paperless. On your phone you can find teaching videos for children, dance and music lessons, and streaming sports games. It's no wonder that the Kaiser Foundation reported that children between the ages of 8 and 18 spend an average of 7½ hours per day with digital media.

The digital world is not going away. I understand that. But it is a huge *distraction* to our journey with God. Distractions of all kinds....SQUIRREL!... can interrupt the concentration needed to pay attention to the nudges and promptings of God. Besides, the stuff on our phones and laptops is funny, colorful, intriguing, informative, and helpful. It's pleasing to the eye.

It's addictive.

Over the past decade, "human moments" have increasingly been replaced by "electronic moments."[4]

And, ALL OF IT IS DISTRACTING. It can take over most all of our attention—attention we should be directing towards God and towards one another. Digital technology becomes safer than actually talking to a live person, and it can be quicker and more expedient.

Again, don't get me wrong: FaceTime and Skype can save hours of driving when the people you want to talk to live far away. I was doing some pre-marital counseling with a couple in the Midwest. The topic turned to finances. The bride-to-be had a lot to say on the matter. As she spoke about a really good plan for saving for a house, a baby, and their future, I could see that her fiancé was closing down emotionally. He crossed his arms, looked away from her constantly, and grunted his responses. It was not going well. In this case, digital technology was very helpful for me, because it allowed me to see body language, thus allowing me to tailor my approach to the couple in question. But technology can also take over our lives.

I wonder if the devil's plan was to not only keep us insanely *busy* all the time, so we'd *hurry* through everything, surround us with *noise* so we can't think, but also, if there's any space left over, fill it with *distractions*. In other words, prevent our minds' focus on what really matters for too long... especially God.

You might think: "If I have to work 8 hours a day, invest some time with my wife and children each day, exercise, serve in my community or church in some way, take some time to relax, and take a day off, when do I have time for spiritual life?" I get it. It's not easy.

As beautiful as this world can be sometimes, Jesus said, "I am *not* of this world." He challenged all of us to live *in this world but not be of it*, meaning: "Don't let the world's ideas of how you should live your life shape you."

Jesus taught instead, "Let Me shape you into My image while you live in this fallen world."

But here's what *distraction* does: *it robs us of what God might be saying to us in the middle of all that stuff we call LIFE.* Spiritual giants from the past have taught repeatedly that we can experience God while changing a diaper, washing dishes, driving to work, talking with your spouse, surfing some waves, jogging in the mountains, and catching up with the news. But distraction never lets us *sit* with anything for any length of time to discover any hidden meaning behind what we're experiencing. Distraction interrupts God's efforts to communicate His attention, His love, His adoring, and His cherishing of you and me. Distraction blinds me to seeing the gifts He's giving me every day because my eyes don't linger long enough to think, *Oh, THAT was a gift from God right there. Thank you God!*

Jesus and Distraction

Jesus told a story that's come to be called "The Good Samaritan" (see Luke 10:25-37). A man is ambushed, beaten and robbed, and left on the side of the road to die. Two religious types are traveling the same road. They see the unconscious man, do nothing, and proceed about their business. (I can picture them looking at the guy and then hearing a "ping" on their cell phone, looking down at the screen, and soon they are out of sight.) These two church staff guys (a priest and a Levite) saw the wounded man as a distraction from what they were supposed to do for God. Their schedules may have been too full to accommodate a wounded person along the way. Maybe they were hurrying to their next religious duty.

"Settled" in the Midst of Distractions

How do we remain settled in the presence of Jesus in the midst of distractions? Or, in the midst of distractions, how do we remain attentive to Christ? We do what Mary, Martha's sister, did. We *make a choice* to sit at Jesus' feet (see Luke 10:38-42). In other words, we make a conscious effort to picture ourselves in His direct presence: with and within us, to the right and left... etc. At Jesus' feet is where the "many things" we are involved in are brought into submission to the "one thing necessary." To Jesus' feet we bring the "many things" in our life for His scrutiny. It is at His feet that we submit our plans, our goals, our work, our opportunities, our schedules, and we ask Him, "Which ones, Lord? Which things do You want me to be about today? In which activities can I serve you best? What work would be the best use of the gifts You have given me?" Then we *wait* for His answer, which often doesn't come right away. That choice to "get busy" or "sit still," to work in the kitchen or to wait at Christ's feet, is essentially a decision whether or not to submit the details of our lives to His Lordship.[5]

Battling Distraction Takes Ruthless Intentionality

At times, combatting *distraction* will take some ruthless intentionality. Being un-distracted is like wearing blinders! Horses who pull buggies and carts wear blinders on their heads so that they can only look forward. They aren't distracted with things to either side of them. They are single-minded in their purpose and direction. In a sense, they are walking in solitude.

I don't know what "spiritual blinders" might look like for you, but they must cut off the distractions pulling at us that would rob us of enjoying and experiencing God in each moment of every day. There is no other way to say it: time on the cell phone, time on the Internet, time on Facebook, video games, TV, and time with constant music are the things we have to put blinders on against, at least sometimes. Otherwise, the cost is that we will miss experiencing Jesus' love and grace to us and for us, as well as missing precious time with each other.

I would hate to get to heaven and have Jesus say to me, "Craig, I had so much I wanted you to experience of Me and know of Me, but I had such a hard time getting your attention and getting you to slow down enough. You were in such a hurry, so busy and so distracted." What distracted you?

Folks, I don't want to answer to the One who created me and died for me, "I was distracted with, ahhh....Facebook? My cell phone? The Internet?" None of us want to give that answer.

I believe that the cell phone is *not only one of the greatest inventions EVER*...and I mean that... but it is *also probably the #1 thing that makes us TOO DISTRACTED to be still, to be quiet, and to pay attention to our relationship with God on a moment-by-moment basis.* So, use that phone! But learn to turn it off. With less distraction, you might just sense Jesus' gentle whisper that says, "You are my beloved child, whom I love and adore with a passion that is unlimited. You are my treasure, my one-of-a-kind, never-to-be-duplicated, apple-of-my-eye whom I celebrate over and cheer for every moment of every day."

The Point

Distraction keeps our undivided attention from any efforts by God to prompt us, nudge us, impress upon us, whisper to us, or sense a leading directed towards us. We can live our lives like the movie *Up* and the talking dog collar:

- God whispers to you, "I want you to know that..." And our response is ...SQUIRREL!
- Your spouse shares something that's bothering him or her, and your response is, "That really matters, honey. Let's sit down and..." Ping of text message arriving...SQUIRREL!
- Your teenage son needs help on his math homework. You say, "Hey, son, let me help you with that..." RING of cell phone. "Let me just answer this, son, real quick." ...SQUIRREL!

Fighting distraction, like fighting hurry, busyness, and noise, will take effort. The devil does *not* want us to have space in our lives to pay attention to God. So, like surfing, it takes a little *effort to catch the wave. Like dancing*, it takes a little *effort* to take the hand of the Savior. The effort we make to fight distraction needs to be intentional and diligent, especially when it comes to technology, the main weapon of distraction in this world. But I'm convinced that God will honor your efforts to fight against distraction and you will experience His presence in the form of His guidance, comfort, and assurances that you are loved, forgiven, and more. Study the "distraction levels" of your own life. Is distraction increasing the busyness and hurry factor of your life? Is it contributing to a decreasing attention span? Do you feel completely naked without your phone? Could you leave your cell phone in the car when you're having lunch with a friend or colleague, or when having dinner with your spouse or family?

What Spiritual Practices Can We Embrace to Counteract the Influence of Our Distraction-Filled Culture?

1. Contentedness

2. Guarding Your Heart and Mind

3. Advanced Preparation

We will discuss these three practices in the chapters of this section of the book.

Try this:

Develop a list of *rules* for yourself that determine how much time you'll give yourself to be on the phone, or to watch TV, or to use the other forms of technology we've just discussed. Develop some rules for not responding to your cell phone—perhaps you'll decide not to respond to it when you're with your roommate, friends, spouse, children, or friends. Intentionally schedule "time outs" from your phone during the course of the day to give yourself a technology break.

Use the decrease in distraction to ask God a question. Then listen, or rest or ponder a verse or story in the Bible, or take on any of the practices in this book, or others like it. What changes do you notice in the speed of your interior life? Share that with someone or write about it in your journal.

So if we have enough food and clothing, let us be content.

- I Timothy 6:8, NLT

Chapter 11: The Practice of
LEARNING TO BE CONTENT

THESE ARE SOME OF THE latest statistics on the debt load Americans carry.[1]

1. 40% of Americans spend up to half their income servicing debt.

2. The average debt of Americans is $37,000.

3. ¼ of Americans, in one particular poll, said they are prone to "excessive" and "frivolous" spending.

4. Consumers say they are spending up to 40% of their income on discretionary purchases such as entertainment, leisure, hobbies, and things they don't need.

5. Cost of living has outpaced income growth over the past 13 years.

It doesn't help that the cost of health care has skyrocketed. Many retired people are faced with the dilemma that the percentage of their hard-earned wages from years of labor which they set aside for their golden years may not be enough. All of these stats, combined with other realities that occur in real life—job loss, a sudden emergency, travel to a loved one's wedding or funeral, a car accident, the cost of a surgery, and other life-surprises—make for an unexpected debt load that may never go away without radical changes in lifestyle. It won't happen unless people address their spending patterns and conclude that "enough is enough."

Why is *learning to be content* a spiritual practice? Because it's something that has to be learned and diligently scrutinized, or it will affect everything in your inner world. Without it, you'll be consumed by worry. The writers of the Bible have a lot to say about contentment. Below is just a very small sampling:

Not that I was ever in need, for I have *learned how to be content* with whatever I have.
- Philippians 4:11, NLT (emphasis mine).

Yet true godliness with *contentment* is itself great wealth.
- I Timothy 6:6, NLT (emphasis mine.)

One more statistic: The Bible used more ink on the topic of *money* than any other topic other than *love*.

There are two frontal assaults on our *contentment factor:*

1. The *myth* of *more*

2. *Worry*

First, let's look at the *myth* of *more!*

One of the world's questions that is constantly forced upon us is: "Are you completely satisfied?"

Operative word: "completely." The truth is we are "completely satisfied" with *nothing!* Because we were made for something the world does not offer.

If that is true then we won't be *completely* satisfied with our house, our car, our job, our retirement fund, the amount of money we have or the size of our big screen TV. We might find ourselves thinking, *I'm not completely satisfied with my spouse. Rather than work anymore on my marriage, I'll just head off into this direction with another partner. I'm sure it will work out for the better.*

The *myth of more* mindset says, "If I just get that one more thing, the 'next' thing, then I'll be happy. If I just had that bigger house, that newer car, the more up-to-date phone or iPad, a newer body, then I'd be happy." *The myth of more says, "The NEXT THING will be IT!"* But eventually, it wears off. We want more. How do we fight the *myth/monster* of *more?* Well, we get there by addressing *worry* first.

Worry

Our culture now has the iPad, iPhone, iHome, iTunes, and more.

What if there was an *iProcrastinate?* This form of technology would have millions of ways to delay what needs to be done and offer billions of excuses for your family, friends, and boss to swallow. Then, how about the *iJudge:* this pad would log all your opinions and assessments about everything you have an opinion on so that if you forgot, you could just look it up then spout your opinion—whether anyone's asking for it or not.

I would own an *iWorry.* This device would keep me abreast of my children, my marriage, my finances, my occupational situation, and my friends' opinions of me. I would touch the button called "children" and up would pop each of their three faces with several "I'm worried about this..." speech balloons attached to each one. I wouldn't even touch the "finances" button. When I was teaching each week as a pastor, I would worry about whether a message would touch people's hearts, about whether anything I said or did was helping people toward a deeper dependency and relationship with God. I worried about the budget, staff hirings, when the next divorce would happen. You name it, I was anxious about it.

Jesus taught about worry. The theme of His teaching was: *You are so valuable to Me that I will supply what you need.* Here is the most extensive address Jesus ever gave about *worry:*

That is why I tell you not to *worry* about everyday life—whether you have enough food and drink, or enough clothes to wear. Isn't life more than food, and your body more than clothing? Look at the birds. They don't plant or harvest or store food in barns, for your heavenly Father feeds them. And *aren't you far more valuable* to him than they are? Can all your worries add a single moment to your life?

And why *worry* about your clothing? Look at the lilies of the field and how they grow. They don't work or make their clothing, yet Solomon in all his glory was not dressed as beautifully as they are. And if God cares so wonderfully for wildflowers that are here today and thrown into the fire tomorrow, *he will certainly care for you.* Why do you have so little faith?

So don't worry about these things, saying, "What will we eat? What will we drink? What will we wear?" These things dominate the thoughts of unbelievers, but your heavenly Father already knows all your needs. Seek the Kingdom of God above all else, and live righteously, and he will give you everything you need.

So *don't worry* about tomorrow, for tomorrow will bring its own worries. Today's trouble is enough for today.

- Matthew 6:25-34, NLT, emphasis mine.

First, Jesus talks about ~~birds~~. They get up each day, look around, fly around, and there's food for them. Presto! God supplies for them and they don't *do* anything to produce it.

Jesus then talks about ~~flowers~~. He says they are more beautiful than most anything on the planet. They don't *do* anything to be so beautiful, they were just made that way. Jesus goes on to say that each one of us is more beautiful to Him than any of those flowers. In other words, God supplies *resources* for the birds. He gifts *value* and *beauty* to the flowers, but His supplying and valuing of each one of us goes far beyond this. He sees each of us as far more beautiful than any sunset, rocky coastline, snow-capped mountain; than Lake Tahoe or the Hawaiian islands. And His attentiveness to each of us is immeasurably more than any of those things.

**Key application: "I, too," (iToo!) "matter that
much more to Him than flowers and birds!"**

Jesus goes on to say that because of my value to Him, He will *supply* what I need. With just a normal dose of responsibility on our part, He will take care of us. Jesus says to *not* do what lots of people *do*, which is to "chase after" this stuff with a worried, stressful mindset. At the end, Jesus says there is one thing worth chasing after: a life where Jesus rules, reigns, teaches, and guides us into a transforming life that reflects Him.

Then Jesus says, "Don't worry about *tomorrow*" (the future) "because just *one day* has enough trouble of its own." He's saying, "Don't borrow trouble. Watch out for the 'what if' mindset." If we worry about what only tomorrow has, we'll be wasting a ton of emotional energy that is needed for who or what is right in front of us at the moment.

I'm in training on debunking the *myth of more*.

I'm working on doing life without my iWorry.

Practices to Gain a Greater Contentedness Factor

The overall principle to keep in mind is: combatting worry and the myth that having more will make me happy is an exercise in *trust*. Can I step back and do an honest assessment and conclude, "You know, I have what I need. Yes, there are issues to face, there always will be, but I believe God is sufficient. I believe I'm one of His valued treasures. He will care for me."

So, am I going to *trust God* or not? *Faith* is *trusting in God's trustworthiness*. Am I going to trust that He can be counted on to supply what I need, in every aspect of life, and not just food, clothing, and shelter?

With a mindset of trusting God, we can increase our contentedness by:
- Practicing the truth of how God sees us
- Practicing *releasing*
- Practicing peace in our hearts and minds.

Let's look at these practices one at a time.

Practicing the Truth of How God Sees Us

We sin, yes. Have we failed? Yes. But instead of staying there, we can practice Jesus' advice to look at birds and flowers. They are pretty happy beings: at peace with who they are and how God has made them. I'm much more valuable to Him than they are—I'm a cherished treasure, in fact. If I live into that, I tend to see the cup of life as being much more than half-full. It makes me feel content that God feels this way about me. Achieving this state of mind and soul might include the practice of *noticing* and *slowing* to observe birds and flowers. Doing this will trigger thoughts of contentedness and a continued *asking* of God to "guard your heart and mind" from worry.

Practicing *Releasing*

This is an exercise with your imagination. Imagine placing whatever is causing the *worry factor* into Jesus' hands on a regular basis. Live into the truth that the person or the situation causing worry is, in fact, in God's good hands.

All of us have a tendency to try to orchestrate outcomes into what we think would be best, whether those outcomes are for a situation, for ourselves, or for our children. To combat this we can employ the practice of *letting go*. I do what I can, pray for what I can, and then release the person or the situation to my loving God, who supplies bountifully for seemingly insignificant creatures like birds, and assigns beauty and value to such a seemingly simple thing as a flower. He cares much more for the people I worry about than I do! It's helpful to picture two huge hands with the object of our worry sitting securely in them, and then to repeat the phrase, "This is safe in God's hands. In fact, I am safe in God's hands." Then, in your imagination, pull your own hands back and let the worry be in Jesus' possession.

One of the things we have to practice releasing is our circumstances. I've found that what causes the most worry to us are people and money. We worry about our children (often rightly so) when they are making self-destructive choices, choosing the wrong friends, making bad decisions, or marrying the wrong person. We worry when things happen *to* them as well…the seemingly random acts of heartache and sorrow. If a child is technically an adult, parents are often left in the position of letting those decisions play out. We want to protect our child from those consequences, but we often can't. We worry about our grandchildren, our parents' failing health, and a friend's heartache. We worry about how our loved ones will handle financial ruin, a divorce or the bad health report about their child. Will God care for my special needs child? Will God provide for me because my husband left me? How am I going to care for my dad who has dementia? These situations cause a lot of worry.

Another thing we have to practice releasing are our money issues.

We worry about money. Will God provide resources for our needs? That's the question. The answer is that "God providing" can have several looks to it.

God provides for Third World problems: Food for the hungry, shelter for the displaced, clothing for the poor, doctors and nurses to stem off illness. Often God's provision comes from His call to the soft hearts of First World people who have money, giftedness, and talents to give to those in need: Syrians fleeing ISIS, African children with limbs removed by radicals, or the homeless. These people issues need the open-handed giving of resources from First World people to meet those needs. Every day, First World people have the choice to say to their spending, upgrading, and acquiring, *"Enough is enough!* I don't really need this; I just *want it."* Third World people don't have enough clean water to drink. I could support well-digging and purification with just a little bit of scrupulous financing.

Rick Reilly, formerly one of the most well-known editorial writers for Sports Illustrated, visited Africa a few years back. He saw the crippling effects of Malaria on the people in many areas. He started a program called "Nothing but Nets." Reilly's program was simple. Ten dollars bought a sleeping net to protect people from mosquitos carrying the malaria virus. It has saved thousands of lives. Rick Reilly, a First World man, essentially said, "Enough with the self-acquiring. I want to help people by raising money for malaria nets and I'm going to use my own resources as well."

God could rain down $20 bills each day from heaven. He could magically build houses, bring clean water out of the ground, or instantly materialize food and wipe out disease. But He doesn't. Why?

First answer: I don't know. Second answer: His dream is that those who "have" would give their time, talents, and treasures to those who "have not." In so doing, both parties win. The giver experiences the joy of sharing what God has given them, having practiced contentedness and defeated the *myth of more*. They have more income to help the poor. The receiver experiences God's gracious provision through the loving hands of those with more. The key: First World people deciding in their hearts and pocketbooks that *enough is enough*. Many Christ-followers have adopted a philosophy of "Stuff-Reduction." They use the resources formerly used to buy "stuff" to help ministries locally and around the world. They simplify.

I was at a Willow Creek pastors' conference several years ago. They brought a man up onto the stage—a regular guy in their congregation, not some famous person. They asked him how he ran his finances. He said, "My wife and I have learned that we can give away 70% of our income to help the poor, support the church's ministries, and support other ministries we are passionate about. It's the greatest feeling to be able to support so many causes for God's Kingdom agenda on earth."

I thought, "How can he do that?" But he said that he and his wife and family figured out what they really needed to live on, and just lived on that. They stayed in their original three bedroom, two bathroom home for over 30 years. They have a strict budget that does include "fun money" each month. They save 10% for the future as well. *They've learned to be content with what they need, like birds do.* After hearing this, the pastors attending were stunned. Frankly, I was ashamed of myself for all the frivolous spending I've done (and continue to do at times), and for giving God the leftovers.

Many years ago, a gentleman in our church had the responsibility for the children's sermon. He brought up as many children as we had and lined them up. He had a tray of brownies. As each child passed by, he gave them a small square of brownie. He told them beforehand that the brownies represented all the money that mommy and daddy had to spend each month. One brownie represented the house payment, another the gas and electric bill, another was cable television, etc., etc. Until it got to the last child...and the tray was empty. As the last child came up to get a brownie, this gentleman said to the lad, "And you represent God." But the tray was empty. (He had a hidden brownie to give to the child later.) The point was driven home: we give God the leftovers, if we decide we have enough. The speaker's point was that God asked for our first check to be written to support His ministry, and then we are to learn to live on the rest and trust that He will provide for the rest, as well as emergencies.

Practicing Peace in our Hearts and Minds

Peace is "shalom," the Hebrew word that indicates that "all is well," even if all around us is heartache, sorrow, loss, chaos, tension, stress, and frustration. How do we *practice peace*? It's not easy, but it begins with Jesus' command to get in the right order and prioritize *what we are seeking after* each day.

If we're seeking to:
• gain a heart like Jesus'
• expand the love quotient in our hearts and
• stay connected to God throughout our day while encountering people, situations, and crises...

then, at the end of the day, we usually feel at peace.

And it may not have looked like a very peaceful day circumstantially. When life's circumstances go south, can I retain a sense of peace that God is still with and within me, above and below, to the right and left, to the front and back? If so, the *I am safe in God's hands* factor stays. I can be content.

What Might You Do, More Practically, to Experience Contentedness?

Go bird watching. Wait, Craig, are you saying that watching birds counts as a spiritual discipline in which I can experience God? *Yes!* Watching birds can remind you of Jesus' words in this chapter. Take your mind to all the ways God supplies for a bird: a tree for a home, seeds everywhere, flight to get around, incredible eyesight to see things far away, and claws to grab prey.

Then tell yourself, "God, show me how you've supplied for me, in any way, shape, or form." I believe He'll show you many, many things about the unique way He's made you, how He's brought certain people into your life, and how He's provided strength, endurance, wisdom, shelter, friends, and fun. You might be brought to your knees.

Do flower pausing (look, admire, marvel, smell). Springtime is a wonderful season to practice this because all the flowers are blooming.

Around where I live, people travel to the desert to see the desert flowers blooming in early spring, simply because they are beautiful.

As colorful and attractive and full of variety as flowers are, Jesus declares that He sees you and me as infinitely more beautiful than any floral beauty. We may have to have some mantras in our minds to trigger these thoughts, like *Jesus, I am even more cherished and attended to and beautiful to You than the flowers I'm seeing and the birds I'm observing. Thank You that You love me that much and will provide for me with such loving attentiveness.*

Jesus' purpose in all of these images is to help us to *relax* with the picture of His attentiveness to us. These images are meant to cut off the debilitating effects of worry. We are safe in Jesus' hands. We can actually be content, moment by moment.

I'd like to trade in my iWorry for an iContent. In the meantime, if you see me pausing to look at a bird for just a lingering second, or if you see me stop and smell a rose for a moment, you'll know why.

More Everyday Life Practices for Contentment

Here are some additional "everyday life" practices that can increase our capacity for contentedness, shatter the *myth of more* and deepen our sense of internal peace.

Speak and repeat phrases in your mind!

1. "Enough."

When you're in a store of any kind, ask yourself: "Do I have enough of these? Do I really *need* it?" If the answer is "yes" to the first, and "no" to the second... leave it. One of the keys is knowing what you are most susceptible to buying in larger quantities than you need. I have an issue with buying more artist pens than I need. It's dumb, I know, but I have to repeat this phrase in my head, or I'll keep buying more than I need. I could feed another child monthly by saying "Enough," with the art supplies.

2. "It could be worse."

It helps to distinguish between, "I *need* that," and "I *want* that." When you observe houses, cars, clothing, and then start comparing yourself with someone less fortunate, you might think, *Man, I have it pretty good: I have a car; they have to take the bus. I own a home; they are renting. I can shop at Target; they go to thrift stores. I have it pretty good.* This type of reflection keeps us from starting the train of thought that says, *I'd like [whatever] in a bigger and better form.*

When I start having a "pity party" for myself, it won't be long until I drive by a homeless person with their shopping cart of stuff and unwashed hair, clothes, and body, and I sometimes think, *It could be worse, Craig. Learn to be content. Stop worrying. Has God supplied? Have you ever missed a meal?*

3. "People are what really matter."

So, *invest in memories!* Remember, whoever you are talking to in the course of your day is someone you may spend eternity with. So, grow *rich* in relationships. Take the initiative with having people over and doing things with families in your church, work and neighborhood. Giving any kind of help to the people in your family, to your friends, or to people God brings to your attention who are in need, reinforces the truth that the only thing lasting past death is people.

4. "What am I passionate about? How have I been gifted?" (i.e., your God-given giftedness.)

Live for the word: *meaning*, not *money*. What's going to keep you energized for the next 10 years? *Money* isn't big enough of a goal. *Meaning* trumps *money!*

5. "My home is in heaven!"

Real contentment comes when you know you're going home someday. Eternal life has nothing to do with money, and we are living *eternal life now!*

Being Content with the People in Our Lives

What about being content with my other circumstances? With the people in my life that I love and am close to?

How do I practice being content when my family blows up, or when my circumstances change? The question I try to always ask myself is this: "No matter how bad the circumstances, am I still in God's hands? Has He gone on vacation? If He's still closer than the air I breathe, then even in these dark circumstances, I am in the hands of My Father in heaven. I am hurting right now, but I'm going to count on His love and grace. Maybe over time the wound I'm enduring will fade, but He will never leave me."

Questions to Ponder:

1. What does it seem you want *more* of even when you don't *need* it?

2. How do you (and your spouse, if you're married) plan out and budget your money so spending doesn't get out of control?

3. What's your strategy with credit cards? Paying off debt?

4. What particular thing causes you to struggle with *envy* the most? What do you do to combat that?

Guard your heart above all else, for it determines the course of your life.

- Proverbs 4:23, NLT

Chapter 12: The Practice of PROTECTING YOUR HEART AND MIND

Here are some ways the nations of the world protect themselves and their people:

1. Switzerland: They have 3,000 points of demolition rigged to blow, in order to cut off any invaders coming by land. Every citizen, starting at age 19, gets military training, then take the guns home with them.[1]

2. Canada: They have one of the best anti-terrorist units in the world. Forty elite soldiers worked alongside U.S. forces to take out 100 high ranking Taliban and Al-Qaeda leaders in Afghanistan over the years of the Afghan war.[2]

3. Vietnam: During the Vietnam War, the Vietnamese Air Force was so good that eight Russian-made MIGs took out 79 American planes.[3]

4. Brazilian Police: These urban warfare specialists fight in the *favelas* (slums), which house 11 million people who lack running water, toilets, electricity, and access to food. These *favelas* have some of the world's highest crime rates. Drug lords rule the area. But these elite police drive urban tanks through the streets and have reclaimed many *favelas* to make the areas more livable.[4]

5. African Union: This federation of 54 African states was created to confront AIDS, malaria, drought, and rulers running lawless states.

They did what the U.S. and U.N. failed to do…twice: clean up Somalia. In four years, they had kicked the bad guys out of Somalia forever.[5]

These are examples of how countries, armed forces, and private companies *guard* and *protect* what is valuable. Jesus and the writers of the New Testament claimed that there are two things more valuable to guard than gold, independence, or a country's borders: our *HEARTS and MINDS.*

Here are a few Biblical passages on the matter:

- "*Guard your heart* above all else, for it determines the course of *your* life" (Pr. 4:23, NLT, emphasis mine).

- "Then you will experience God's peace, which exceeds anything we can understand. His peace will *guard your hearts and minds* as you live in Christ Jesus" (Phil. 4:7, NLT, emphasis mine).

- "Watch out! Be on your *guard* against all kinds of greed; life does not consist in an abundance of possessions" (Luke 12:15, NIV, emphasis mine).

- "So letting your sinful nature control your *mind* leads to death. But letting the Spirit control your *mind* leads to life and peace" (Romans 8:6, NLT, emphasis mine).

What Are the Things We Need to Protect Our Minds and Hearts From?

Jesus and Paul spoke a lot about "mind and heart" issues. They knew that from these places come actions that can be wonderful or, potentially, self-destructive. Their combined lists of things that we need to be on alert for are:

Achievements (they can inflate our ego), inattentiveness to the Bible and prayer, possessions, money, attraction for another person's spouse, greed (desire for another's beauty, stuff, spouse, child), lust (pornography), gambling, alcohol, gossip, lying (stretching the truth or outright warping it).

How do we defend our life with Jesus from these things that can slowly erode our relationship with Him?

In other words, what does guarding your heart and mind look like?

1. Know your weaknesses. Know where you are vulnerable to moral failure OR know what things have a strong pull on you.

In battle, the commanders are always saying to "watch your flank" (that's the area to either side of what's in front of you). These are the subtle attacks, not direct attacks. So, in what areas are you more vulnerable: Money? Hurry? Busyness? Distraction? Noise? Spending? Gossip? Arrogance? Self-reliance? Pride? Envy? Greed? Self-control? Flirting? Anger? Demeaning words? Negativity? Escape? In what area do you need to "not get caught asleep at your post"? So, know the weak points in your flank, and develop a defense or counter-attack that works for you.

For some, "protecting your spiritual flank" involves having one confidant that you can share with when one of your weaknesses is being attacked. AA was built on this. If you desire a drink, call your sponsor. Getting the temptation out in the open disarms its power. For others, being in a small group where you are learning from the Bible, sharing how life with God is going and praying for one another brings strength to combat your vulnerabilities. It also requires saying "the last 10%." This portion of what we share is the part where we are most exposed to another; the part where we feel the most shame.

For some, a wonderful worship service makes the attacks you've been fighting seem conquerable. Singing songs, praising, praying, listening to teaching—all these help to give strength for the battle against what would be our ruin. For others, protecting their spiritual flank means solitary study of the Bible, silent meditation on God's grace, love, and forgiveness. Some can do a mini-quiet retreat in their office or room. Some carry around a few biblical passages in their memory to recall when their thoughts start going in a bad direction. Whatever it is that keeps your heart and mind alert to God's presence with and within you, lean into that. It will protect you from being overrun by temptations that could hurt you.

2. Know that temptation and sin start small, then grow big!

This is the "falling asleep at your post" syndrome. We relax our alertness level and so we miss possible dangers coming our way. Evil's approach is usually slow and gradual, planting a small thought that says, "Ah, what's the harm in a little gambling; with letting off some steam at the bar every night. What's the harm in a little twisting of the truth, a little lie, a little deception? I'm not doing something really big."

Usually, this comes with a lot of internal rationalization: "I work hard, I deserve this, so I'm going to buy that thing. I'm going to click that mouse." This type of rationalization indicates our guard is down.

One Tool to Help: Know Yourself!

Stay alert to any step toward sin *at the start*. Don't wait till you're in deep. Get it out in the open with a real human being so it doesn't gain power by staying hidden. It takes diligence and alertness to stand guard against what would ruin our souls. We have to stay alert to what might cause distance in our relationships with God and others. So, study yourself. We must admit and then own our areas of weakness. There's no need to feel shame. We all have at least one, if not many, areas where we are particularly vulnerable. One person's weakness may be another person's strength area. God understands and He will help you with internal warnings. You'll sense "flashing red lights" inside your soul whispering, *"Danger! Danger!"* Listen to them. Run from the danger. And be careful not to place yourself in positions where you'll be exposed to your area of weakness. Taking action in this way is a spiritual practice that is just as important as any other practices in this book.

Taking the Offensive in Guarding Your Heart and Mind

God has given us *weapons* for guarding our hearts and minds. In other words, we don't just sit around and wait for the evil one to attack us. We don't just play defense with our heart and mind. We can play offense too. There are a few things we can take on to keep our souls at peace. These include scripture memorization, making room for fun, making room for rest, and always going back to the basics. Remember: God will use *any* effort on our part to build stronger protection for our hearts and minds. So let's look at four practices that anyone can do at any time.

Have Scripture Memorized in Your Head and Heart!

I haven't addressed the role of the Bible much in this book. As I mentioned in the introduction, many authors have expounded on the importance of knowing God's story, knowing the people He interacted with throughout history, and most important, knowing the story of God coming to earth in the person of Jesus. I chose not to repeat their work, but let me say this: biblical illiteracy is at an all-time high. People are simply not reading the Bible on their own. Maybe they are relying on a pastor or speaker to do the reading and application for them. Maybe they read it and don't really understand what is going on and feel defeated. Maybe they understand but can't figure out how it applies to their everyday life. To all this I say, "I get it." I'm seminary-trained and I have to work at the "what does this mean for my regular, weekly life?" question, too.

Now, if you're the "typical, everyday Joe and Joan," what can you do to gain application of the Bible's stories? One possibility is to get in a small group so the application and implications can be discussed and sorted through. You might want to get an understandable commentary on the Bible book you're reading to help you understand what's going on and what's being said. You could grab someone you know who's further along in biblical knowledge and experience and ask them to help you out on a regular basis as you go through, for example, the story of Jesus in Luke.

When we understand the application of the Bible, then memorizing small portions of the Bible has real impact. The following are a few samples of biblical texts you could memorize. I've added a brief explanation and application so that the memorized truth can have meaning for you in real life.

SALVATION:

"He saved us, not because of the righteous things we have done, but because of his mercy. He washed away our sins, giving us a new birth and new life through the Holy Spirit" (Titus 3:5, NLT).

Application: We cannot do enough good behavior to counteract our bad behavior. We cannot change our heart's condition by behavior modification. Jesus took on His body my moral failure and paid the penalty I deserve. I'm now morally clean. I can live each day not trying to balance moral scales, but *receiving* His undeserved favor and love all day long.

"Everyone who calls on the name of the Lord will be saved" (Romans 10:13, NLT).

Application: When I rely on what Jesus did for me and not on what I may do for Him, I'm in the right mindset. Jesus saved my life, here and in eternity. That's a fact I can count on and live into every day.

ASSURANCE:

"There is no condemnation for those who belong to Christ Jesus" (Romans 8:1, NLT).

Application: Condemnation is "having the last word." My moral failures, the devil, and my past do *not* have the last word on my life. Jesus does. And He has given His life for me. Therefore, His continuing statement about me is, "Not guilty! I have paid your debt! Be glad!"

"Since we have been made right in God's sight by faith, we have peace with God because of what Jesus Christ our Lord has done for us" (Romans 5:1, NLT).

Application: Because I've embraced the fact that Jesus has made me right with Him, I can relax and know that I am loved and cherished. So, rather than wondering if God likes me, I am assured I'm constantly adored by Him.

FEAR:

"If God is for us, who can ever be against us?" (Romans 8:31, NLT).

Application: The Creator of all things, the most Powerful being of all, the One who created all forms of life, is *on my side*. He's rooting for me, cheering for me, encouraging me, and forgiving me in my failures. With Him on my side, what's to worry about?

"Don't be afraid, for I am with you. Don't be discouraged, for I am your God. I will strengthen you and help you. I will hold you up with my victorious right hand" (Isaiah 41:10, NLT).

Application: Jesus is closer than the air I breathe. He is with and within me. He will encourage me, and give me moral, emotional, and spiritual strength to face what comes my way with His attentive love.

TEMPTATION:

"The temptations in your life are no different from what others experience. And God is faithful. He will not allow the temptation to be more than you can stand. When you are tempted, he will show you a way out so that you can endure" (I Corinthians 10:13, NLT).

Application: I'm not alone in my struggles. God won't shy away from me when I'm choosing self-destructive things. He'll be with me more than ever. He intends for me to win over my struggle. And when I feel most trapped, He'll show me a way to disarm temptation's power, most likely by confessing to another live human being.

TRIALS:

"And we know that God causes everything to work together for the good of those who love God and are called according to his purpose for them" (Romans 8:28, NLT).

Application: No matter what tragedy, loss, or betrayal may come to me, no matter what I may do to hurt others or destroy myself, God is always working to redeem, forgive, heal, comfort, guide, encourage, and empower my life. This is true whether life sucks or is great.

PRIDE:

"Humble yourselves before the Lord, and he will lift you up in honor" *(James 4:10, NLT).*

Application: I don't know it all. Act like it!

"Live in harmony with each other. Don't be too proud to enjoy the company of ordinary people. And don't think you know it all!" (Romans 12:16, NLT).

Application: Never look down on people. If I am, I'm not "looking up" to God. Every person, in any circumstance, in any physical or mental state, matters to God. Treat them like they matter to you as well. Janitors, bus boys, restaurant greeters, waitresses, secretaries, the laundromat employee, the checker at the store, the bagger at the store, a car mechanic: they are all God's treasures.

ANGER:

"Anger will not help you live the right kind of life God wants" (James 1:20, NCV).

"Don't sin by letting anger control you. Don't let the sun go down while you are still angry." (Ephesians 4:26, NLT).

Application: Find the reasons behind my "anger triggers" so I understand why I respond to certain situations with anger. Be open about my anger with someone else, so anger's power can be disarmed. Practice one sentence from I Corinthians 13:4 for a month: *Love is patient.*

When these verses constantly linger in your brain, you will have guidelines for handling any decision, conversation, temptation, or reaction. God will then help you respond and think like Him. If memorizing isn't your "thing," write these verses on index cards and place them in places where you'll always see them: bathroom mirror, refrigerator, car dashboard. Or make a verse for your screensaver.

Build Genuine *Fun* into Your Life!

Being all-work or all-ministry or all-responsibility equals burnout and an unhealthy soul. Real fun results in a joyful heart. Therefore, pursuing genuine joy protects your heart from false fun; from fun that promises joy but doesn't deliver (e.g., alcohol, gambling, drugs, pornography).

What is life-giving for *you?* Genuine fun and rest make life-draining temptation seem shallow and small. What do you do on a regular basis that's simply *fun*; not necessarily *productive?* Do you live into the truth that you are loved by God when you're not *doing* for God, but also when you're having fun? Is it hard to imagine that God is just as pleased with you when you're playing freeze tag with your grandchildren as He is when you're building a house for the poor? He is!

Examine your life. Do you have any real "fun for you" time built in? Not fun for your spouse; fun that's really fun for *you*. You'll be surprised to find that when you experience legitimate fun, your heart quickly turns to God in gratitude.

Build Genuine *Rest* into Your Life

Rest gives you strength to do battle with spiritual warfare. In other words, *go off duty* in some way. Build some *no-responsibility* time into your life.

Even soldiers on guard duty take shifts. If we get run-down, burnt-out, fatigued, and over-worked, we are sitting ducks for an attack on our flanks from the evil one. The devil loves people with an unhealthy sense of duty. He can work very well with someone who grows weak from not taking time to unplug and rest. He hates it when people give themselves permission to rest, reflect, remember God's love and grace, and *then* go back at it. The choice facing us is: will we give ourselves permission to rest? To be unproductive? To simply *be?*

Do you have time set aside when you are truly *unavailable?* For everyone else's sakes and for yours, it's better you have a true day off, or at least some sort of extended, regular time to rest each week. In addition, God is encouraging you to take vacation time throughout the year. Unless taking vacation time to work on your home is what energizes you, *don't do it!* Give yourself permission to rest in the way that's real rest for you. Have retreats away from home, a regular time of napping, a favorite spot in creation. *Do it!* God's cheering for you to.

Never Stop Practicing the Fundamentals of Life with God!

Think of physical training. If we stop or slack off for any length of time, we can get "out of shape." This happens in our life with God as well. Athletes never stop practicing the fundamentals of their sport. Why? It keeps them at their best. When we practice the fundamentals of faith, it keeps us at our best. Think of the fundamentals needed in each of the following:

- *Baseball players* constantly practice to improve running speed, fielding, arm strength, and hitting.
- *Basketball players* never stop practicing shooting, rebounding, passing, dribbling, quickness, speed, and strength.
- *Musicians* never abandon practicing scales, proper fingering, and loud-to-soft tone dynamics.
- *Soldiers* run, lift weights, study battle strategy, do target practice, and practice hand-to-hand combat, mapping, and adapting. They never stop practicing.

If you want to master anything, there's no way around that old adage: practice, practice, practice! When these players, musicians, and soldiers have put in the time and energy and have seen to their nutrition and rest, they are ready for "game time."

What are the fundamentals that we should never stop practicing in life with God? Let me point out five (though there are more depending on how you're wired up):

- *Church.* In some way, shape or form, doing life with God together is a practice that keeps us sharp and spiritually alert.
- *Spiritual Practices.* Like athletes, musicians and soldiers who keep practicing the fundamentals, Christ-followers must keep practicing the fundamentals of connecting with God, being taught by God, and being corrected and encouraged by God. Therefore, we must take that "one step" of opening that Bible, getting on our knees to pray, taking

266

private and quiet "alone time," and privately worshipping, celebrating, and serving. The practices in this book are spiritual practices you can do as well. There's just no way to maintain an "alert status" to God's presence other than regularly practicing these things.

- *Small group.* Our desire to do battle with temptation, spiritual laziness, and complacency can be ignited when we hear how others are practicing the presence of Jesus in their lives. Don't think that "going to church" is enough. It isn't.

- *Discover and serve with your SPIRITUAL GIFTS.* Some soldiers shoot with more accuracy. Some do sneak attacks with more stealth and skill. These skills, discovered and used, make the platoon a force to be reckoned with. It is absolutely essential that you and I discover the spiritual gifts God has given to us: teaching, leading, administration, helping, discerning, knowledge, intercessory prayer, encouraging, and more. Do you know the "special abilities" God has given you? If not, find a course or take an online survey to get started on it.[6] Then get in there and try it out. And, once you've discovered it, practice it and improve it, knowing God gave it to you to forward His kingdom. What a shame it would be to show up in heaven having not discovered or put into play the special ability(s) that Jesus gave to you so you'd feel the thrill of being used by God. Using your "divine ability" in an area of service that you care about and which is matched perfectly with your unique temperament makes you feel "in the zone." You can't help but experience God's presence when you're feeling, *God, this is why I'm here on earth. I'm in my sweet spot of my role in advancing Your kingdom. Thank You!* See, your heart becomes aware of His presence in that He had "unique you" in His mind before the world was ever made. Enjoying that uniqueness leads to enjoying Jesus.

- *Give to the poor.* Giving a portion of our *time, talents, or treasures* protects our hearts from greed and arrogance. My wife and I served in an area of Port-au-Prince in Haiti for about eight weeks. In the poverty-ridden slum of Simon-*Pelé*, several organizations had joined together to help build a school. Karen and I served as hosts for Ameri can groups that came each week. We joined together with the Haitians to build the school. For eight weeks we observed how people searched and scavenged for food, how eight people slept in a 10'x10' room, how people formed shanty homes from scrap-wood and discarded pieces of aluminum roofing. No electricity. No running water. No sewage system. At the time, the average *daily* wage was $3.45.

Needless to say, our money and our possessions soon faded in importance. A sense of "wanting things" seemed to go away. We realized that people are what really matter to God. Investing in their future by helping to build a school made my heart softer, more empathetic, and heavy with the enormous struggle to survive that will never go away for the Haitians. Never before had I seen in living color the words of Jesus, "The poor you will always have with you" (Mark 14:7, NIV).

Remembering this experience has kept my greed in check, debunked the "myth of more," and softened my heart to those who go without for most of their lives. I believe Jesus wants our hearts to be this way. Whether it's the homeless and poor in our communities, or experiencing the poverty of people in other countries, a steady diet of getting out of our normal world to see how others less fortunate than us struggle to escape the cycle of poverty is always an exercise that increasingly forms our hearts into a reflection of Jesus' heart.

Dangers of "Over-Serving"

Never get into a serving position where it "all depends on you." Maybe you've been in a serving position that has, over time, become too taxing or heavy with too much responsibility. It is not God's wish or assignment for you to bear all the responsibility all the time. Learn to ask for help. Learn to trust others to do as good a job as you. Learn when to bow out and give yourself permission to rest. This battles the mindset of "I guess no one's going to do this like I could so I'll just do it myself."

I learned the hard way on this one. When I was a pastor, I hesitated to ask for help because I felt I was inconveniencing people. I listened to them lamenting their busy schedules and packed lives and thought, *I can't ask them to volunteer for this need. I'll just be adding to their stress level. I'll only be adding more busyness and fatigue to their lives.*

You can see, I was answering for them. I never gave them the chance to answer for themselves. Add up a long line of these types of decisions and soon you have a pastor who is doing too much, adding to his stress level, and soon crashing and burning. Which I did. I made the mistake of making too many things dependent on me. Big mistake. Why? I soon became too tired at my post. I fell asleep on caring for my soul. With my heart and soul unguarded and emotionally emptied, I allowed spiritual enemies to attack my flanks. And I paid a price for it: I had a seizure and landed in the hospital. The cause: overwork, causing extreme stress and exhaustion. All of it my own doing. I neglected to give myself permission to care for myself. As a result, the first thing I had let go unattended was my own personal soul care, my own relationship with Jesus, all in the name of serving Him. How ironic.

Jesus never asked for this from me. I don't know why I was asking it of myself. The crash and burn led me to leaving my senior pastor position and beginning a long journey towards health. Habits of caring for my heart and soul were restored. Emotional energy returned. I have the energy to be on full-alert for the devil's tactics. Don't let your soul care go unattended for long. Don't follow my example and over-serve in the name of Jesus. It's ok to take care of yourself.

What is Your Unique Temperament?

A critical question for protecting your heart and mind is, "How did God wire you up?" One aspect of how you are wired up is: Where are you on the introvert-extrovert scale?

Obviously, God made people different from one another. Wherever you are on the introvert-extrovert scale really matters with guarding your heart and mind. Why? If you're someone who tends to say "yes" to jobs, volunteering and attending social gatherings, and you're an introvert, eventually you'll discover that many of these things are not a good "fit" for you.

At a recent wedding I officiated, I was talking with one of the site coordinators. Besides this job, she had another job in sales. I could tell just by talking with her that she was rather quiet and reserved; an introvert. She recharged emotionally with stretches of time alone. Further probing revealed that she hated sales. She said, "I've found out it's not what I'm good at, so I'm looking around."

Everyone is located on a certain spot in this spectrum. Everyone is somewhere between really introverted (energized by being alone) or really extroverted (energized by being with people). For many, they might be closer to the middle (at times energized by people and at times energized by being alone). Others may be closer to halfway from the middle to the extreme. Wherever you are, knowing this (and your spouse knowing this, if you're married) helps you understand why you feel the way you feel after a party, or after an afternoon alone. Introverts can be the life of the party...*for a while!* But when they are "done," you can tell. Knowing this also helps you understand why you might connect with God better with more private practices than with group practices.

I enjoy long periods of time being alone. I can go days not talking to anyone. I'm a self-starter. No one needs to tell me to get to work. No wonder God made me a more extreme introvert!

Where are you? Knowing this shows you how you connect with God best, thus increasing your alertness factor to God, which increases inner strength, which is critical to protecting your heart and mind from what might be life-draining. Knowing these types of things guards your heart.

Don't Minimize Your Feelings

At the crisis point of my ministry life, I was told by a counselor that I wouldn't know a feeling if it hit me. That wasn't really true. I just never paid attention to what I was feeling, nor understood what I was feeling. As a basketball player, I had been taught to be non-emotional. Also, I didn't see much emotional expression growing up. So, I had to learn how to identify and put words onto what I was feeling, and how to communicate them appropriately.

Not being in touch with my feelings really hurt me while in ministry. I didn't feel the permission to say, "I don't like doing that." People might reply, "What? Don't you care about this? I do!" I wanted to say, "Well, I don't. Not as much as you do." Of course, I never did. And it sucked the life right out of me. Eventually, the accumulation of doing things that were life-giving to others, but not to me, drained me to a point where I was very vulnerable to "escape behavior." My guard was way down, in part, because I didn't know what I was feeling, nor did I feel I could own it as part of how God wired me up.

I am still learning to identify a feeling when it hits me and to embrace it as something important rather than to minimize it. I didn't realize that too many ignored feelings lead to resentment and anger.

So, I encourage you to do a little "focus on yourself" time, and when you find out how God made you, embrace it as His gift to you. He'll never ask us to be someone we are not. Powerful speakers can convince us to get excited about their agenda with their enthusiasm and with their spiritual gift-edness, but don't fall for it until God convinces you that it's an agenda that fits "unique you." Find out who you are and be that person, not someone else. Over time, you'll continue to grow stronger in emotional energy, and be able to guard your relationship with Jesus from tiredness, fatigue, and a lack of emotional energy.

Try This:

You know yourself better than anyone. What activities have you learned that best help protect your heart and mind? Bible memorization? Recalling a song? Picturing yourself in Jesus' loving presence? A photo of your family? All of heaven's angels cheering for you? A walk on the beach? Time with a close friend? Identify them. Then, practice them on a regular basis.

Be prepared.

- Boy Scout motto

Chapter 13: The Practice of
ADVANCED PREPARATION

It was nearly 30 years ago: my wife's 30th birthday. I wanted to surprise her. The Internet had just been born, so I mailed the invitations, arranged the location, the food, the formation of the people for the actual surprise, and the program for the party. I arranged the volunteer help I'd need, notified my friends about what types of gifts to bring, and arranged a clean-up crew. Then I planned how to get her there unsuspectedly. Surprises take a lot of advanced preparation.

ANY SUCCESSFUL EVENT—A MARATHON, A high school football game, teaching a class full of students, a dinner in your home, a meeting with volunteers, a house-building project, a meeting with your employees, your vacation, or a weekend of handing your young children off to the grandparents—all require *advanced preparation*.

Think of the last event for which you did a lot of advanced preparation. What did you do? Was it a holiday? A big dinner at your home? A family gathering? Think of all the things you had to do in advance. How did that advanced planning contribute to the success of that event?

Jesus and Advanced Preparation

Jesus used *advanced preparation* for one of the most meaningful events in recorded history—an event we still remember and re-create today.

Jesus was nearing the end of His life. The countdown had begun on the final week of His life on earth. Each day of the week after Palm Sunday, Jesus walked into Jerusalem in the morning and retreated to nearby Bethany each evening. Then came Thursday.

Thursday began with Jesus asking Peter and John to go into Jerusalem (a very large city packed to three times its normal capacity because of Passover). When they entered the city, Jesus told them to look for a man carrying a water jug on his head. "Follow him," Jesus said, "and then ask the owner of the house if everything's been prepared."

I can imagine Peter and the fellas looking at each other and asking Jesus, "Let me get this straight, you want us to walk into town, follow a guy with a jar on his head, then invite ourselves over for a dinner for 12 hosted by this person we've never met?"

"You got it," said Jesus. Lo and behold, when they entered Jerusalem things happened just as Jesus had said.

(Note: In ancient times, the task of water carrying was exclusively a woman's job, so singling out a man carrying a water jar would be as obvious as spotting a Raiders fan dressed and painted in black and silver at a San Diego Chargers home game. Still, the timing of their entry and seeing this guy was miraculous.)

When the preparations were made for The Last Supper, and everyone was reclined at the table. Jesus said, "I have been anxious to celebrate this Passover with you." Then Jesus continued to give the last instructions on how to celebrate and remember His life for all time. What is *not* written in the Biblical text is when Jesus met with the homeowner, asked for the upper room to use, and asked if he'd set the table and purchase the food. And, finally, asked if one of his male servants might do the "water jug carrying thing" as a signal for Peter and John when the time came.

Like I did for my surprise party for Karen, Jesus did a lot of advanced preparation in order for His friends to experience a moving, memorable, and monumental event that would be seared on their hearts for all their lives (and for all time). Communion (sometimes called "The Lord's supper" or "the Eucharist"), has been repeated through the centuries as our primary reminder of Jesus taking our sin and moral failures upon Himself.

Advanced Preparation Is a Legitimate Spiritual Practice

How can it be that some forms of *advanced preparation* can be called a spiritual practice? What kinds of spiritual *advanced preparation* make it increasingly easier to have some deep and meaningful experiences with Jesus? How could we go about our regular day and use *advanced preparation* in ways that would result in being:

- reminded by God that we are loved
- made aware of His closeness
- taught or guided by Him?

How can we use every day experiences as an advanced training practice so that we're even more aware of God's communication with us? What sort of reminders of God's presence can we be more alerted to if we prepare, in advance, to receive them? Here are some ideas.

Advanced Preparation to Face Our Day!

What do we do to get ready for the day?

- Get up
- shower
- put on clothes
- look in the mirror
- eat breakfast…

…maybe more.

What if we looked at each of those everyday actions as triggers to turn our minds to the truth that God is *with* and *within* us? (I addressed a couple of these actions in the chapter on "Thinking Things Through," but the approach here is a "prayer approach," rather than a "thinking approach.") For example:

- *Getting up*: "God you have given me the gift of another day. Thank you!"
- *Showering*: "Jesus, because of your sacrifice for me, I am washed clean from my sin. Help me to live into the truth that I am forgiven and you see me as white as snow."
- *Putting on clothes*: "Lord, may I put on love, joy, peace, patience, kindness, self-control, helpfulness, graciousness, and gentleness and give those good things to the people you bring my way today."
- *Looking in the mirror*: "Jesus, may I see myself as You see me: Your precious child, Your cherished treasure, Your one-of-a-kind master-piece."
- *Eating breakfast*: "Jesus, fill me (like this food does) with an awareness of Your presence, Your love, and Your grace for me."

Advanced Preparation for Reading Your Bible

You're about to read your Bible. Wait! Do you feel rushed? Do you only have a certain amount of minutes? Are you distracted? Is your to-do list on the forefront of your mind?

Why not do a little advanced preparation before reading the Bible? Do you know that God has something *personal* to say to you in the text you're reading? A little advanced preparation will help you recognize that just-for-you whisper from God.

Here's a prayer I've used to help *slow me down* and to focus on what I'm reading in the Bible, which increases my chances of hearing from God:

My Father, Lord Jesus, Ever-Present Holy Spirit...I believe the text I'm reading today has something utterly personal to say to me for the shaping of my life with You. I believe it is Your Word for Christ-followers in general, but also for me individually.

I am here to expose myself to Your word. I pray that You would address me personally. I believe it is not only Your Word for the world, but Your Word for me. So please:

Teach me, so that I'll be formed into Christ-likeness.

Confront me. Shine a light on my thoughts, intentions, and actions to see if there be any wicked way in me.

Correct me to get me back on course with You.

Train me. Educate, nurture, and grow me into maturity so I can be a clearer reflection of You to others.

There may be information to learn today, but may Your Word *form* me into one who increasingly thinks, feels, responds, acts, discerns, dreams, and speaks like You. Help me to see myself correctly...as You see me... and to be humbled and delighted in how much You love me. I am your student. You are my Teacher. Please be my Teacher today."

Pausing like this, before exposing yourself to the Bible, increases your chances of sensing that a portion of the text you're reading is something God wants you to pay attention to. You might read it and think, *Huh. I wonder why that's causing me to pause? Why that phrase or sentence is grabbing me, jumping out at me?* Ask God, "What is it that you want to show me in this?" Maybe the phrase is meant to encourage you, assure you, teach you, remind you, comfort you, or confront you. Recognizing these leadings from God largely depends on a bit of advanced preparation of your mind, soul, and spirit so you can be fully present to God, your Teacher.

Advanced Preparation for Church

Most often we enter into a church service with many things on our mind:

- *I'm late again and I still have to get my children into their programs. I have to go grocery shopping after church and I don't have a list.*
- *I'm not ready for that meeting on Monday.*
- *I have to work with my child on that report that's due on Monday.*
- *I know my wife and I are not getting along right now and we have to talk. I'm dreading the confrontation.*
- *We're running low on money.*

Here's an idea: why not set the clock a little earlier so you arrive at church a little early? You won't be in such a *hurry*. The devil loves it when week after week, people arrive at church feeling rushed, and then leave in a hurry to get on with their busy lives, and never pause to reflect on what they just experienced or to talk with anyone afterwards.

While waiting for the service to start you might pray something like, "God, I want to be fully present here in this service. If I think of something that I need to do, or start getting anxious about anything, may I simply put it aside, maybe write it down and not beat myself up about that thought, but then return to the fact that I am in your Presence and You have something for me today. Bring to my attention anything You want me to hear that is from You: the lyrics of a song, a conversation with someone, the message, an announcement. And help me to *rest* in Your presence." Imagine what state your heart and mind might be in if you entered a church service like that!

Many times God brings a person to mind that I need to call, write to or get together with. Sometimes, I see someone and God nudges me with, "Ask how they are *really* doing." Other times, I'm talking with someone after church and something comes up that's significant and I sense a whisper saying, "Ask them to lunch."

A prayer of, "Make me attentive to what You may bring my way," is a wonderful prelude to entering a church service.

Advanced Preparation for Attending a Small Group

I've been leading a small group for a few years now and I noticed that our gang was just showing up. Recently, I gently asked, "How many of you read the text before you came tonight?" Silence. Then I said, "You know, if you read the text that I send out before you get here, the chances of hearing from God go up exponentially, because your mind is already set on that text."

For many churches, small groups are a critical part of connecting with others and experiencing God's presence. It is here that people share what's really going on with their personal lives, once they feel safe. This is where people, hopefully, feel free enough to express doubts about God, or to express disappointments, setbacks, and sadness. It is here that group members can encourage with words, looks, and touches. They can support with prayer and hugs, and follow up with acts of compassion and love.

But, if there was just a little practice of *slowing* and *pausing*; a little expectation that God will show up *before* entering the door where you're meeting, we would be consistently ready to respond with love and care. We'd be able to listen more intently and respond as Jesus would. With a little advanced preparation, I believe we'd sense more leadings and promptings.

Advanced Preparation for Going to Work

You may be white collar or blue collar; the boss or the employee. You may be self-employed or work for a giant conglomerate. You may facilitate board meetings or staff meetings. You may do construction or work in a restaurant. You may do childcare or drive for Uber. You may work at a school, at Home Depot, or at someone's home doing repairs. It doesn't matter. How might you do advanced preparation for doing your job?

Again, it takes a *pause* and thinking it through, and seeing that what you are doing is an opportunity to model and express all the wonderful attributes of Jesus without saying a word about Him. You can really listen to someone so they feel heard and valued. You can work diligently and ask if there's any other way you could help, above and beyond what you were asked to do. You could pray in advance for your attitude, so that the love and grace of Jesus you've received, can be seen on your face.

As I mentioned, I officiate weddings. Sometimes, an enthusiastic Christ-follower will ask me, "So how do you weave in the 'God-thing' during the service? You are obligated to let them know you're all about Jesus. They know you're a part of the clergy. They need to hear about that!" I tell them, "I don't mention Jesus' name or talk about God. That would be inappropriate. It's *their* wedding, not a chance for me to express a hidden agenda. Instead, I believe Jesus can be seen behind my words. If I talk about how sacrifice and forgiveness are two keys to a successful marriage and I talk about how that's fleshed out in regular, everyday real life, I'm talking about biblical themes without announcing it. Who knows what He's prompting the guests with?"

Whether the words hit home or not, I want to give people a positive experience with a professional minister, because so many have had negative experiences with church staffs, parachurch organizations, and overbearing Christ-followers who feel it's their duty make sure the word "God" or "Jesus" is mentioned. If I can give all the guests, families, wedding party, and the bride and groom a positive impression and experience with a pastor/minister/reverend, it goes a long way for them being open, later, to yet another impression of a Christ-follower who may come their way down the line.

Imagine guests leaving a wedding feeling bored, "preached at," and not understanding the "churchy language." Imagine people leaving a wedding feeling that the notion of church, Christians, and pastors is just what they thought: irrelevant. What if they left thinking this instead: "Hey that was fun and yet meaningful. He looked very organized. It was personal. He knew the couple. It didn't seem like he phoned it in. I understood what the guy was saying. It was practical and down-to-earth. He described the 'real life' of what it means to be married. And he seemed genuinely humble."

I have trained myself to pray a type of prayer before and after a wedding. Whether it's the couple's first, second, or third or whatever number wedding, on the way to the wedding I pray, "Jesus, I believe this is going to be their last wedding day. I could treat it as 'just another wedding' for me. But I pray I wouldn't phone it in or treat this as routine. Grant to me the strength and alertness and energy to be a representative of You. This is a joyous occasion. Remind me to be joyful with them. And I pray that what I'll be saying are words from heaven. May the people hear them as words from You and may their hearts grow increasingly intrigued with checking You out."

After the wedding, I pray, "God, please guide and protect their marriage. More importantly, may they come to know You as the loving and gracious God that You are. I know You'll never give up on them. May they see Your extended hand of invitation to do life with You and take it."

I believe that a life speaks louder than words. I believe that in my short time to make an impression at a wedding I can leave a good taste in people's mouths about a Christ-follower, and a key tool in leaving that impression is being well-prepared in my mind and heart for the event. I want the focus to be on the bride and groom, not me. I'm reminded that when Jesus healed a paralyzed man by a pool of water, that man had no idea it was Jesus who did it until much later. Jesus was perfectly fine with helping someone, then slipping away, without all the attention being on Him or having the blind man know it was Him.

What if we prayed before any of our job situations or the day at work itself, "Lord, this isn't a throwaway job; I get to give a first impression to everyone I meet, and it may be someone's first time meeting and interacting with a Christ-follower. I may be the only example of a Christ-follower that this person sees up close and personal. Help me to see everyone I lock eyes with as Your precious treasure and let me treat them accordingly. Let my words, facial expressions, and listening skills tell people that they matter to me. And I pray that something I do or say might be one event that will lead them to coming to know You one day." *The person who prays that* is ready for work!

I teach small groups and classes. I do a lot of material preparation, but I pray before each group I'm with, "God, I have some stuff prepared, but You might have another agenda for the people who are coming. May I sense when I need to go off script and see it as a divine interruption from You."

Or, you might pray, "God, people in this meeting or event are coming in with something on their minds and hearts. They may be tired, discouraged, and worn-out. Grant me the strength to empathize. Help me to *listen* carefully and be slow to *speak*."

Advanced Preparation for Re-entering Your Home After a Day of Work!

You have no idea what your spouse's day has been like or how it made them feel. You are coming home from a rough day; maybe a long day too. Maybe your spouse did childcare all day and they want to pull their hair out. As you're walking up the pathway to your door, what about doing a little *advanced preparation* for coming home? Try something like:

> "God, I have no idea what I'll encounter when I go through that door. I've given a lot of energy to my job today. But the people on the other side of that door are the ones I love, and they love me. Don't let me give them my leftovers. Grant to me strength, patience, and power to be others-oriented, to ask about my spouse's day first and to listen intently. I know we'll get around to me eventually. May I give to my spouse, kids, (roommates, for you single people), those looks, words, actions, and touches that let them know they are treasures."

I think the evening might go better.

Advanced Preparation for Tragedy, Crisis, and Loss

How do we prepare for surprise crises: unexpected news, tragedy, death, illness, financial loss, and more?

- *Know* that your time will come for any of these life situations.
- *Know* that God doesn't protect Christ-followers from facing the heartaches, betrayals, and hits that come to all people.
- *Know* that Jesus understands every type of pain (physical, emotional, mental, and relational) because He experienced all of them. Therefore, He not only understands our pain but He deeply empathizes with us as well.

In one sense, there is no preparation for life's tragedies. Even though we go to funerals for children and teenagers; even though we watch someone lose their house; even though we see a child born with a birth defect. We know those things happen, but it's a much different thing when it happens to you personally. Now, the heart that is stabbed is yours, not your friend's. Now, you have to live with it every day. Now, you're the one who's thinking, *How am I going to handle this? This is awful. And there's no way out.* This is true. There is no escape from your crisis. You can only go through it.

In my experience of walking with people who have experienced an awful event, the ones who have done the advanced preparation of reading, studying, pondering, and applying the Bible to their lives *before* the crisis hits, have a much better chance of coming through it with their marriage and faith still intact. We must know how Jesus handled crisis, and what God's assurances in crises are. We must know the lives of biblical figures who faced crisis and how they handled it, and how God comforted them in it.

Just to be clear, part of advanced preparation is giving yourself permission to *not* be strong; to *feel helpless, find no solutions, be so hurt you are unable to pray,* and still say in your heart, "I'm still here, God."

Advanced Preparation for Heaven

Death is tragic. Frankly, it sucks. I've officiated many funerals and memorial services: some for the elderly; some for people who would be in the category of "gone before their time." There's simply nothing good about a young person dying, or a mother of three young children falling to cancer, or a husband dying in a car accident. In most cases, there isn't a day that goes by where the survivors don't remember that their child, their spouse, or their family member is now gone. Death *sucks!*

However, death isn't the ultimate tragedy. In one sense, death is the ultimate healer of a failing body. And, most wonderful of all, death is the way home, to the place where we finally meet Jesus face-to-face. Let me quickly say: even this image is not completely helpful to the ones left behind, because

283

we still miss our loved ones. We think of a life cut short. We think of all the things they will never experience. Depending on how old they were when they died, they'll miss their first kiss, their senior prom, walking down the aisle of their wedding day, having a child, making new friends, seeing beautiful places in the world, serving others. And most of all, the survivors will miss the normal conversations about mundane news, how things at work are going, what are they doing for fun, what they are doing for the weekend. These are all the things we take for granted, until death suddenly steals it away.

In one sense, there are no great methods to do advance preparation for the end of our lives. No matter how much we look forward to heaven, there is a built-in instinct to stay in the land of the living. If people believe that this life on earth is all there is, then staying alive for as long as possible is the goal. But for the Christ-follower, this world is not all there is. In fact, Jesus said that our lives here are relatively short compared to our life in eternity. We are given one and only one life. Then, for time never-ending, we get to revel in and enjoy heaven, where there is no more death or sorrow, where every tear is wiped away, where there is only pure joy, where we have healed bodies and where we see Jesus with our own eyes.

If eternity awaits us, is there any way we can prepare in advance for it? Is it okay to fill our minds with images of being with Jesus and being in our eternal home?

Long ago, I heard a statement, "They are so heavenly minded, they are no earthly good." It was a statement meant to cut off daydreaming about the days to come in eternity and to encourage us to keep our focus to the agenda of the kingdom of God on earth. We have a role to play, spiritual gifts to discover, needs to meet, people to feed, ministries to get started, and service to do. I have this voice in my head constantly whispering, "What are you going to do with your one and only life?" Am I going to waste it away on the pursuit of money, or on possessions, pleasure, and self-service? Or, am I going to spend all my energy, efforts, and giftedness forwarding the Kingdom of God on earth...one life at a time?

The answer is: This is not an either/or thing. It's a both/and thing. It is an error on both sides to emphasize one over the other. Yes, I want to get to the end of my days on earth and be able to say, "I gave it my best to love people as Jesus would if He were in my place. I discovered and put into play my spiritual gifts for the sake of introducing people to the aroma of Jesus. I did my best to model the words, actions, looks, and touches of Jesus. I was given the privilege of teaching about the life of Jesus and how God worked, and continues to work, in human history."

But while I'm doing all that on earth, I've learned that God invites me to dream, to be still, to be quiet, do nothing, and enjoy His presence with and within me while not accomplishing anything. In many of these times, I dream of being without physical pain. I've had three spine surgeries, one knee surgery, one foot and ankle surgery, and bladder surgery. I have a pacemaker. I'm 62. I dream of a healed body. I dream of just an hour without significant pain in my back. My surgeon said most of the discs in my spine are crunched and unhealthy. Fixing one area throws off the rest of the discs. And he told me before each surgery that he can bring the pain from a "9" to a "4-5." He said, "Now, before surgery, you can't stand on your feet for more than five minutes without experiencing significant pain, but after surgery, I can give you 20 minutes." I wish I could say the surgeries worked to that degree. The pain is lessened a bit, but it never goes away. It's been that way for 30 years. Ask me if I long for heaven.

But, do I want to live long enough to see my grandchildren graduate from high school and college and get married? Of course I do. But do I want to go through that agony of a brain tumor or pancreatic cancer? Heck no! But do I have times I wish I could leave this world of sorrow, heartache and pain? Yes. But not until my job is done for Jesus on earth, whenever He deems it done. See, it's the "both/and."

If I had to summarize how to prepare in advance for heaven:

- *Practice dreaming of heaven.* It's okay if you're wrong about your dreams when you get there. But, embrace the truth that this world is not our home. It's not your home. Imagine life in eternity.

- *Practice that you matter.* Embrace the truth that anything you do, say, think, or feel is used by God to make Jesus known to the people around you in everyday life. Nothing is wasted in the Kingdom of God. Do not minimize yourself. You matter here on earth as you will matter in heaven. Embrace your life as an essential puzzle piece in God's economy of the world at this time.

- *Do everything in your power to practice the presence of Jesus.* There will be a lot of surprises in heaven (as far as who makes it there, which is none of our business), but experiencing the presence of Jesus in our normal lives is a taste of heaven. Jesus described a picture of heaven as a huge banquet table full of the best kinds of food ever, enjoyed with all types of people. I don't know if that's literal or symbolic, but if it's a picture of enjoying time with Jesus, then we have a veiled sense of that here on earth by practicing this truth of His constant invisible presence in us.

This is advanced preparation. I don't always do all these categories well, but when I do, I experience Jesus' presence in ways I wouldn't if I hadn't done a little prep work with Him. Advanced preparation for your day, your arrival home, your day off, your day at work, your evening dinner date *counts* as a spiritual practice.

Try This:

Choose *one* of the categories above and do some advanced preparation for it. Do it for a month. Write down or recall if doing the preparation heightened your awareness of Jesus' presence with you.

Be still, my soul, the Lord is on your side.
Bear patiently the cross of grief or pain.

- Song adapted from Psalm 46:10 in 1752 by Katharina Amalia Dorothea von Schlegel (1697–1768) and translated into English in 1855 by Jane Laurie Borthwick (1813–1897).

Epilogue: Experiencing Jesus in Sadness, Loss, Trauma, Debilitation, Setbacks, and Being Wounded

YOU CAN'T HURRY THE PROCESSING of pain...

Look at the title of this epilogue. If you are reading this chapter you have experienced at least one of these words: tragedy, sadness, loss, trauma, debilitation, setbacks, or being wounded. And if you haven't, you will.

Annie has parents and relatives who told her she was ugly for most of her childhood and adolescence. Now, as an adult about to get married, her husband needs to know that her self-esteem has been shattered time and again. She carries this negative image of herself that needs to be undone every day. She was *wounded by words*.

Katy was born with severe Down's syndrome. She will never talk in her lifetime. She needs a strict, simple routine for her day. She's eight years old and has no interest in being potty-trained. Her parents may watch her entire life go by never knowing what she's thinking, never hearing her voice, and maybe never seeing her have a friend. Her parents are *wounded by loss* of what might have been.

Mary was wedded to Gene for 25 years. As they were getting ready to go on a big anniversary trip, Mary found a condom in Gene's pants pocket. When Mary confronted him about it, Gene blamed his 16-year-old son. "He put it in my pants to shift blame to me." When the son was confronted he had no clue what they were talking about. Eventually, the truth came out that it was Gene's. He had been having affairs through

289

most of their married life...with men. At the same time this news came out, Mary was diagnosed with a severe form of breast cancer. She had a double mastectomy. She was tested for AIDS and other diseases. She was clean. A divorce ensued. In a matter of two months, her world went from "Happy Anniversary" to "Tragic Real Life." She was *wounded by betrayal.*

Candy was a high school student I knew years ago. At the time, her mom was 41. Her mother was diagnosed with pancreatic cancer. She died two months later. A high school junior was now motherless for the rest of her life. She was *wounded by death.*

Ken was a sophomore in high school. He was adopted by a wonderful couple. He had two other adopted brothers. One by one, each of the brothers died in tragic accidents, so Ken was the only one left. He was riding in the back of a truck, standing up and holding onto the roll bar, joy-riding in the mountains with his buddies. Lots of bumps, potholes, sudden drops in the road. While Ken was standing in the back, the truck hit a rock and launched Ken over the front of the truck. He hit his head on a rock and died instantly. The last adopted son was gone. Ken's parents were *wounded by tragedy.*

Richard and Debbie were riding high in the early 2000's, but then the economy crashed. They were upside down on their home, so it was foreclosed upon. Richard was laid off. Debbie had three young children at home. Richard had a hard time finding work. They had to move in with her parents. Richard became depressed and after two years of trying to find work, closed in on himself and stopped talking to Debbie. He felt like a total failure. Debbie had to find work to get some sort of income coming in for the family. They've struggled for six years to get back on their feet. They were *wounded by life's circumstances.*

What Causes Injury and Pain to Our Souls, Hearts, and Minds?

- Loss: of a home, a job, and friends
- A bad medical report. (Cancer, Alzheimer's, dementia, tumors, Autism)
- Divorce
- Financial ruin
- Death of a loved one
- Betrayal by a friend or a spouse
- Gossip or rumors that are untrue
- Personal moral failure
- The pain of a wayward child…

…and more.

In all of these real-life situations that I have experienced with these people, I find myself having nothing to say. I have no clue why God allowed each of these situations to happen. I wouldn't even venture a guess. Who knows the mind of God? Not my teeny-weeny brain. Besides, as we've said, we wouldn't like God's answer to the *"Why* did this happen?" question anyway.

How Does Someone Experience God While Being Wounded?

What's one to do when personal tragedy, loss, sadness, and woundedness come your way?

The overall answer to this is: *Be Gentle on Yourself.* That's your spiritual practice. Give yourself *time* and *space* to be "wounded" with the tragedy and loss.

A pastor I know had a son in his sophomore year of high school. For some reason, he tried to cross a three-lane road at night and was hit by a car and killed. To say that the pastor and his wife and family were devastated is selling it short. After the funeral, this pastor continued with his duties for one year. At the one-year mark of his son's death, he resigned. Not only did his church handle this pastor with compassion and grace, but this tragedy became a defining moment that changed his career path. He lives with severe woundedness. He continues to give himself time and space to grieve his son's loss.

Analogy to Being Physically Injured

Athletes get injured. Soldiers get wounded. There are specific regimens, processes, and orders for recovery when we are physically injured or have surgery. Every one of them comes with a specific plan for recovery. But in all of those different plans, these three things are usually required:

- Therapy
- Time
- Rest

Your recovery plan for emotional injuries should include the same three things.

Being Gentle on Yourself

What's the recovery process look like when one of life's hard hits comes your way? What does the spiritual practice of *Being Gentle on Yourself* look like? Recovery from this type of event may include some things you need to "do," but mostly, we will do a lot of "being," because there is simply no emotional energy or motivation to "do" much of anything.

One father I know, who lost his son, spent a lot of time playing video games to pass the time. You might think, "Shouldn't he have been in mourning, pondering and reflecting?" He was. But sometimes he just needed something to occupy his mind with a rather mindless thing. He was gentle on himself, not feeling like he was wasting time. So, be gentle with yourself on the use of time.

Be *Gentle* on Yourself as You Re-engage with People

Just getting out of bed each day may be a huge victory. Something even more victorious might be going to the store, walking the dog, or fixing yourself lunch. Do not feel badly that you don't want to see or visit certain people. *Your job is yourself* for a time, and most people don't give themselves the time or energy to care for their hearts and souls, let alone their bodies. Serving in the community or the church may be distracting and helpful, but again, go easy on yourself. You may want to drop out of participating and serving in church activities for a season. I know many people who take an extended vacation from church after a divorce or the death of a loved one because they don't want to cry or talk about how they are doing with their friends at church. In fact, I've noticed that when there's a divorce, one of the two spouses "gets" the church (gets to stay at their home church). When a child dies, a huge percentage of the parents end up getting divorced, not because of blame, but they simply have no emotional gas to give to each other. If time is not taken to process and care for yourself when tragedy hits, things often don't go well in years following.

Be Gentle on Yourself Regarding Time for Recovery

Depending on the "hit" it may take a long time to reengage with God and people. What's the timeline on recovery from finding out your spouse had been having an affair for years? What's the recovery time for a widow or widower? For a parent who's lost a child? There is no timeline. A friend of mine lost his 33-year-old daughter. Eight months later, some people were asking him why he was still so deeply wounded. Are you kidding me?

Your injury usually leaves a scar. (Those scars can be emotional, relational, or to your self-image.)

Often people don't know what to say or do with someone who's in the middle of experiencing tragedy, betrayal or loss. In their effort to be empathetic or comforting, they say stupid and irritating things. Here are a few:

- "I thought you might be over this by now."
- "I didn't realize you'd still be feeling this way."
- "Five years from now, you'll have a lot to say to people who go through the same thing."
- "Someday the sting of this hardship will fade."
- "God will heal your wound someday."
- "This event will eventually increase your faith and trust in God."
- "Someday, you'll look back on this event and see that all things work together for good for those who love God."

These statements may come true someday, but when the wound is fresh, or even after some time, these statements are *not* helpful and must not be said. Some of you are thinking, *Oh my gosh, how could someone say such things?* They probably didn't intend to be hurtful. They just weren't thinking it through from the wounded one's perspective. The truth about being hit with a life-jarring event is that it always leaves a scar. The pain of the event is always just under the surface. There isn't a day that goes by when the tragedy is not thought of. When someone is suffering, don't project the future into their present.

Walk Alongside the Wounded: Don't Try to Talk Them Out of It

If someone loses a child, that pain never goes away. Its intensity may lessen over time, but the sorrow remains. There's not a day that goes by when the parents and family don't think about their dead child, brother, or sister. They wake up every day with the memory of loss. Can Christ-followers allow people to "be" in that place of grief, sorrow, and even despair for as long as they need to be? Even better, could Christ-followers stay committed enough to walk with someone through this kind of event, not just for a couple of months, but for a long time? The grief-stricken do feel like taking their own lives at times. It's that serious. There's no special spiritual trick for staying present to someone in this terrible event. It's just the loving thing to do.

294

What *Be-ing* May Look Like for the Suffering One

For the grieving, just *be-ing* doesn't mean sitting around and staring out the window. For many, if they did that, they'd go crazy. Some jump right back into work because they need to stay preoccupied with doing something. Many exercise rigorously and more often. That can help.

If you are reading this and you are in this category, your prime directive from Jesus is: Do or not do whatever it is you feel you need or want to do. That includes doing nothing or doing something or somewhere in between those two. Whatever positive and life-giving activity you might land on that helps, go with that. Then stay with it for as long as you need. One warning: being in suffering circumstances makes you susceptible to harmful "escape" coping mechanisms like alcohol, drug use or excessive TV watching. Watch out for this. Get help and support if this happens.

Often, people who lose a child can't keep attending the church they've been going to. It reminds them of where they were when they lost their daughter or son. It sometimes results in leaving the church. It's not the church's fault. The memories stirred in that place are simply too much. Again, are we going to allow them to let that be a part of their process, and who will stick with them even if they leave the church? I hope someone would.

There is no way out of grief. We simply have to go through it. Loss and betrayal leave a scar for life. But a loving friend willing to walk with someone through their pain is a treasure from God.

Matching Someone's Emotional State

A spiritual practice for one who's coming alongside a friend who's been hurt in some way is the practice of *matching their emotional state*. You can't completely understand what they're going through, but you can listen for the feelings behind the words and then match their emotions with matching empathy. They may be quiet one day. Be quiet with them. They may want to talk only about "surface-y" stuff. Do that with them. They may want to escape to movies, trips, experiences, or activities. When possible, go with them. When they want to talk about their pain, listen hard. Don't stay in your brain. Go to your heart and feel with them as best you can. Nod a lot. Make empathizing facial expressions. If you speak, make it be "I'm listening" type of phrases: "Oh geez, I can't even imagine…" or "There's no way I could understand the depth of your pain. I'm so sorry." Or, ask a *depth-ing* question that lets them know you're listening, like, "When you feel this way, what do you end up doing with that? What do you think about doing with those thoughts? Or "Is there anything that you do or don't do that seems to help you?"

They are scarred. Whenever you are present to them you (symbolically) put your hand on their scar, letting them know that you are a safe person to spill their guts to, because they know you'll feel with them. In a sense, your hand is Jesus' hand placed on the wound of their heart. Don't be shocked if all that you offer doesn't immediately result in someone gaining hope. Count on this truth: You are being Jesus to them, and it really matters. You will be the human expression of the Comforter; the Holy Spirit coming alongside someone to heal and give hope. This is the type of person I want around me when loss comes my way. I want someone who can match their emotions to what I'm feeling.

The Spiritual Practice of *Rest* and *Receiving*

Wounded people don't have a lot of energy for talking. They usually experience a new way of looking at the world. They see all the things people go after in life as rather silly. Acquiring "things," traveling to the new and interesting places in the world, and even eating out doesn't really do it for people who are the victims of tragedy, loss, betrayal, and sadness. Emotionally, people are wiped out. They can be wiped out for long periods of time. They may not feel motivated to practice their hobby or to do anything fun. If you are in this kind of scenario, allow yourself to be "given to" rather than being the giver. Give yourself permission to be in this place for as long as you need to. Especially, give yourself permission to experience feelings of grief long after the event. If you are the one who's been hit with a tragedy, loss, or sadness, will you do the practice of *receiving* the love, the gifts, and the presence of these people who are "Jesus in the flesh"?

I don't like to receive. I would much rather give to others than have them give to me. I feel unworthy, indebted, and undeserving. But I've taken my share of hits in life and when I did, the one thing I really needed to heal was *rest*. I also had to allow people to say words of comfort and empathy. I had to receive their presence and not feel obligated to send them home because I didn't feel worthy. I'm slowly learning to embrace the truth that, at times like these, I need to rest and receive.

Do What Works for You

In addition to giving yourself permission to disengage with certain people or to lie down or to "waste" time, pay attention to what really helps you to recover and rest. There are many ways people can experience God while being hurt. Inviting God to love you, comfort you, assure you, or weep with you is a good start. If you find you can't pray, don't. Then don't beat yourself up about it. Let others pray for you. God understands. And don't put pressure on yourself to come up with amazing, grief-filled prayers. Just blurt stuff out. "I'm out of bed, Lord." Or, "I can't talk today, Lord," or "Hold me, Jesus."

Being Injured Sometimes Includes Professional Help to Recover

At various crisis points in my life, I needed to seek out a professional counselor to figure out what was going on with me. It costs money. But I ask again, "How much is your soul worth? How much is it worth to have help in putting your life back together?" ANSWER: Everything you've got.

Physical injury needs a physical therapist; emotional/relational injury may require seeing someone you respect that has wisdom, experience, and a lot of life-under-their-belt training. Someone whose opinion and advice you *welcome*. If you go to someone who's *not professionally trained*, it better be someone who:

- *Listens* before *speaking.*
- *Asks good questions.*
- *Draws out your feelings.*
- *Values your anger towards God.*
- *Allows you* to *be* in whatever state or stage you're in.
- *Encourages* you to *stay* in the place you are at in your injury recovery process and encourages you to invite God to meet you *there*, not where you think you *"should"* be.

We tend to put pressure on ourselves to "get over" this event; to hurry through grief. Months, or even years after the event, we think, *I should be over this by now.* We wonder why we still have sneak attacks of grief while doing the most mundane of things. When we feel this way, it really helps to have a spouse or close friend nearby who allows you to feel this way. This person can speak words of hope.

The Spiritual Practice of *Dependency*

We are taught and trained to be *independent.* However, in times of grief, sadness, sorrow, pain, and loss, it's time to be *dependent* on the people God brings our way. So please: BE GENTLE WITH YOURSELF. Being gentle…

- Could mean practicing: Giving yourself TIME to be non-productive.
- Could mean practicing: Getting out of bed and taking one step at a time.
- Could mean practicing: RECEIVING (counseling, empathy, mercy, encouragement).
- Could mean practicing: Allowing God to love you; comfort you; assure you; weep with you.
- Could mean staying active physically.
- Could mean spending time with a safe person with whom you can be raw and speak unedited thoughts and feelings.

Your spiritual recovery regimen for now is somewhere between:
BE …………………………and …………………………DO!

Final Thoughts

Any spiritual practice that works for you while you are in any of these conditions of sadness, abandonment, or life-hits that come, is not only perfectly legal, but God is wanting you to do it. Remember, probably the hardest thing for Americans to do is to give themselves time to accomplish nothing. We can't *hurry* grief. The spiritual practices of rest, receiving, dependency, or being gentle on yourself or doing a lot of *be-ing* when tragedy and loss come your way, are all God-directed thoughts. So please, go easy on yourself when life turns on a dime. Know that Jesus is very close to you, holding you and whispering "I'm here. I'm here...with and within you."

Acknowledgments

A GREAT BIG THANK YOU to Jessica Snell who made this book so much better with her editing. To Deborah Stocco at MyBookDesigner.com for her patience on designing this book with a rookie author. To Christine Lee Smith for her wonderful book cover design. To Larry Warner who kept pestering me to write.

I'd like to thank the people that God brought my way, those who really want to follow Jesus more closely, but felt defeated about how to do anything about that. For all those who felt so guilty about not following Jesus like they thought they should, thank you for being honest. Your transparency with me over the years was a stimulus for writing this book.

I'd also like to thank the people who have supported me emotionally, spiritually, and financially. You have never wavered in believing in me: Karen, Kristi, Kelsey, Tyler, Carolyn, Stan and Marie, Tic and Terrie, Randy and Lyne, Jeff and Li-an, Tom and Liza, Rick and Cathy, Scott and Becky, Scott and Tracy, Bill and Janny, Lee and Sandy, Nate and Amanda, John and Susie, Curt and Rebecca, Gail, Dan and Kelly, Barry and Colleen, Dale and Beth, Casey and Beth, Andy and Miriam, Bruce, John and Penny, John and Gwen, Tim and Stanna, Scott and Linda, Scott and Beth, Kevin and Sherri, Mark and Lynda, Al and Mary, Bob and Gina, Dan and Nicola, Greg and Jan, Tim and Robin, Paul, Doug and Jean, Bev, C.T., Bill and Beth, Rob and Norma,

Clay and Lani, Mark and Beth, Rick and Joyce, Mark and Kathy, Cody and Danielle and the many unnamed people from Community Covenant Church and Young Life down through the years.

I am the richest man in the world because of you!

Endnotes

Introduction: God's Dream for Doing Life with Him

1. Koessler, page 19.

2. "Training vs. Trying" is a concept found in John Ortberg's book, *The Life You've Always Wanted*. A fabulous book that I highly recommend!

Part 1: HURRY (Too Fast!)

1. Response of Dallas Willard upon being asked, "What's the most important thing in a vibrant life with God?" John Ortberg, "Ruthlessly Eliminate Hurry," *CT Pastors, Christianity Today*, July 2002.

2. Adapted from *An Unhurried Life* by Alan Falding, pages 38-39.

3. Henderson, page 31.

4. Adapted from *The Busy Christian's Guide to Busyness* by Tim Chester, page 45.

5. Chester, page 47.

6. *https://bible.org/illustration/milan-cathedral*. Feb. 2, 2009.

Chapter 1: The Practice of SLOWING

1. http://www.businessinsider.com/startup-founders-going-off-the-grid-for-weeks-at-a-time-2017-11. Nov. 15, 2017.

2. Falding, page 52.

3. Henri Nouwen, quoted in article found at https://richerbyfar.com/2016/11/13/daily-riches-interruptions-henri-nouwen-c-s-lewis-and-frederick-buechner/. Nov. 13, 2016.

Chapter 2: The Practice of BEING USELESS

1. Chester, page 117.

2. Adapted from *The Busy Christian's Guide to Busyness* by Tim Chester, page 31.

3. Koessler, page 10.

4. *Ibid*, page 118.

Chapter 3: The Practice of WAITING

1. Patterson, Ben, *Waiting*, p.11

2. Romans 5:2, NKJV (emphasis mine).

Part 2: BUSYNESS (Too Much!)

1. Kelsey, page 21.

2. List taken from *Crazy Busy* by Edward M. Hallowell, M.D., pages 8-10.

3. Adapted from *Crazy Busy* by Edward M. Hallowell, M.D., page 18.

4. Chester, page 89.

Chapter 5: The Practice of NOTICING

1. Gire, page 11.

2. *Ibid*, page 29.

Chapter 6: The Practice of BEING ALONE

1. Koessler, page 118.

Part 3: NOISE (Too Loud!)

1. Noise Level Chart, www.noisehelp.com. (Look up "decibel charts.")

2. Prochnick, page 99.

3. Noise Level Chart, www.noisehelp.com.

4. Prochnick, page 15.

5. *Ibid*, page 60.

Chapter 8: The Practice of BEING QUIET

1. Prochnick, page 283.

2. Prochnick, page 27.

3. *Ibid*, page 4.

Chapter 9: SENSING LEADINGS from God

1. Points 1-5 adapted from Bill Hybel's *The Power of a Whisper*, pages 98-106.

2. Willard, page 39.

Chapter 10: The Practice of THINKING THINGS THROUGH

1. Tomeo, page 27.

2. Gire, page 22.

3. Tomeo, page 27.

4. Adapted from Ken Gire's *Seeing What is Sacred*, pages 91-92.

Part 4: DISTRACTION (Too Many!)

1 and 2: adapted:https://www.businessnewsdaily.com/8098-distractions-kiling-productivity.html and https://www.thetoptens.com/top-ten-distractions-from-real-life/

3. Hollowell, page 83.

4. Hollowell, page 81.

5. Adapted from *Seeing What is Sacred*, Gire, pp. 122-123

Chapter 11: The Practice of LEARNING TO BE CONTENT

1. Sources: www.marketwatch.com, April 30, 2017; www.nerdwallet.com, Erin El Issa, December 2016.

Chapter 12: The Practice of PROTECTING YOUR HEART AND MIND:

1. "Switzerland's Military Defense Involves Blowing Up All Roads into the Country." Walter Hickey, Business Insider, June 22, 2012.

2. "JTF2 is the 'Jewel in the Crown' of Canada's Special Forces." Bruce Campio-Smith, the-star.com, Ottowa Beureau, June 26, 2016.

3. "North Vietnamese Aces." Diego Zampini, AcePilots.com, March 22, 2012.

4. "Inside Rio's Elite Police Force," Michael Bucher, TIME, Aug 10, 2016,

5. "African Union Mission in Somalia." Globalsecurity.org, August 3, 2017.

6. Recommended online spiritual gifts tests:

 - www.lifeway.com/lwc/files/lwcF_MYCS_030526_Spiritual_Gifts_Survey.pdf.

 - giftstest.com/test.

 - https://mintools.com/spiritual-gifts-test.htm.

 - https://gifts.churchgrowth.org/spiritual-gifts-survey/.

Works Cited

Tim Chester. *The Busy Christian's Guide to Busyness*. Downer's Grove, IL: IVP, 2006.

Alan Falding. *An Unhurried Life*. Downer's Grove, IL: IVP, 2013.

Ken Gire. *Seeing What is Sacred*. Nashville, TN: Thomas Nelson, 2006.

Edward M. Hallowell, M.D. *Crazy Busy*. New York: Ballyntine Books, 2006.

David Henderson. *Tranquility*. Grand Rapids, MI: Baker Books, 2015.

Bill Hybels. *The Power of a Whisper*. Grand Rapids, MI: Zondervan, 2010.

Jan Johnson. *Enjoying the Presence of God*. Colorado Springs, CO: Navpress, 1996.

Kirk Byron Jones. *Addicted to Hurry*. Valley Forge, PA: Judson Press, 2003.

Morton Kelsey. *The Other Side of Silence,* Missionary Society of St. Paul, New York, 1997

John Koessler. *The Radical Pursuit of Rest*. Downer's Grove, IL: IVP, 2016.

John Ortberg. *The Life You've Always Wanted*. Grand Rapids, MI: Zondervan, 1997.

Ben Patterson. *Waiting*. Downer's Grove, IL: IVP, 1989.

George Prochnik. *In Pursuit of Silence*. New York: Anchor Books, 2010.

Richard Swenson. *Margin,* Navigators Press, Colorado Springs, CO. 2004

Teresa Tomeo. *Noise*. West Chester, PA: Ascension Press, 2007.

Dallas Willard. *Hearing God*. Downer's Grove, IL: IVP, 1984.

Alli Worthington. *Breaking Busy*. Grand Rapids, MI: Zondervan, 2016.

About the Author

HE'S TALL. HE'S BALD. HE'S not famous. This is his first book. It took five years of hounding from friends and family to convince him to write this book. He used to play basketball, but now he's a broken-down shell of his former self. Finally, he's failed in a lot of areas of life, so he's just like everyone else.

Besides that, he was on the Young Life Staff for 12 years, a high school teacher and coach for five years, and senior pastor of Community Covenant Church in El Cajon, California for 19 years. Now, he's a Minister-at-Large and officiates weddings all over San Diego county with the creative business title: Craig Does Weddings (http://www.craigdoesweddings.com).

Made in the USA
Coppell, TX
02 August 2020